The Stage Liv

The Stage Lives of Animals shows what it means to make theater beyond the human. In this stunning collection of essays, Una Chaudhuri engages with the alternative modes of thinking, feeling, and making art that are offered by animals and animality, bringing insights from theater practice and theory to the emergent academic field of animal studies as well as exploring what animal studies can bring to the study of theater and performance.

As our planet goes through what scientists call "the sixth extinction," and we become ever more aware of our relationships to other species, *The Stage Lives of Animals* traces a theatrical path toward understanding how other animals make us who we are. Chaudhuri offers a highly original perspective on the "animal imagination" of well-known plays, performances, and creative projects, including works by:

- Caryl Churchill
- Rachel Rosenthal
- Marina Zurkow
- Edward Albee
- Tennesee Williams
- Eugène Ionesco

Covering over a decade of explorations, a wide range of writers, and many urgent topics, this volume demonstrates that an "interspecies imagination" deeply structures modern drama, theater, and performance.

Una Chaudhuri is a Professor of English, Drama, and Environmental Studies at New York University. She has lectured and published internationally on modern drama, performance theory, animal studies, and eco-criticism.

The Stage Lives
of Animals

Zooësis and Performance

Una Chaudhuri

Routledge
Taylor & Francis Group

LONDON AND NEW YORK

First published 2017
by Routledge
2 Park Square, Milton Park, Abingdon, Oxon OX14 4RN

and by Routledge
711 Third Avenue, New York, NY 10017

Routledge is an imprint of the Taylor & Francis Group, an informa business

British Library Cataloguing-in-Publication Data
A catalogue record for this book is available from the British Library

Library of Congress Cataloging-in-Publication Data
Names: Chaudhuri, Una, 1951- author.
Title: The stage lives of animals : zooësis and performance / Una Chaudhuri.
Description: Milton Park, Abingdon, Oxon ; New York : Routledge, 2016.
| Includes bibliographical references and index.
Identifiers: LCCN 2016002710 | ISBN 9781138818453 (hardback) |
ISBN 9781138818477 (pbk.) | ISBN 9781315745237 (ebook)
Subjects: LCSH: Animals in the performing arts. | Human-animal relationships in the performing arts. | Animal welfare.
Classification: LCC PN1590.A54 C47 2016 | DDC 791.8--dc23
LC record available at http://lccn.loc.gov/2016002710

ISBN: 978-1-138-81845-3 (hbk)
ISBN: 978-1-138-81847-7 (pbk)
ISBN: 978-1-315-74523-7 (ebk)

Typeset in Sabon
by Saxon Graphics Ltd, Derby

For Mike, cat whisperer and paragon of animals

Contents

Figures

Preface

Tracking the Stage Lives of Animals

The title of this book pays homage to one of a pair of works that have accompanied and inspired me in my fifteen years of journeying between the field of Animal Studies and the arts of Theater and Performance. J.M. Coetzee's *The Lives of Animals* makes many appearances in the pages that follow, as does its unforgettable protagonist, Elizabeth Costello. An Australian novelist visiting a small American liberal arts college where she has been invited to give a lecture, conduct a seminar, and participate in a debate, Costello departs from convention by making her subject neither her writing nor herself—as is customary for novelists speaking in public—but rather the lives, and often horrific deaths, of animals. Her presentations are further dismaying to her academic audience in that they use the lingua franca of the academy—rational argumentation—to expose its own woeful limitations, and for the apparent simplicity—and hence apparent ill-placement—of her thesis: "open your heart."

I am not alone among women of my generation in feeling a sisterhood with "Elizabeth"—as we like to call her, marking both our affection for her as well as our willing suspension of disbelief in her fictionality. Elizabeth's vulnerability and resilience, her commitment to voicing harsh truths while also registering the personal costs of doing so, have made her a hero to many of those, like me, whose feminist politics eventually led us beyond the realm of the social, to a concern for lives beyond the human: the lives of animals, of course, but also the lives of other species, and even the fate of inanimate but vital earthly forces, like the climate. Those concerns are increasingly shared by many people, from many political and theoretical backgrounds, and addressing them has included recognizing how important, how complicated, and how challenging it really is for us—as individuals, groups, nations, and as a species—to truly respond to Elizabeth's injunction.

The essays in this book were written in the first decade and half of this new century, a century that began, for me and my fellow New Yorkers, with a trauma destined to launch not only countless analyses but also, as we now know, a new kind of endless conflict. In an article I wrote for the *Village Voice* a month after 9/11, I envisioned an expansive theatrical response to the catastrophe, indulging a utopianism that the scale of the event seemed to permit:

> The theater I dream of would invite our playwrights to look beyond the American horizon. It would encourage them to bring their insights and compassion [...] to the intersections between this culture and others, whether forced, or fortuitous, or fearsome. [...] This would then also be, automatically, an ecological theater, contesting our leaders' denials of the link between our lives and the deaths of species and ecosystems.

The title of that essay, "The Birds are on Fire," now links it, in my mind, not with utopian artistic programs but with the escalating violence to humans and other species that characterizes our times. The first—and most brilliant—theatrical treatment of this subject that I encountered was Caryl Churchill's *Far Away*, the second of the works that has guided and inspired my thinking about animals in performance. Though the play is the explicit topic of only one chapter here, the complex challenge it poses to anthropocentric ideology, and the way it ruptures dramatic form to pose that challenge, has made it my primary theoretical source—its brevity and fictionality notwithstanding. Not least of that play's values to me is that it contains the line (my favorite in all of world drama): "The cats have come in on the side of the French" (5). That such wild humor can erupt from a play of otherwise unrelieved desolation captures one of my abiding convictions about animals and animality: they are subjects that shift many of the established grounds of both artistic experience and knowledge production—affective, stylistic, disciplinary, and institutional. They uncover surprising spaces for feeling and thinking anew and askew.

The essays are presented here more or less in the form in which they were originally published. As such, they reflect the evolution of my concept of zooësis from its early focus on the figure of the animal to an increasing interest in the idea of species life, including the species life of human animals. This evolution has brought me—along with many other scholars—to a heightened awareness of an unprecedented challenge that species life faces in the present moment, in the age of climate chaos. The earlier essays (1 to 5, originally published between 2002 and 2007) engaged the question posed by Alan Read, "What might it mean to practise, think, and write theatre beyond the human?" The later essays (6 to 11, originally published between 2011 and 2016) respond to a changed question: How might we practice, think, and write theater—and make art—that is aligned with the turbulent planetary present, in which not only humans and other animals but also rivers, oceans, coastlines, topsoils, groundwater, forests, ice, air, and the atmosphere itself are in a state of constant crisis? Or, to put it in terms favored by the great eco-performer and feminist Rachel Rosenthal: How can art connect us to the Big Picture? In gathering together the essays—and a creative project—in which I've tried to engage with this question, I want to contribute a few brush strokes to the rich canvas of ecological hope that is unfolding all around us today.

Acknowledgments

I am proud to join—and I warmly thank—all those who dedicate their work to the health of our planet and that of the other animals we share it with. I have especially been grateful to, and inspired by, the creative, critical, and theoretical animal works of Ralph Acampora, Wendy Arons, Melissa Boyd, Jonathan Burt, Matthew Calarco, Marla Carlson, Meiling Cheng, Cynthia Chris, Caryl Churchill, Emilie Clarke, Jane Desmond, Kristin Dombek, Lori Gruen, Donna Haraway, Martin Harries, Holly Hughes, Dale Jamieson, Coin Jerolmack, Nina Katchadourian, Baz Kershaw, Michelle Lindenblatt, Susan McHugh, Kim Marra, Theresa May, Lourdes Orozco, Jennifer Parker-Starbuck, Michael Peterson, Anat Pick, Martin Puchner, Alan Read, Nicolas Ridout, Erika Rundle, Peta Tait, Deke Weaver, David Williams, and Cary Wolfe.

In addition to the dear friends and colleagues named above, I am deeply grateful to the following people for their intellectual comradeship and unfailing friendship over many years: Jacqueline Allen, Awam Amkpa, Bill Blake, Eliot Borenstein, Marvin Carlson, Mary Carruthers, Jessica Chalmers, Gabrielle Cody, Helen Cook, Catherine Coray, Patricia Crain, Prasenjit Duara, Deb Levine, Elinor Fuchs, Ernest Gilman, Claire Glietman, Benjamin Goldberg, Wendy Goldberg, Charles Grimes, John Guillory, Philip Harper, David Hoover, Julia Jarcho, Imad Khachan, Linda Lowell, Maureen McLane, Charles McNulty, Jane Malmo, Judy Miller, Veena Oldenburg, Peggy Phelan, Ruben Polendo, Mary Poovey, Marc Robinson, Amit Shah, Lytle Shaw, Alison Summers, Diana Taylor, Gauri Visvanathan, Bob Vorlicky, Hana Wirth-Nesher, and Ted Ziter.

I warmly thank my graduate assistants, John Lindstrom and Mercedes Trigos, for their careful and painstaking work on preparing the manuscript. Mercedes's steady and thoughtful presence made the final push almost enjoyable!

My treasured creative collaborators, Fritz Ertl, Steven Drukman, Shonni Enelow, Oliver Kelhammer, and Marina Zurkow have taught me more about animals, species, art, and performance—and, for that matter, about homo sapiens and life—than words can convey. To them, as well as to the extraordinary creative teams of Youth in Asia, the Animal Project, Queeraq, and the Ecocide Project, I offer lung-filled pant-hoots of thanks.

To my family and friends in India, I owe four decades of happy homecomings and continued belonging. Thank you forever Bella, Baby, Bobby, Alka, Harsh, Sher, Simi, Subu, Viraj, Sanam, Paully, and Renee.

For making my new country feel like home from the very beginning, I thank Peggy Estela, my conspecific.

For sharing their lair and their lives with me, and for all the mutual grooming over the years, I thank Mike, Natty, Sonu, and Cat. Nesting with them (to shift animal metaphors) has undoubtedly made me a better human.

Funding Acknowledgment

The author is grateful for a grant from the Abraham and Rebecca Stein Faculty Publication Fund of the Department of English, New York University.

Publishers' Acknowledgments

The publishers wish to thank the following for their permission to re-publish Una Chaudhuri's work in full or extracts.

1 "(De)Facing the Animals: Zooësis and Performance," *TDR/The Drama Review* 51 no. 1 (Spring 2007), pp. 8–20. © 2007 by New York University and the Massachusetts Institute of Technology.
2 "Animal Rites: Performing Beyond the Human," in *Critical Theory and Performance* (revised and enlarged edition), ed. Janelle G. Reinelt and Joseph R. Roach. Ann Arbor: University of Michigan Press (2007), pp. 506–20.
3 "Animal Geographies: Zooësis and the Space of Modern Drama," *Modern Drama* 46 no. 4 (Winter 2003), 646–62. Reprinted with permission of Toronto University Press. www. utpjournals.com. DOI 10.3138/md.46.4.646
4 "AWK!" Extremity, Animality and the Aesthetic of Awkwardness in Tennessee Williams's *The Gnädiges Fräulein*," in *The Undiscovered Country: The Later Plays of Tennessee Williams*, ed. Philip Kolin. New York: Peter Lang (2002), pp. 54–67.
5 "Zoo Stories: 'Boundary-Work' in Theatre History," in *Theorizing Practice: Redefining Theatre History*, ed. W.B. Worthen with Peter Holland. London: Palgrave Macmillan (2004), pp. 136–50.
6 "Becoming Rhinoceros: Therio-Theatricality as Problem and Promise." *The Routledge Human Animal Studies Handbook*, ed. Susan McHugh and Garry Marvin. Oxford: Routledge (2014), pp. 194–207.
7 "Bug Bytes: Insects, Information, and Interspecies Performance." Copyright © 2013 Johns Hopkins University Press. This article was first published in *Theatre Journal* 65 no. 3 (2013), pp. 321–34. Reprinted with permission of Johns Hopkins University Press.

8 "The Silence of the Polar Bears: Performing (Climate) Change in the Theatre of Species," in *Readings in Performance and Ecology*, ed. Wendy Arons and Theresa J. May. London: Palgrave Macmillan (2012), pp. 45–57.

9 "Queering the Green Man, Reframing the Garden: Marina Zurkow's *Mesocosm (Northumberland, UK)* and the Theatre of Species." *Scapegoat: Architecture/Landscape/Political Economy*, no. 02: *Materialism* (December 2011), pp. 6–8.

10 "Embattled Animals in a Theatre of Species," in *Performing Animality: Animals in Performance Practices*, ed. Lourdes Orozco and Jennifer Parker-Starbuck. London: Palgrave Macmillan (2015), pp. 135–49.

11 "Interspecies Diplomacy in Anthropocenic Waters: Performing an Ocean-Oriented Ontology," in *The Routledge Companion to the Environmental Humanities*, ed. Ursula Heise. Oxford: Routledge (2016).

Illustrations

The publishers thank all those credited in the figure captions for their permission to reproduce illustrations.

Introduction

Animals and Performance

> And of all nonsensical things, I keep thinking about the horse!
> Not the boy, but the horse, and what it might be trying to do.
> —Peter Shaffer, *Equus*

People in Animal Studies speak of the "laugh test," that moment when you inform someone that you, who are not a scientist but a humanist, are working on animals, and are met with an incredulous giggle or dismissive snort. For someone in the humanities to take animals seriously seems, as Shaffer's unhappy protagonist says, "nonsensical." As that play glosses the role of animality in psychoanalysis, to put the horse before the boy is to violate the anthropocentric grammar of the "normal." A similar assumption of animal irrelevance has characterized not only the humanities but also public culture, although in that sphere the assumption is comfortably camouflaged by such ubiquitous and unexamined "animal-loving" practices as pet-keeping, bird-watching, safari-going (for the wealthy), and (for the rest of us) the reverential watching of wildlife movies. In academia, the relegation of animal study to the sciences was so strictly enforced for so long that the advent of Animal Studies in the humanities and social sciences was prefigured as a joke, as Kathleen Kete delightfully reminds us: back in 1974, an article entitled "Household Pets and Urban Alienation" by one "Charles Phineas," spoofed the then-emerging trend in social history to attend to the history of everyday life. As Kete notes, the article narrowly preceded a host of publications that would soon establish the human–animal relation as an important topic and lens for the study of European social history. Not coincidentally, one of the books that the satirical article also narrowly preceded was Peter Singer's *Animal Liberation*, the book that launched the current phase of the historical animal rights movement.

Attempts to turn the animal lens on theater, and vice versa, are not so much mocked or resisted as they are constrained by a history of firmly fixed animal positions. Theater animals tend to congregate in two broad genres, children's performance and musicals, herded there by a tacit agreement with the cultural consensus that to take animals seriously is nonsensical. The inquiry represented by essays like the ones presented here, therefore, must acknowledge that history while refusing to observe its carefully maintained divisions. As Theater and Performance Studies join other disciplines in making what has been called "the animal turn" in contemporary thought, the animal energies released will surely reconfigure both the genres and the aesthetics that have produced the anthropocentric theater we have known so long, the theater which, as Nicholas Ridout says, "rigorously excludes nature" (98). Just as "Charles Phineas" was registering a development that he was also resisting, the theater animals of today reflect a history of segregation that they will also, I believe, inevitably reform.

Around the time I began thinking seriously about animals, a production of Stephen Sondheim and Nathan Lane's adaptation of Aristophanes' *The Frogs* was on stage at Lincoln Center. Watching those fabulous amphibians dancing on stage (in brilliant choreography by Susan Strohman), I mused on the long line of stage animals who have delighted audiences since theater began, momentarily distracting them from the antics of that most self-absorbed of animals, the human being. While *Cats* had by then ceded its appearance of immortality to *The Lion King*, the live camels, sheep and donkeys of the Christmas show at Radio City Music Hall marched on, part of a tradition that linked the Lincoln Center frogs to their originals in ancient Greece and, beyond them, to the sacrificial animals of the rituals from which Western theater itself arose.

The frogs whom Nathan Lane encountered on his journey to Hades had one striking feature: they were not only gorgeous to behold, but also unexpectedly naturalistic, even scientific. The brilliant colors and varied markings on their costumes seemed to be based on careful empirical observation and to celebrate the marvelous diversity of the real creatures they represented, who happened to be the subject of a special exhibit a few blocks away at New York's Museum of Natural History. Intentionally or not, the designer, William Ivey Long, had subtly departed from the long-standing practice of distorting the animal figure on stage—usually in the direction of cuteness and sentimentalism. These frogs were dazzling and entertaining, as stage frogs should be, but the inevitable anthropomorphism of the stage animal seemed to be tempered, in their case, by a powerful connection to actual animality, and so to the mystery of the non-human. The naturalistic elements of the frogs—conveyed mainly through their costumes but also in the choreography—opened a thematic link between the play's humans and animals, linking them in a frenzied encounter with death and drama.

Historically, of course, Western theater has not had much use for the *mystery* of the non-human. On those rare occasions that human-animals bring their non-human cousins on stage (in other than the two animal-permissive genres mentioned above), they tend to treat them as mirrors for themselves. Even the most powerful animal presences on stage have a hard time resisting the urge of their interpreters (whether spectators or playwrights, directors or critics, actors or dramaturgs) to recast them as symbols of human behavior and allegories for human preoccupations. So it is common to hear that Edward Albee's extraordinary animal play, *The Goat*, is "really" not about bestiality at all but about homosexuality, and Ionesco's classic play of animal-becomings has nothing whatsoever to do with rhinoceroses but is actually all about fascists. Similarly, Eugene O'Neill's hairy ape is "actually" the proletariat, and Peter Shaffer's *Equus* is "really" a pagan god, or the collective unconscious, or the return of the repressed. More generally, animality stands in for all that is repressed by culture, as exemplified by Harold Pinter's remark about the "menacing" quality of his plays: they are, he famously said, about "the weasel under the cocktail cabinet."

The animals who have shared the stage with human actors through the ages—usually only as verbal images and references (drama, like language itself, teems with animal imagery and simile), sometimes as costume, movement, and behavior, and, on rare occasions, in their own organic persons—have generally been taken for granted, no more attended to or specially considered than their countless offstage counterparts. From Aesop to Disney, talking animals have been used to delight and instruct, and the most satisfying lesson they teach is the tacit one of human superiority. They are a kind of language we use both to flatter ourselves as well as to denigrate our enemies. To call someone an animal is the easiest way to insult them (and then to justify mistreating them). At the same time, to fill children's books with suited, booted, and frilled talking animals is to suggest a gracious willingness on our part to tolerate—even to enjoy—these inferior beings. But no matter how quickly the animal presence is deflected by anthropocentric allegorizations, the passage from human to animal and back again is always thrilling, complicated, full of possibility. Shakespeare captured it in a single line: "Bless thee, Bottom! Thou art translated!" The human encounter with animality is both terrifying and exalting. For the actor who embodies it, like Bottom, or for the spectator who witnesses it, like Quince, it is like crossing into another culture, hearing a strange language, experiencing a frightening recognition that is at the same time a delicious bafflement.

The shared contingency of humans and animals has never been more evident than it is today. Not surprisingly, then, a growing group of artists, activists, and academics are responding to the urgent recognition of how much the future of our species and our planet depends on changing our attitudes to the non-human, and learning to live in what the philosopher David Abrams calls "the more-than-human world." In recent years, perhaps in response to the accelerating extinction of species, and certainly galvanized by the animal rights movement, cultural consciousness about animals has undergone a sea change. In painting, film, literature, photography, video, and theater, animals seem to be speaking back, rejecting their rhetorical exploitation, challenging us to think anew about them and about our relationship to them. Animal lives, they seem to be suggesting, are not as distant or unconnected to ours as we think—they are not, as the title of Caryl Churchill's disturbing animal drama puts it, so "far away." And they are not figments of our imaginations: they have independent existences and real lives as rich and valuable as our own.

Animal plays like Mark Medoff's *Prymate*, A.R. Gurney's *Sylvia*, Elizabeth Egloff's *The Swan*, Mabou Mines's *Animal Magnetism*, to name just a few, have provided rare opportunities for actors to explore and convey other ways of being, to answer, through performance, a version of the question now famous in Animal Studies, asked by American philosopher Thomas Nagel: "What is it like to be a bat?" Nagel's article opened up a discussion that holds much promise for theater makers—actors, playwrights, designers, directors—looking for larger frameworks within which to locate their explorations of human life. These plays challenge the unthinking anthropocentrism of drama and theater, and ground a growing art practice that thinks humanity beyond the human. This practice, writes Allan Smith, "seems so deeply the product of a vision in which the fates of humanity and animality coincide, that we are confronted not with a program but nothing less than a new creaturely imaginary" (156).

The "animal acts" I write about in the essays presented here are part of this "new creaturely imaginary," as is the field of Animal Studies which has inspired them. My own term for this phenomenon is *zooësis*, intended to refer broadly and comprehensively to the discourse of species in art, media, and culture. The term echoes both Platonic *poesis* and Aristotelian *mimesis*—both commonly used in literary and dramatic theory to designate modes of construction and representation—but is more directly inspired by *gynesis*, a term proposed in the 1970s by feminist theorist Alice Jardine to refer to "the putting into discourse of 'woman' [. . . and] the valorization of the feminine, woman, and her obligatory, that is, historical connotations, as somehow intrinsic to new and necessary modes of thinking, writing, speaking" (Jardine 25). Zooësis (from the Greek *zoion* = animal) refers to the ways the animal is put into discourse: constructed, represented, understood, and misunderstood. In proposing the term I also share Jardine's progressive ambition of contributing to new modes of thinking and writing that would valorize the animal and bring a heightened ethical attention to human–animal relationships.

The ubiquity of animals in theater, as in all the arts, is ripe for new theorizations. Jean-Marie Pradier puts it on a continuum with uses of animals as resources for clothing, shelter, and nourishment: "The presence of animals in the bodily practices of humans is inseparable from the teeming symbolic significations in countless myths, fables, poems, stories, and dramatic texts in which animals with human or superhuman attributes take the leading roles" (14). Steve Baker, following John Berger's seminal diagnosis of the disappearance of the real animal and the proliferation of the animal effigy in capitalist modernity, finds a "postmodern animal" coming into view by extricating itself from the symbolism and allegory of its modernist incarnation. Jonathan Burt proposes that attention be shifted from issues of animal death and considerations of sacrificial logics, which he regards as anachronistic, and be focused instead on modes of co-living among species, to arrive at "an aesthetic of livingness."

While Burt's thesis echoes zoontology's interest in animal life, it is animal death that has commanded the American stage in recent years. Animal carcasses played central roles in three important plays, edging the animal figure into dramatic theory and criticism. The first is Edward Albee's eponymous goat, its shocking appearance concluding the latest investigation, by a leading American playwright, of a subject of abiding interest to modern drama—namely, the possibility of modern tragedy. Albee's goat is linked implicitly, explicitly, and etymologically to the *tragoidia* ("goat song") of ancient Greece. By contrast, the second carcass, that of Mad Padraic's cat Wee Thomas in Martin McDonagh's *The Lieutenant of Inishmore*, is—its mangled, blood-soaked condition notwithstanding—a figure of pure farce, destroying all order around it yet itself cheating death. Finally, another animal cadaver on stage looms large and literal in Sam Shepard's *Kicking a Dead Horse*, an object of rueful comedy as well as an allegorical figure for the tragedy of America.

While all three of these animals serve largely to structure the human stories that dominate this most anthropocentric of the arts, each in its own way also participates in a dawning realization about the limits—and consequences—of humanist doctrines. By virtue of their sustained engagement with the animal,[1] the plays offer the kind of "interruptive encounter" that Matthew Calarco identifies as the proto-ethical foundation of Jacques Derrida's thinking about animals, that soul-shaking "exposure" that Cora Diamond describes as "a sense of astonishment and incomprehension that there should be beings so like us, so unlike us, so astonishingly capable of being companions of ours and so unfathomably distant" (Calarco 118; Diamond 61). And, in their renditions of the familiar yet mysterious terms of the human–animal relation, they contribute to one of the key programs of contemporary zooësis: to counter the tendency in Western philosophy, "since at least Plato's Cave, of seeking systematically to transcend or impugn the ordinary in existence" (Cavell 96).

A taxonomy of the animal in performance could pose, at one extreme, the actual, living animal (whether on stage or in extratheatrical cultural performance): individualized and "matrixed" animals, like Launce's Crab, the dog of Montargis, Mazeppa's "wild horse of Tartary," and Bartabas's Zingaro but also more generic visitors—the mouse who appears on stage unbidden, that stray fly on the upstage scrim.[2] At the other extreme would be the offstage animal—heard perhaps (Juliet's nightingale or Romeo's lark), but more frequently spoken of, described, loved, hated: the blinded horses of *Equus*, Jerry's dog in Albee's *Zoo Story*, the warring animals of Caryl Churchill's *Far Away*. Between these extremes lie innumerable representational possibilities: the actor in full animal costume and using realistic behavior, as in Shakespeare's *Winter's Tale* when Antigonus must "Exit, pursued by a bear" (3.3) or when Eugene O'Neill's Yank is locked in a deadly embrace with the hairy ape whose effigy has haunted him; the actor in animal mask or using other animal stylizations, including behavioral and vocal ones (e.g., the *Equus* chorus); the talking animal, as in countless children's plays; the human changed into animal (Bottom "translated" [*MND* 3.1.110–11]); the human in the process of transformation (e.g., Ionesco's *Rhinoceros*); the human as animal (e.g., Beckett's *Act without Words I*).[3] To step beyond the Western dramatic canon from which my examples are drawn and to include the popular, folk, and children's theatrical and dance forms of world culture, as well as the numerous performative dimensions of cultural animal practices (including activism, fashion, sports, and spectacle), is to recognize how immense a trove of material performance offers to Animal Studies for analysis.

The animal in performance can both reveal and obscure the animality *of* performance, its capacity for moving—animating—its participants, performers along with spectators. The dead horse in Shepard's latest play propels the living human who confronts it into a self-examination in which the contours of personality give way to those of ideology: the lone man begins to speak as the historicized people who have betrayed the land and its inhabitants (*Kicking*). On the surface, the protagonist's jeremiad rings familiar: a distinctly masculinist lament for the robust values and healthy pleasures of a mythic American past of freedom and natural living. Delivered as a monologue to a realistic animal form,[4] however, the rant begins to resonate beyond its clichés. As the speaker hurls himself at the huge dead weight in anger and frustration, the human figure diminishes in power yet somehow grows in stature (one feels this play should have been an opera, so constrained is its epic vision by its quasi-realist trappings, a Beckettian gloss notwithstanding). The animal he contends with activates in him an unexpected animality of his own, played out as a lively repertoire of voices, gestures, exertions, clowning, prop jokes, and pratfalls. The bland allegory of the basic situation is underlined by every violent kick delivered to the unyielding corpse, but it is also undermined by the literalness of the animal form and the force of the performer's animality. This is an "interruptive encounter" with a vengeance, and through it (as the actor who created the role puts it) "Shepard dismantles the imagery that distinguishes the previous body of his work" (Rea xi–xii).

Indeed, *Kicking a Dead Horse* offers vivid evidence of the animal's ability to dismantle moribund structures of thought and language. The dead horse here recalls and revises an earlier Shepard play, *True West*, in which a story of men and horses on the prairie served to ironize the myth evoked by the play's title.[5] Another, more naive and unironic version of that myth was also invoked in that play, by reference to its generic repository, the Hollywood Western. Lee, the lost-soul character of the play, recounts the part of *Lonely Are the Brave* in which a cowboy dies "from the death of his horse" (19). The circumstances of this telling (he's trying to impress a Hollywood producer) already inaugurate the ideological unraveling that concludes in *Kicking*, where the mythology of the Wild West runs aground in a harsh judgment on its role in American history.

Even more interesting than what the animal figure dismantles is what it brings into view: a dawning recognition of other histories, other relations. Because, as Donna Haraway writes, embodiment is always "ongoing, dynamic, situated and historical"; its life in performance not only reflects its cultural context but also may transform it, producing the new thinking that animates contemporary zooësis (2008: 249). In Shepard's play, the man pleads with the empty prairie to reveal the ghosts that centuries of violence must surely have left behind. Exchanging his cowboy paraphernalia for an Indian blanket, he unwittingly transforms himself into one of the ghosts he needs to see. While doing so, he slowly renounces the beloved and iconic accoutrements of horsemanship: saddle, bridle, spurs, cowboy hat. As he lovingly admires these fetishistic objects before ritualistically sacrificing them, a complex and lengthy shared history is acknowledged, one that reminds us how much we humans are, in Haraway's inspired formulation, a "companion species." As this rich history of the human–animal relation comes into view, the anthropocentrism of traditional performance comes to feel less compelling—even, perhaps, "nonsensical."

Notes

1 The shortest of the three plays is an hour long, the longest, double that. In all three, the animal dominates the stage picture, or the conversation, or both.
2 Michael Peterson has usefully applied the concept of matrixing (theorized by Michael Kirby) to animal performance (2007: 34). Launce's Crab is

that most famous of Elizabethan stage canines, from *The Two Gentlemen of Verona*. Dragon, the faithful hound who detected and arrested the murderer of his beloved master, was the hero of the most popular of the many nineteenth-century dog dramas, *The Dog of Montargis* (1814). In the title role of *Mazeppa*, a play adapted from a poem by Byron (itself adapted from a folktale), the American actress Adah Isaac Menken caused a sensation by being tied to a real horse while wearing only a short tunic and tights that made her legs look naked (Brooks 2006: 167). The story of the "mouse in the house" launches Nicholas Ridout's fascinating recent discussion of the animal on stage (2006: 96).

3 Beckett's play provides the focus for Martin Puchner's important theorization of a negative mimesis, which exposes the anthropocentric prejudices of literary and theatrical representations.

4 The scene description reads, "The dead horse should be as realistic as possible with no attempt to stylize or cartoon it in any way. In fact, it should be a dead horse" (8).

5 Lee, the vagabond brother in the play, forces his screenwriter brother, Austin, to type a screenplay he dictates to him. The story involves two men chasing each other across the prairie on horses. When Austin objects that "people don't conveniently have horses with them when they run out of gas! And they don't run out of gas either!" (22), Lee insists that they do in his "true-to-life Western" (19).

Works cited

Albee, E. (2000) *The Zoo Story*. London: Cape.

—— (2003) *The Goat, or Who Is Sylvia?* New York: Dramatists Play Service.

Baker, S. (2000) *The Postmodern Animal*. London: Reaktion.

Beckett, S. (1994) *Endgame* and *Act without Words*. New York: Grove.

Brooks, D.A. (2006) *Bodies in Dissent: Spectacular Performances of Race and Freedom, 1850–1910*. Durham: Duke UP.

Burt, J. (2008) "The Aesthetics of Livingness." *Antennae: The Journal of Nature in Visual Culture* 5: 4–11. Online.

Calarco, M. (2008) *Zoographies: The Question of the Animal from Heidegger to Derrida*. New York: Columbia UP.

Cavell, S. (2008) "Companionable Thinking" in S. Cavell et al., *Philosophy and Animal Life*. New York: Columbia UP, 91–126.

Churchill, C. (2001) *Far Away*. New York: Theatre Communications Group.

Coetzee, J.M. (1999) *The Lives of Animals*. Princeton: Princeton UP.

Derrida, J. (2008) *The Animal That Therefore I Am*, ed. Marie-Louise Mallet, trans. David Wills. New York: Fordham UP.

Diamond, C. (2008) "The Difficulty of Reality and the Difficulty of Philosophy." *Philosophy and Animal Life*. New York: Columbia UP, 43–90.

Haraway, D. (2003) *The Companion Species Manifesto: Dogs, People, and Significant Otherness*. Chicago: Prickly Paradigm.

—— (2008) *When Species Meet*, vol. 3. Minneapolis: U of Minnesota P.

Ionesco, E. (1960) *Rhinoceros*. New York: Grove.

Jardine, A.A. (1985) *Gynesis: Configurations of Woman and Modernity*. Ithaca, NY: Cornell UP.

Kete, Kathleen (2002) "Animals and Ideology: The Politics of Animal Protection in Europe" in *Representing Animals*, ed. Nigel Rothfels. Bloomington: Indiana UP.

McDonagh, M. (2003) *The Lieutenant of Inishmore*. New York: Dramatists Play Service.

O'Neill, E. (2008) *The Hairy Ape*. Studio City: Players.

Peterson, M. (2007) "The Animal Apparatus: From a Theory of Animal Acting to an Ethics of Animal Acts." *TDR/The Drama Review* 51, no. 1: 33–47.

Pradier, J.-M. (2000) "Animals, Angels, and Performance." *Performance Research* 5 no. 2: 11–22.

Puchner, M. (2007) "Performing the Open: Animals, Actors, Philosophy." *TDR/The Drama Review* 51, no. 1: 21–32.

Rea, S. (2008) Foreword to Shepard, S., *Kicking a Dead Horse*. New York: Vintage, ix–xii.

Read, A. (ed.) (2000) "On Animals," *Performance Research* 5, no. 2.

Ridout, N. (2006) *Stage Fright, Animals, and Other Theatrical Problems*. Cambridge: Cambridge UP.

Shaffer, P. (1977) *Equus*. New York: Penguin.

Shakespeare, W. (1997) Collected works in *The Riverside Shakespeare*, ed. G.B. Evans and J.J.M. Tobin. Boston: Houghton.

Shepard, S. (1981) *True West*. New York: French.

—— (2008) *Kicking a Dead Horse*. New York: Vintage.

Smith, A. (2007) "Bill Hammond's Parliament of Foules" in *Knowing Animals*, eds. L. Simmons and P. Armstrong. Brill.

Chapter 1

(De)Facing the Animals
Zooësis and Performance

Figure 1.1 Damien Hirst, *A Thousand Years*, 1990, steel, glass, flies, maggots, MDF, insect-o-cutor, cow's head, sugar, water, 83.9 x 168.1 x 83.9 in (213 x 427 x 213 cm) DHS1814. Installation view, Gagosian Gallery, London, June 2006.

How can an animal look you in the face? That will be one of our concerns.

(Jacques Derrida)[1]

Did your food have a face?
(People for the Ethical Treatment of Animals poster, 2001)

As my two epigraphs suggest, the burgeoning field of animal studies encompasses a vast cultural territory, ranging—contentiously[2]—from philosophy to activism, and including anthropology, sociology, history, psychology, art history, cinema, and literary studies. This special issue of *TDR* [*The Drama Review*, Spring 2007] extends an exploration, begun several years ago,[3] of the intersections of this new field with performance studies. In proposing the term "zooësis" to designate the activity at these intersections, I am conscious of indulging a neologistic impulse that has become a characteristic of animal studies; a symptom, perhaps, of its desire to intervene radically in established discourses and their terms of art. Coinages like "zoontologies" (Wolfe), "zoopolis" (Wolch), "petropolis" (Olson and Hulser), "carno-phallologocentrism" (Derrida 1991), even "zooanthropology" and "anthrozoology" run the gamut of disciplines and suggest a shared program of creative disciplinary disturbance.

To speak of zooësis is, at the very least, to index the history of animal representation that stretches, in the Western literary tradition, from Aesop's Fables to Will Self's *Great Apes* (1998); in the Western dramatic tradition, from Aristophanes' *The Frogs* (405 BCE) to Edward Albee's *The Goat, or Who Is Sylvia?* (2000); in film, from Eadweard Muybridge's "zoogyroscope" in 1879[4] to Werner Herzog's *Grizzly Man* (2005); in popular culture, from Mickey Mouse to the Animal Planet TV channel; and in popular performance from gladiatorial contests to the Las Vegas duo Siegfried and Roy. Beyond that, to speak of zooësis is to acknowledge the manifold performances engendered by such ubiquitous or isolated cultural animal practices as pet keeping, dog shows, equestrian displays, rodeos, bullfighting, animal sacrifice, scientific experimentation, species preservation, taxidermy, hunting, fur wearing, meat eating— each with its own archive and repertory, its own spatialities and temporalities, its own performers and spectators.[5]

The neologisms that frantically signal the need to "take animals seriously" reflect a new pressure on what an influential anthology calls "The Question of the Animal" (DeGrazia; Wolfe). The double meaning of this phrase is important for my understanding of zooësis: the question of the animal is raised in and by philosophy *for* us (with increasing contentiousness since Descartes's pronouncement that animals were nothing more than machines), but it is also a question put *to* us—individuals and disciplines—*by* animals, with increasing urgency as their disappearance from modern life and extinction from the planet accelerates beyond denial.

The ethical value and urgent need for an approach to animals that is imbued with the traits of performance—embodiment, presence, expressive encounters in shared time–space—is suggested by one of the contemporary classics of animal studies, J.M. Coetzee's *The Lives of Animals* (1999), a work that adds generic distortion to the disciplinary disturbances characteristic of this field. Having begun its life as the 1997/98 Tanner Lectures at Princeton, the novel thematizes and fictionalizes its origins: it is a narrative about two lectures delivered at an American college by Coetzee's intriguing creation, the novelist Elizabeth Costello. The first of these lectures is the subject of a chapter entitled "The Philosophers and the Animals"; the second one is entitled "The Poets and the Animals." The disciplinary trajectory thus encapsulated begins with an attempt to tackle "the question of the animal" with the instruments of reason— an attempt Costello deems necessary but that ultimately proves to be fruitless—and progresses to the effort to discover and enlist other faculties, notably the poetic imagination, in this endeavor.

The novel itself seems pessimistic about Costello's quest for a renewed relation between humans and animals: it ends on a note of exhaustion and disappointment, with the aging novelist reduced to tears, trembling in her grown son's arms. But while Elizabeth herself may feel tired and hopeless, one achievement of her effort is quietly recorded in the titles of the chapters and of the novel itself: the insistence on the plural form of all the key ideas—poets, philosophers, lives, animals—anticipates a crucial admonition in Jacques Derrida's exclamation upon the human arrogance of the use of the singular noun to refer to the myriad living beings and species with whom we share this planet: "The Animal," says Derrida, "what a word!" In this word Derrida locates the origins of logocentric humanism:

> *Animal* is a word that men have given themselves the right to give [...] at the same time according themselves, reserving for them, for humans, the right to the word, the name, the verb, the attribute, to a language of words, in short to the very things that the others in question would be deprived of, those that are corralled within the grand territory of the beasts: the Animal.
> (2002: 400)

In pluralizing the words in his title *The Lives of Animals*, Coetzee hands Costello a victory she herself despairs of: the plural marks her lectures as a step in the long journey it will take to face the consequences of the gigantic gap between our singular insensitivity to animals and the vast numbers of different species and individuals upon which that insensitivity has been wreaking havoc, now almost to the point of extinction.

Yet numbers do crop up regularly in contemporary discourse on animals: stunning, numbing numbers, often in a citational form I think of as "cows per hour, chickens per minute." Besides sheer quantities, discussion of contemporary animal practices uses statistics regarding proportions and distribution in ways that invariably mark this subject as one that lies well below the threshold of cultural awareness. For example, most people would be surprised to know that 98 percent of all animals with whom humans interact in any way, even including pets and zoo and circus animals, are farmed animals—that is, bred for human use (Wolfson and Sullivan 206). An amazing statistic indeed: not only does it tell us that we eat animals much more than we do anything else with them; it should also help us to recognize that the self-identification as animal lovers that we perform every day in our homes (and on Sundays when we drag the kids around the zoo) is part of a paper-thin but rock-hard veneer on an animalculture[6] of staggering violence and exploitation.

Whether approached with the tools of rationality or those of imagination—both of which Costello deploys—the lives of animals as currently configured generally resist meaningful cultural visitation on any significant scale. The search is therefore on, in the arts and the humanities, to identify new means of seeing, showing, and knowing the animals. The trajectory Costello follows is not just from philosophy to poetry but also from one kind of poetry to another. Contrasting two famous animal poems—Rainer Maria Rilke's "The Panther" (1902) and Ted Hughes's "The Jaguar" (1957)—she identifies embodiment as the principle of a potentially meaningful human–animal discourse. Unlike Rilke's panther, which is presented for our gaze, Hughes's jaguar, she says, is given to us as an organism, alive in muscle, breath, and sinew like our own, a living stage for human–animal encounters of a deeper kind. Costello's distinction between the seen animal and the somatically shared one provides an obvious invitation to performance and performance studies—with their emphasis on the body, on presence, and on shared experience— an invitation to join her quest for a reawakened animalculture.

That this invitation is also an opportunity for us to rethink certain key concepts of theater and performance is suggested in Albee's play *The Goat, or Who Is Sylvia?* Even before the published script of the play overdetermined the direction of critical analysis by featuring, on the title page, the parenthetical phrase, not quite a subtitle, "Notes toward a Definition of Tragedy," critics had begun to discuss the interplay of genres evoked in the title—tragedy, from the Greek word for goat, *tragos*, and pastoral comedy, evoked in the play's subtitle: "Who Is Sylvia?" which appears to quote Shakespeare's *The Two Gentlemen of Verona*. There is certainly no doubt that Albee is interested here, as he has been before, in the question of modern tragedy. Early in the play, a character says, "I hear a kind of ... rushing sound, like a ... wooooooosh! Or ... wings, or something." Martin, the protagonist, jokes: "It's probably the Eumenides." His more practical friend responds: "More like the dishwasher. There; it's stopped." "Then it probably wasn't the Eumenides," says Martin, "they don't stop" (22). It is one of many references to actual tragedies, ancient and modern, in the play, as well as to elements of tragic structure, including a hero at the pinnacle of his life, poised for a fall. In Martin's case this pinnacle is, like so much else in the play, literal as well as figurative, with the literal being insistently associated with animality. Twice in the play, Martin tells the story of his first encounter with Sylvia and describes driving up to the top of a hill. Both times his listeners interrupt to correct him: "crest" they say, meaning that that is the right term for the top of a hill (38). The second time the interruption is uncanny enough to make Martin ask, in bewilderment, "Who are you?" (38). The question has several answers: the one supplying the correct word is not just his well-spoken wife, it is also the playwright, aspiring to tragedy, and beyond that, the conventions of a dramatic genre in which disaster befalls the hero at the crest of his fortunes. The presence of the animal, however, destabilizes those conventions and subverts those intentions.

The Goat is the story of Martin and Stevie, a sophisticated, successful and happy Manhattan couple whose perfect life is shattered when Martin confesses to an unthinkable transgression, his love affair with the enchanting but unfortunately non-human Sylvia. In the play, Sylvia is initially experienced as a smell. This sensory challenge to the ocularocentric medium of theater acutely deploys Freud's sensory etiology of civilization, his account of the derogation of the "lower senses"[7] (touch and smell), and the privileging of sight in the human evolution from quadruped to biped, from rooting about in the dirt to scanning the skies. So incongruous is animal odor in the space of drama (and in the sanitized, deodorized dwelling of these classy New Yorkers), that it is almost immediately displaced, and Sylvia is quickly transformed into a preposterous joke. Those to whom Martin reveals the affair invariably respond, first, by failing what people in animal studies call "the laugh test"—that initial refusal to take the subject seriously at all. Martin's friend Ross is sure he's kidding when he shows him a photograph of the person he's having an affair with, and Stevie just roars with laughter at his confession. Later, Martin's relationship to Sylvia is firmly framed as perversion, complete with calls for therapy and support groups. Martin admits to having found such a group (online, of course!) and to having attended meetings and shared stories and twelve-step resolutions with other troubled animal "lovers." All these reactions to Sylvia teeter on the edge of wild hilarity, and much has already been written about Albee's astonishing feat in drawing genuine pity and fear from a subject that is referred to in the play, repeatedly and hilariously, as "goat-fucking."

This carnivalesque dimension of the play's rhetoric makes its concluding assault on the logic of tragedy all the more devastating. In the final moments of Albee's play, Stevie comes on stage, dragging behind her the slaughtered and bloody body of Sylvia. It is as shocking a stage image as the ending of Sam Shepard's masterpiece *Buried Child* (1978), when Tilden walks on stage holding the tiny, mud-covered corpse of the play's title. Like Shepard's image, this one uses literalization to exceed and expose the conventions of its putative and contested genre, modern tragedy. The actual buried child, like the actual slaughtered goat, poses a powerful threat to the self-consciously metaphoric edifice upon which modern tragedy depends. The abjected animal body intervenes in a system of equivalence that has been painstakingly established both within the play[8] and beyond it.[9] By putting the goat back in scapegoat, as it were, and by doing so in the context of a self-conscious exploration of tragedy, the play brings the animal into relationship with other key elements of the "definition of tragedy," including recognition. Aristotelian recognition, the kind that occurs late in the action, with or without reversal, is earnestly sought by the play's characters, who embark upon a sustained investigation worthy of Oedipus himself. That kind of clarifying recognition, however, is never achieved. Perhaps it has been displaced, from the outset, by another kind of recognition, played out, in a scene twice described (haltingly, with many interruptions) by Martin of his first encounter with Sylvia:

... and it was then that I saw her. Just ... looking at me [...] And
there she was, looking at me with those eyes. [...] It was ... it
wasn't like anything I'd felt before; it was so ... amazing, so
extraordinary! [...] I'd never seen such an expression. It was pure
... and trusting and ... and innocent; so ... so guileless. [...]
I went over to where she was—to the fence where she was, and
I knelt there, eye level ... and there was a ... a what!? ... an
understanding so intense, so natural ... [...] that I will never
forget, [...] And there was a connection there—a communication—
that, well ... an epiphany, I guess comes closest ... .

(42–43, 80–82)

This account stands in stark contrast to every other character's
attitude toward Sylvia in the rest of the play, where the fact of her
animal body utterly outstrips any interest in her face. No one shows
any willingness to join Martin in pondering the meaning of his
epiphany. In the play's dialectic of animal body and animal face,
the latter—the face, Sylvia's face, her eyes, her gaze, the look that
Martin believes they exchange—all this is almost entirely effaced by
her sexually forbidden body. And yet this moment in the narrative
indexes a special kind of knowledge, a non-Aristotelian recognition,
which lies at the heart of contemporary zooësis.

The experience Martin describes—the face-to-face encounter
with the animal—is, in fact, one that animal studies and animal
art invoke compulsively. It is even enshrined in the title of one of
the seminal texts of the discourse, John Berger's 1980 essay "Why
Look at Animals?" which initiated many key formulations of
animal studies: the animal as Other to be faced, the animal face as
inscrutable mask, the animal gaze as a window on to alternative
epistemologies, even ontologies. Before locating Albee's
recognition scene in relation to contemporary cultural modes of
"facing the animal," it is crucial to note the fate of modernity's
first sustained gaze upon the animal face. In 1872, Charles Darwin
published his extraordinary study, *The Expression of the Emotions
in Man and Animals*. The author being already well known and
highly respected, the book was an instant bestseller: nine thousand
copies sold in the first four months. Thereafter, however, not only
did sales fall off dramatically, but, in the words of the volume's
most recent editor, the book was "virtually forgotten for ninety
years" (qt. in Darwin, xxix). Among the five main factors Paul
Ekman identifies in trying to understand "how could this happen

to such an illustrious author, writing on an intriguing topic with such an enticing title?" is one that is particularly relevant to my inquiry here: in the eyes of modern science, says Ekman, Darwin's conviction that animals had emotions made him "guilty of the sin of anthropomorphism" (xxx). As Jeffrey Masson writes when he takes up Darwin's topic after a century-long hiatus, "So persistent are the forces that militate against even admitting the possibility of emotions in the lives of animals that the topic seems disreputable, even taboo" (1–2). Why do modern scientists actively blind themselves to a phenomenon that most lay people have no trouble accepting and that every pet owner would vigorously affirm: that animals have feelings like fear, anger, happiness, and sadness? The conversation that follows Costello's lectures reveals much of what is at stake for various individuals and disciplines in refusing Darwin's fundamental premise that emotions and their expression are not unique to humans. Not only does such refusal help to sanction practices like animal slaughter and experimentation, it also maintains the human–animal boundary that fuels what Giorgio Agamben calls the "anthropological machine" of Western philosophy (33).

More recently, the animal's face initiated one of contemporary philosophy's most searching explorations of animality, in an article that begins with what is surely one of the strangest scenes in philosophy—the philosopher in his bathroom, naked, watched by his cat:

> The animal [can] be looked at, no doubt, but also—something that philosophy perhaps forgets, *perhaps being this calculated forgetting itself*—it can look at me. It has its point of view regarding me. The point of view of the absolute other. And nothing will have ever done more to make me think through this absolute alterity of the neighbor than these moments when I see myself seen naked under the gaze of my cat.
> (Derrida 2002: 380)

Besides being an instance of the face-to-face encounter and look, Derrida's bathroom scene also involves one of modernity's most successful relationships with animals: the pet. Berger had identified the pet as one of the modern world's two major monuments to the vanishing animal (the other being the zoo creature). Anticipating Gilles Deleuze and Félix Guattari's notorious critique of the pet as the quintessential "oedipal animal," Berger locates the pet symptomatically, within a distinguishing feature of consumer societies, "that universal but personal withdrawal into the private small family unit, decorated or furnished with mementoes from the outside world," human-made replicas of nature that narcissistically reflect "their owners' way of life" (233, 14). From this perspective, to write about one's cat, as Derrida does, might be to participate in the anthropomorphizing tradition that runs from ancient beast fables to Donald Duck. But of course it is precisely as a potentially unassimilable Other that Derrida is interested in his cat—a radical Other sharing one's most intimate moments and spaces. Unlike the "animal familiars" cultivated by New Age neoshamanism, Derrida's cat belongs in a philosophical project of animal *de*-familiarization, of gradually discovering the contours of a vast and self-serving misrecognition of animals by humans.

A very different kind of animal recognition is prompted by a reference to the animal face in a famous PETA poster, which asks the question that gave me my second epigraph: "Did your food have a face?" The scene being initiated by this question stages an act of violent re-recognition, an attempt to force people to "face up" to some of the realities of the one animal practice that is more widespread in contemporary culture than pet keeping: meat eating. PETA's question is accompanied by an image that complicates the question of the animal Other as much as Derrida's cat does. The image is not of a face at all: it is of the head of a carcass, skinned and bloody. It is an image of a *missing* face, aptly representing the disappeared animal of the modern meat industry, which invests hugely in suppressing such images, and which systematically and literally keeps its operations, its vast animal factories, hidden—and keeps us, the consumers, in the dark.

The apparently simple rhetoric of the PETA poster gets more complicated when it is inserted into the field of contemporary zooësis. Reading it in relation to a work of art that it resembles closely—Damien Hirst's *A Thousand Years* (1990), which also features the severed head of a cow—opens another perspective on the complexities involved in facing the animal. In *A Thousand Years*, a rotting cow's head lies on one side of a glass partition; on the other side are maggots from which live flies hatch, then fly though a small hole in the glass partition to feast on the carcass. The side of the glass box that contains the severed head also has an ultraviolet insect electrocuting device, in which many of the flies are incinerated.

Figure 1.2 People for the Ethical Treatment of Animals poster, 2001.

Photo by Giuseppe Fassino; courtesy of PETA.

Like the PETA poster, *A Thousand Years* makes shock and revulsion one pole of a dialectic set off in the spectator. The other pole here, however, is not political action, but rather philosophical reflection. According to the Saatchi Gallery, where the work was displayed:

> *A Thousand Years* is a universe under scrutiny. Breeding a colony of flies from scratch, maggots can be watched feeding on a severed cow's head, turning into flies, only to have their miraculous metamorphosis prematurely terminated by their inevitable contact with the insect-o-cutor. Hirst's flies are a crude parody of the life-cycle of man—a cruel joke played out in microcosm.

The viewer who can endure the sight is being asked to face an allegory of life and death, a drama of chance and determinism.

Might one's participation in this scene eventually alter—even slightly—one's next experience of a summer backyard barbecue, burger in one hand and flyswatter in the other? Perhaps. But Hirst's intention is quite different than—maybe even the opposite of— PETA's: it is to restore our lost relationship to our own carnality, to our fleshly being in a material world. His use of the animal head is similar, it seems to me, to an idea reported by Andre Gregory in *My Dinner with Andre* (1981), about returning the real to performance:

> When I was a young director, and I directed *The Bacchae* at Yale [in 1969], *my* impulse, when Pentheus has been killed by his mother and the Furies, and you know, [...] they rip him to shreds and I guess cut off his head—*my* impulse was that the thing to do was to get a head from the New Haven morgue and pass it around the audience. I wanted Agave to bring on a real head and that the head should be passed around the audience so that people somehow realize this stuff was real, see. (qt. in Shawn and Gregory 84).

For Gregory as for Hirst, the putrefying head is a way to face both our mortality and all the devices through which we deny it. Hirst is, we might say, animalizing humans, reminding them, as his fellow British artist Francis Bacon once put it, that "we are meat, we are potential carcasses" (qt. in Sylvester 23).[10] If the post-Enlightenment subject is constructed through a distancing from his animality, the process Slavoj Žižek calls "desubstantialization," animal art like Hirst's and Bacon's belongs in a posthumanist program of *re*-substantialization, a task the posthumanist philosopher John Gray calls "*removing* the masks from our animal faces" (Žižek 81; Gray 38, emphasis added).

PETA, on the other hand, is in the business of *humanizing* animals, although for a very different purpose from that of the anthropomorphizing tradition regularly decried in animal studies. In seeking to give our food a face, PETA is cleverly deploying the protocols of identity politics, the politics of visibility and representation. In the introduction to her book *About Face*, Dorinne Kondo writes:

> Face is our primary external, bodily locus of identity, as David Henry Hwang's farce of mistaken racial identities, *Face Value*, suggests. For him, face as skin colour literally masks a more genuine and vulnerable self. In its more liberatory senses, face signifies the construction of new, contestatory identities by

people on the margins, as exemplified in Gloria Anzaldua's anthology, *Haciendo Caras/Making Face, Making Soul* (1990).

(25)

To give animals a face, as PETA tries to do, would seem to be to give them what Descartes denied them, a soul, a place in our moral universe, and the opportunity to be seen and known as our fellows. One great obstacle to this project, however, becomes clear in the conclusion of the passage from Kondo quoted above:

> Those of us on the margins are trying to "write our faces" with the tools at our disposal: theatre, design, cultural production, political organizing, academic writing. Our faces, in turn, can speak back to Orientalist hegemonies.
>
> (25)

Unlike others "on the margins," animals cannot "speak back"—to humanist hegemonies or to anything else. To make them speak is not to write their faces; it is usually to write ours, to indulge that anthropomorphic reflex that is all too often rooted in an anthropocentric outlook.

In the sense that the animal cannot write its face (and in this sense only), the animal can be characterized as faceless. Could this facelessness also be understood, more positively, as a freedom from what Deleuze and Guattari call "faciality," their word for the reductive individuality of modernity's enforced conformities? The face, for Deleuze and Guattari, is a deadening social mask imposed on the modern subject: It "can cover the whole body, indeed the whole world; it is a grid, a diagram, a binary machine, and is in its very nature despotic; it takes the human animal and makes it Man; it takes the lover and makes her Citizen; it takes the animal and makes it bestial" (176).[11] The animal is free of faciality, immersed in the very condition that makes the animal so threatening to individualistic humanism: its multiplicity, its membership in a herd or pack in which individuals are not readily distinguishable. This is the multiplicity so brilliantly and paranoically evoked in Eugène Ionesco's *Rhinoceros* (1958), perhaps the paradigmatic antianimal work in modern drama, where the indistinguishability of one animal from another is the occasion for a derogation as easily accepted as the one based on their notorious lack of language. Another characteristic routinely used to denigrate animals is appearance. It is not surprising to find that the "beauty myth" has been enlisted in speciesism as much as it has in sexism and racism. One of the great moments of unintended irony in dramatic animal representation is the spectacle of the Elephant Man, face and head shrouded, insisting—illogically but all-too-comprehensibly: "I am not an animal. I am a human being" (Lynch 1980). His disavowal of his animality bespeaks his investment in faciality and its rigid aesthetic. In a chapter entitled "Faces Unlike Ours," nature writer David Quammen suggests that it would be by learning to look—really look, eye-to-eye—at so-called "repulsive" animals that we might begin to engage the fundamental question of "how human beings should behave towards the members of other living species" (3).

The face-to-face relation is central to the thinking of Emmanuel Levinas, whose insistence that alterity is fundamental to the ethical relationship appears to promise the project of animal ethics a way beyond the impasse between the Kantian and utilitarian models.[12] Levinas's narrative about a poignant animal encounter has attracted a lot of attention in animal studies (see Clark 1997; Steeves 2005; and Wolfe 2003). Writing about the dog who befriended him and his fellow inmates in a concentration camp, and whom they named Bobby, Levinas says that this dog was "the last Kantian in Nazi Germany," because his joyful greetings reminded the prisoners of their human dignity (50). Yet, when questioned closely about the ethical status of non-human animals, Levinas is reluctant to ascribe to animals that "ethical face" which he elsewhere has called (as Martin calls Sylvia's face) "an epiphany." By contrast, says Levinas, the animal face is merely "biological," incapable of demanding the ethical response (57–58). Levinas denies that the dog can have a face in the ethical sense: "the phenomenon of the face is not in its purest form in the dog," he writes. "I cannot say at what moment you have the right to be called 'face.' The human face is completely different and only afterwards do we discover the face of the animal" (49). In an article subtitled "Levinas Faces the Animal," Peter Steeves, with gentle irony, stages another face-to-face encounter between Levinas and Bobby, asking the philosopher: "What could Bobby be missing? Is his snout too pointy to constitute a face? Is his nose too wet? Do his ears hang low, do they wobble to and fro? How can this not be a face?" (24).

A pro-animal zooësis faces the following dilemma: How to perform the animal *out of* facelessness (a political necessity that organizations like PETA have responded to with hundreds of images of appealing—in both senses of the word—animal faces) without burdening it with an oppressive and necessarily anthropomorphic faciality. Or: How to face the animal Other without either defacing it (as when it starts singing "I wanna walk like you, talk like you") or entirely effacing it. This was the challenge that Costello tried to meet by journeying from philosophy to poetry and from one kind of poetry to another. Albee's *The Goat* stages another trajectory, related to Costello's but also in some ways its inverse: from animal face to animal body, from the face-to-face encounter and exchange of looks to the violent reduction of the animal to the condition of pure physiology. However, unlike the carcasses in the work of Hirst and Bacon, which seek to animalize the human, the animal body at the end of Albee's play seems to animalize the animal, a maneuver made necessary by its endless figural transformations, not least in this play itself.

The urgent dialectic of the animal face and the animal body gets something of a definitive statement in *The Goat* during a particularly bizarre section of the conversation between Martin and his outraged wife Stevie on the subject of the gender of the goat he is involved with. When Martin insists it is female, like Stevie herself, she is further outraged by this strange compliment, "So long as it's female, eh? So long as it's got a cunt it's all right with you!" Martin roars: "A SOUL!! Don't you know the difference!? Not a cunt, a soul!" When Stevie whimpers, "You can't fuck a soul," Martin roars triumphantly: "No, and it isn't about fucking" (86). Martin's insistence that his bond with Sylvia is more than physical returns us to their recognition scene and to the animal face, to that exchange of looks across what Berger has so memorably called "the narrow abyss of non-comprehension" between human and non-human animals (5).

The role of the animal—its face, body, being, meaning—in the constitution and defacing of performance genres is a vast project, to which these comments are the sketchiest preface. To finish the sketch, I turn now to two animal moments from another brilliant dramatic meditation on genre, Derek Walcott's metatheatrical comedy *Pantomime* (1980). Set in the postcolonial Caribbean, *Pantomime* stages a day in the life of an English hotel owner, Harry Trewe, and his native servant, Jackson, as they struggle over the form and content of some "Night Entertainment" with which Harry hopes to attract visitors to his establishment (98). Harry has chosen *Robinson Crusoe* as the subject of the play within the play; needless to say, the two men bring vastly different perspectives to bear on this most Eurocentric of myths, as well as on the genres available to them, which Jackson refers to, at one point, as "codemy" and "tradegy" (152) (the literary tradition defaced, as it were). For the Englishman, the story is an occasion for romantic self-dramatization. A speech he has written goes as follows:

> O silent sea, o wondrous sunset that I've gazed on ten thousand times, who will rescue me from this complete desolation? … Adam in paradise had his woman to share his loneliness, but I miss the voice of even one consoling creature, the touch of a hand, the look of kind eyes. […] Even Job had his family. But I am alone, alone, I am all alone.
>
> (142– 5)

Jackson, the Caribbean servant, listens to the speech and comments: "Touching. Very sad. But something missing. […] The goats. You leave out the goats" (145–46). He then proceeds to act out, in excruciating pantomimic detail, Crusoe's encounter with the animal, which covers the same path as Albee's goat, from the exchanged gaze to the violated body of the animal:

> He not sitting on his shipwrecked arse bawling out […] "O silent sea, O wondrous sunset," and all that shit. No. He shipwrecked. He desperate, he hungry. He look up and he see this fucking goat with its forked fucking beard and square yellow eye just like the fucking devil, standing up there … (*Pantomimes the goat and Crusoe in turn*) smiling at him, and putting out its tongue and letting go one fucking *bleeeeeh*! And Robbie ent thinking 'bout his wife and son and O silent sea O wondrous sunset; no, Robbie is the First True Creole, so he watching the goat with his eyes narrow, narrow, and he say: "*Blehhh*, eh? You muther-fucker, I go show you *blehhh* in your goat ass, and vam, vam, next thing is Robbie and the goat, *mano a mano*, man to man, man to goat, goat to man, wrestling in the sand, and the next thing we know we hearing one last faint, feeble, *bleeeeeeeeeehhhhhhhhhhhhhhhh*, and Robbie is next seen walking up the beach with a goatskin hat and a goatskin umbrella, feeling like a million dollars.
>
> (148)

If Albee puts the goat back in scapegoat, exposing the sacrificial logic of humanism, Walcott's "First True Creole" puts the goat, one might say, back in goat curry, and celebrates the animal as provisioner, resource, and raw material—not sacrificed to fantasies of human exceptionalism and transcendence but engaged within a struggle for survival, yielding understanding, respect, and gratitude.

Jackson's unsentimental celebration of Crusoe's mastery of his world through mastery of the animal body is contrasted with Trewe's reaction to an animal killing by Jackson himself. Throughout the play, Jackson has complained about the hotel's resident parrot, who, he says, taunts him with racist epithets. Harry merrily denies the allegation, saying that the parrot is not insulting Jackson but only repeating the name of a former owner of the hotel, a German named Heinigger! When Jackson finally wrings the parrot's neck and throws its body into the ocean, Harry's anger leads him to make the following exceedingly unusual insult:

> You people create nothing. You imitate everything. It's all been done before, you see, Jackson. The parrot. Think that's something? It's from *The Seagull*. It's from *Miss Julie*. You can't ever be original, boy.
>
> (156)

He might have added, it's from *The Wild Duck*, it's from *Trifles*—birds drop like flies in modern drama. But the curse of unoriginality is upon Harry Trewe more than it is on Jackson: he is the one who compulsively reproduces Crusoe as the figure of a lonely humanism, unable to see and hear the animality in which he participates. Jackson, by contrast, seems to want to listen to the animal, take its measure, and respond to it as a being rather than a symbol. He has, in these two moments, faced the animal. The blood on his hands, like the blood on Stevie's dress at the end of Albee's play, stains the pristine surface of a desubstantialized humanism and its enabling genres.

Notes

1 Derrida 2002: 377.
2 Richard Kahn gives a lucid account of the fundamental ideological split—between political advocacy and postmodern cultural studies, between activism and ideological analysis—that became painfully apparent during the now notorious "Representing Animals" conference (Kahn calls it "a minor scandal") that was held at the Center for 20th-Century Studies at the University of Wisconsin–Milwaukee in 2000.
3 *Performance Research* vol. 5 no. 2 was an issue "On Animals," guest edited by Alan Read (2000).

4 The importance of animals in the development of early film technique has been documented by Jonathan Burt and compellingly theorized by Akira Lippit.

5 A number of these practices have been the subject of studies that pay attention to their performative aspects: pet keeping (Kete 1994), hunting (Marvin 2000), spectacle (Davis 1997; Desmond 1999), rodeos (Lawrence 1990), taxidermy (Desmond 2002), and zoos (Malamud 1998; Mullan and Marvin 1999; Hanson 2002; Rothfels 2002).

6 I derive the term animalcultures from Donna Haraway's inspired term "naturecultures" (2003), itself derived on analogy with the ubiquitous "technoculture."

7 Freud 1961.

8 For an excellent discussion of the play's dense intertextuality, see Kuhn 2004.

9 The printed *Playbill* to the Broadway production of the play included an insert in the form of a faux newspaper named the *Goat Gazette*, in which the goat was explicitly related to the scapegoat and characterized as "symboliz[ing] the powers of procreation, the life force, the libido, and fertility" (2002). This gave the audience a convenient—and in my view, regrettable—handle for grasping the animal presence; regrettable because it handed them, as it were, the wrong end of goat—its metaphoric end, etymologically and mythologically certified.

10 In an analysis of the role of animality and meat in Francis Bacon's art, Deleuze observes that Bacon "pursues a very peculiar project as a portrait painter: to dismantle the face" (2005: 19).

11 Alphonso Lingis's Deleuzian account of the face also makes the connection to animality: "The face extends down the whole length of the body [...] Everything animal in the body must be covered up, with clothing that extends the face, the blank surfaces of the business suit and the tailored two-piece suit of the career woman [...]" (2003: 180).

12 An excellent discussion of these positions is provided by Donald Turner, who identifies Levinas's idea of the face as being particularly helpful in formulating an alternative to a foundational assumption shared by Immanuel Kant and Jeremy Bentham: that for another being to qualify for direct ethical consideration, it is both necessary and sufficient to identify some essential aspect of similarity between the other being and the deliberating self (2003: 19).

Works cited

Agamben, G. (2004) *The Open: Man and Animal*, trans. Kevin Attell. Stanford: Stanford UP.

Albee, E. (2003) *The Goat, or Who Is Sylvia?* Woodstock: The Overlook Press.

Berger, J. (1991) *About Looking* [1980]. New York: Vintage Books.

Burt, J. (2000) *Animals in Film*. London: Reaktion Books.

Chaudhuri, U. (2003) "Animal Geographies: Zooësis and the Space of Modern Drama." *Modern Drama* 46, no. 4: 646–62.

Clark, D. (1997) "'The Last Kantian in Nazi Germany': Dwelling with Animals after Levinas," in J. Ham and M. Senior, *Animal Acts: Configuring the Human in Western History.* London: Routledge, 165–98.

Coetzee, J.M. (1999) *The Lives of Animals.* Princeton: Princeton UP.

Darwin, C. (1998) *The Expression of the Emotions in Man and Animals* [1872], introduction, afterword, and commentaries by Paul Ekman. New York: Oxford UP.

Davis, S. (1997) *Spectacular Nature: Corporate Culture and the Sea World Experience.* Berkeley: U of California P.

DeGrazia, D. (1996) *Taking Animals Seriously: Mental Life and Moral Status.* Cambridge: Cambridge UP.

Deleuze, G. (2005) *Francis Bacon: The Logic of Sensation*, trans. and with an introduction by D.W. Smith. Minneapolis: Minnesota UP.

Deleuze, G. and Guattari, F. (1987) *A Thousand Plateaus: Capitalism and Schizophrenia*, trans. and foreword by B. Massumi. Minneapolis: U of Minnesota P.

Derrida, J. (1991) "'Eating Well' or the Calculation of the Subject," in E. Cadava, P. Connor, and J.-L. Nancy (eds), *Who Comes After the Subject?* New York: Routledge, 96–119.

—— (2002) "The Animal That Therefore I Am (More to Follow)." *Critical Inquiry* 28, no. 2: 369–418.

Desmond, J. (1999) *Staging Tourism: Bodies on Display from Waikiki to Sea World.* Chicago: U of Chicago P.

—— (2002) "Displaying Death, Animating Life: Changing Fictions of 'Liveness' from Taxidermy to Animatronics," in N. Rothfels, *Representing Animals.* Bloomington: Indiana UP, 157–79.

Freud, Sigmund (1961) *Civilization and its Discontents*, trans. J. Strachey. New York: W.W. Norton.

Gray, J. (2002) *Straw Dogs: Thoughts on Humans and Other Animals.* London: Granta Books.

Hanson, E. (2002) *Animal Attractions: Nature on Display in American Zoos.* Princeton: Princeton UP.

Haraway, D. (2003) *The Companion Species Manifesto: Dogs, People, and Significant Otherness.* Chicago: Prickly Paradigm P.

Kahn, R. (2005) "Is That Ivory in That Tower? Representing the Field of Animal Studies." *H-Nilas, H-Net Reviews*, February. Online.

Kete, K. (1994) *The Beast in the Boudoir: Petkeeping in Nineteenth-Century Paris.* Berkeley: U of California P.

Kondo, D. (1997) *About Face: Performing Race in Fashion and Theatre.* London: Routledge.

Kuhn, J. (2004) "Getting Albee's Goat: 'Notes toward a Definition of Tragedy.'" *American Drama* 13 no. 2: 1–32.

Lawrence, E.A. (1990) "Rodeo Horses: the Wild and the Tame," in R. Willis (ed.) *Signifying Animals.* London: Unwin Hyman, 222–38.

Levinas, E. (1988) "The Paradox of Morality: An Interview with Emmanuel Levinas," trans. A. Benjamin and T. Wright, in R. Bernasconi and D. Wood *The Provocation of Levinas: Rethinking the Other*. London: Routledge, 168–80.

Lingis, A. (2003) "Animal Bodies, Inhuman Faces," in C. Wolfe *Zoontologies: The Question of the Animal*. Minneapolis: U of Minnesota P, 165–82.

Lippit, A.M. (2000) *The Electric Animal: Toward a Rhetoric of Wildlife*. Minneapolis: U of Minnesota P.

Lynch, D. (1980) *The Elephant Man*, film in black and white, 124 minutes, screenplay by C. De Vore, E. Bergren, and D. Lynch, produced by J. Sanger. Hollywood: Paramount Pictures.

Malamud, R. (1998) *Reading Zoos: Representations of Animals and Captivity*. New York: New York UP.

Marvin, G. (2000) "Natural Instincts and Cultural Passions: Transformations and Performances in Foxhunting," in "On Animals," ed. A. Read, *Performance Research* 5 no. 2: 108–15.

Masson, J.M. and McCarthy, S. (1995) *When Elephants Weep: The Emotional Lives of Animals*. New York: Delacorte P.

Mullan, B. and Marvin, G. (1999) *Zoo Culture* [1987], 2nd edn. Urbana: U of Illinois P.

Olson, R.J. and Hulser, K. (2003) "Petropolis: A Social History of Urban Animal Companions." *Visual Studies* 18 no. 2: 133–43.

Quammen, D. (1988) *The Flight of the Iguana*. New York: Touchstone.

Read, Alan (2000) "Editorial: On Animals," in "On Animals," ed. A. Read, *Performance Research* 5 no. 2: iii–iv.

Rothfels, N. (2002) *Savages and Beasts: The Birth of the Modern Zoo*. Baltimore: Johns Hopkins UP.

Self, W. (1997) *Great Apes*. London: Bloomsbury.

Shawn, W. and Gregory, A. (1981) *My Dinner with Andre*. New York: Grove Press.

Steeves, H.P. (2005) "Lost Dog, or, Levinas Faces the Animal," in M.S. Pollock and C. Rainwater *Figuring Animals: Essays on Animal Images in Art, Literature, Philosophy, and Popular Culture*. New York: Palgrave Macmillan, 21–35.

Sylvester, D. (1987) *The Brutality of Fact: Interviews with Francis Bacon, 1962–1979*, 3rd edn. New York: Thames and Hudson.

Turner, D. (2003) "Altruism Across Species Boundaries: Kant and Levinas on the Meaning of Human Uniqueness," paper presented at the Metanexus Conference. June. Philadelphia, PA.

Walcott, D. (1980) *Remembrance and Pantomime*. New York: Farrar, Strauss and Giroux.

Wolch, J. (1998) "Zoöpolis," in J. Wolch and J. Emel (eds) *Animal Geographies: Place, Politics, and Identity in the Nature–Culture Borderlands*. London: Verso, 119–38.

Wolfe, Cary (ed.) (2003) *Zoontologies: The Question of the Animal.* Minneapolis: U of Minnesota P.

Wolfson, D. and Sullivan, M. (2004) "Foxes in the Hen House: Animals, Agribusiness, and the Law: A Modern American Fable," in C.R. Sunstein and M.C. Nussbaum (eds) *Animal Rights: Current Debates and New Directions.* New York: Oxford UP, 205–33.

Žižek, S. (1992) *Enjoy Your Symptom!: Jacques Lacan in Hollywood and Out.* New York: Routledge.

Chapter 2

Animal Rites
Performing Beyond the Human

The dividing line between nations may well be invisible; but it is no less real. How does one cross that line to travel in the nation of animals? Having traveled in their nation, where lies your allegiance? What do you become?

(Sy Montgomery)[1]

The animal is the sign of all that is taken not-very-seriously in contemporary culture: the sign of that which doesn't really matter.

(Steven Baker)[2]

Caryl Churchill's play *Far Away* takes the final of its many disorienting turns when a character blandly declares, "The cats have come in on the side of the French" (35). The concluding scene of the play is a shocking elaboration of the possibility this line contains: the possibility that the politics of division and aggression that have defined human history for so long will finally infect the non-human world as well. In the world that results, animals enter into alliances with human groups, themselves now bizarrely divided along postnational lines: "Portuguese car salesmen. Russian swimmers. Thai butchers. Latvian dentists" (36–37). Conflict has become the defining feature of society, the rule rather than the exception. New reasons for hatred and new opportunities for alliance abound: "Mallards are not a good waterbird. They commit rape, and they're on the side of the elephants and the Koreans. But crocodiles are always in the wrong" (39). In *Far Away*, Shakespeare's "universal wolf" seems to be on the prowl. All creation partakes of division, discord, and violence. Even the weather "is on the side of the Japanese," and "we are burning the grass that wouldn't serve" (43).

Churchill's extraordinary vision of an ecocidal free-for-all, in which nature is violently divided within itself as well as against a violently divided humanity, has more than a general ecological background. In the years immediately preceding its appearance, Britain experienced an ecological and epidemiological disaster of unprecedented proportions. From 1996 onward, the discovery of BSE (bovine spongiform encephalopathy, popularly known as "mad cow disease") in British cattle caused a national crisis that was also, in a sense, a crisis of nationalism, of national identity. The three-year-long European ban on British beef hurt more than the British economy: given the symbolic status of beef in the construction of English identity, national pride was deeply wounded as well. And when four million cows had to be destroyed, it was not just confidence in Britain's scientific and agricultural institutions that was shaken: the image of the idyllic English countryside, so deeply inscribed in the mythology of British imperialism, suffered a traumatic blow as well.

Among the thousands of articles and opinions that the BSE crisis elicited, two strike me as particularly generative for ecocritical inquiry. That both are from unexpected sources, European philosophers George Steiner and Jean Baudrillard,[3] simply illustrates the fact that ecocriticism is a matter of new disciplinary alliances and fertile cross-theorizings. In a BBC interview, Steiner suggested that instead of destroying the infected cattle far from public view (as was being done), they be "sacrificed" in huge pyres by the side of main roads and major highways, where people could experience, firsthand, what was after all an entirely man-made disaster, a result of the practice of feeding meat by-products to cattle. The hideously unnatural process that had turned herbivores not only into meat-eaters but cannibals[4] might be ritually—that is performatively—acknowledged by the spectacle of the burning carcasses. As Alan Bleakley puts it, Steiner's proposal suggested that our health—our physical, psychological, and ecological health—may depend on supplementing our current notions of animal rights with an understanding and practice of animal *rites*.

My subject in this essay is animal representation and performance as reconceived within postmodernism and ecology. Postmodernism comes to the animal as it does to other categories that have been "backgrounded"[5] by, or altogether excluded from, the dominant discourses of humanism. It comes to the animal as it has previously come to the lunatic, the child, the freak, the woman, and the deviant, seeing these as contentiously oppositional categories rather than as reliably and innocently descriptive ones. Beyond that, and in a more positive vein, postmodernism comes to the animal "as a reminder of the limits of human understanding, and also of the value of working *at those limits*" (Baker 2000: 16). The emerging figure of this exploration, which Steven Baker has dubbed "the postmodern animal," is the cultural product of a post-Cartesian, ecological, and neototemistic[6] worldview that rejects dualist thought and oppositional taxonomies in favor of models that emphasize complexity and dynamism.

Postmodernism comes to the animal as to a figure capable of inspiring and guiding a new journey—a postmodern shamanism, if you like, across the ideological borders within which modernism has kept the human separate from its many "Others." While traditional shamans undertook their spirit travels in the company of animal "familiars," postmodern travelers favor odd and ungainly beasts, with strange— and strangely powerful—forms. I invite one such "animal unfamiliar" along on my journey here: Emily Mayer's *Corvus corium* (fig. 2.1).

Figure 2.1 Emily Mayer, *Corvus corium*, 1995, leather, steel, wood, rubber. 117 x 76 x 44 cm (HxWxD).

Courtesy of the artist.

This imposing yet oddly melancholic creature articulates—quite literally so—the fundamental principle of animal rites: the *interpenetration* of human and non-human animals. Using man-made objects—rusty pipes, an old boot, parts of a leather saddle, petrified wood—Mayer creates an organic form that both acknowledges and exceeds its cultural resources. *Corvus* encapsulates the difficult yet essential double relation (a relation also captured in the term *human animal*) that is at the heart of ecopolitics and must guide the project of animal rites. Such rites would be, then, the enactment of the vision that the sculpture embodies, the vision of a reciprocal animality, binding us to "the creatures among whom we move and in whom we have our being as they do in us" (Wheeler 5).

From the point of view of performance, the idea of a reciprocal animality operating within and around human experience has received its most intriguing formulation in French philosopher Gilles Deleuze's notion of "becoming-animal." One of many transformative "de-territorializations" of fixed identity that Deleuze proposes, this "becoming" is conceived as a process that is performative and transactional without being in any way mimetic. It is not a matter (as Deleuze says in a famous example) of imitating a dog, but something much more fluid, aleatory, creative, temporary, and fleeting:

> Not imitating the dog, but putting together its organism with *something other*, so that from the composite whole particles will be emitted that are canine... . It goes without saying that this something other can vary a great deal and can be more or less tied to the animal in question: it can be the animal's natural diet (the earth and the worm), it can be its outer relations with other animals (one becomes a dog in the midst of cats, or a monkey with a horse), it can be a machine or a prosthesis that the human straps about the animal (a muzzle, reins, etc.), it can be something that really has nothing to do with the animal in question.
>
> (274)

This Deleuzian becoming-animal offers a framework for theorizing animal rites, beginning with Churchill's bizarre animal act, where the divisions among the animals themselves, as well as between animals and humans, require something that goes beyond a traditional dialectics of "self" and "other." By virtue of its emphasis on change and dynamics, Deleuze's model of becoming-animal also goes beyond the important psychoanalytical recognition that in all human–animal encounters, invariably, "deep identifications and violent denegations are acted out" (Ham and Senior 2). Using terms like "surfaces," "molecular swarms," "folds," and "convections" (borrowed from "the idioms of chemistry, of Lucretian philosophy, of biology, and Leibnizian monadology"),[7] this model for performing the encounter with alterity suggests a rethinking of encounter itself, as an event involving not whole entities but rather *facets* or *zones* of various identities. The bizarre divisions and unlikely alliances of *Far Away* are an apt image for this notion of an encounter that is simultaneously fragmenting and conjoining, simultaneously creating and destroying unities, simultaneously producing continuity and separation.

The notion of "animal rites," of a new form of ritual performance that would engage with, diagnose, and heal the historically complex relationship between humans and other animals would be one answer to the question posed in an issue of *Performance Research* focusing on animals: "What might it mean to practise, think and write theatre beyond the human?" (Read iii). Animals are a conduit into those "excluded sites" from which, according to the emergent discourse of posthumanism, the definition of humanness is carved.[8] But animals, surprisingly, have not been the main focus of recent explorations beyond the borders of the human: machines have. That exemplary figure of posthumanism, the cyborg, seems a little more kin to us than do the living creatures with whom we share both a long history and an inconveniently essentializing biology. Perhaps it is not so surprising, after all, that the cyborg is preferred over the animal. Unlike the animal, whom popular misreadings of evolutionary theory have coded as hopelessly atavistic, the human–machine hybrid is cheerfully forward-looking: "The cyborg has no origin story in the Western sense … [It] would not recognize the Garden of Eden; it is not made of mud and cannot dream of returning to dust" (Haraway 68). Unfettered by originary nostalgias, the human–machine offers new fields of play for identity, new liberations from old discursive formations. The animal, on the other hand, tiresomely reminds us of a nature that we have quite lost the taste for.

When, how, and why we came by our current aversion to nature have been subjects of foundational interest to contemporary ecology, generating numerous eco-etiologies that function as lightning rods for the inherently complex and controversial nature of the issue.[9] From a performance studies perspective, perhaps the most provocative such formulation is the ironic one offered a century ago in J.-K. Huysmans's novel *À rebours* (translated as *Against Nature*). Huysmans's hero holds the following proto-Baudrillardian view of our alienation from nature:

> Nature, he used to say, has had her day; she has finally and utterly exhausted the patience of sensitive observers by the revolting uniformity of her landscapes and skyscapes. After all, what platitudinous limitations she imposes, like a tradesman specializing in a single line of business; what petty-minded restrictions, like a shopkeeper stocking one article to the exclusion of all others; what a monotonous store of meadows and trees, what a commonplace display of mountains and seas!
>
> In fact, there is not a single one of her inventions, deemed so subtle and sublime, that human ingenuity cannot manufacture; no moonlit Forest of Fontainebleau that cannot be reproduced by stage scenery under floodlighting; no cascade that cannot be imitated to perfection by hydraulic engineering; no rock that *papier-mâché* cannot counterfeit; no flower that carefully chosen taffeta and delicately colored paper cannot match!
>
> (11–12)

According to this ironic formulation, the roots of our ecological crisis lie in mimesis, particularly the literalistic mimesis upon which the modern theater's most successful aesthetic—realism—rests. As technologies of artificial replication and reproduction generate ever more seductive and spectacular sound- and color-saturated versions of reality, nature itself recedes into a drab, inexpressive, and uninteresting silence.

Ironic though it may be in Huysmans's original, the idea of ecological malaise as a pathology of mimesis sustains a model of ecoperformance as revelation, exposure, and disclosure. The impulse of this model is to pull back the curtain of artifice behind which nature has been shrouded, to break the "vast, eerie silence which surrounds our garrulous human subjectivity" (Mannes 16). Rachel Rosenthal's 1984 performance piece *The Others* is an ambitious example of this model of ecoperformance; much about it, not least the fact that it includes forty-two animals, would seem to qualify it as a promising (and rare) example of animal rites.

Before turning to it, however, I want to invoke another perspective on animals, one that vastly complicates the powerful fantasy of an art that would "speak for" nature, that would give voice to the suffering of animals.

Jean Baudrillard reacted to the BSE crisis with a trope even more surprising than Steiner's: he spoke of *revenge*. Calling the disease "an act of terrorism through the virus," he suggested that the cows were reacting to a history of abuse, to having been "exploited, dismantled, and damaged." This shocking idea—so like Churchill's shocking characterization of animals in *Far Away*—took one long step beyond Baudrillard's earlier discussion of the discursive role of animals in modernism. The exclusive ascription of reason to human beings, Baudrillard had previously argued, was bought at the cost of an active dehumanization of the animal: "animals were demoted to the status of inhumanity as reason and humanism progressed" (133). Characterizing modernity as a betrayal of "the divine and sacred nobility" that all previous ages conferred on animals, Baudrillard had (in one of his most original and important moves) singled out animals as the only category of "Other" that modernity has not succeeded in rendering discursive. The fundamental fact about animals, says Baudrillard, the fact that finally accounts for our boundless cruelty toward them, is that they *do not speak*. All other "Others" have capitulated to the discursive imperative of modernity:

> The mad, once mute, today are heard by everyone; one has found the grid on which to collect their once absurd and indecipherable messages. Children speak, to the adult universe they are no longer those simultaneously strange and insignificant beings—children signify, they have become significant—not through some sort of liberation of their speech, but because adult reason has given itself the most subtle means to avert the threat of their silence. The primitives also are heard, one seeks them out, one listens to them, they are no longer beasts.
> (129–41)

For ecoperformance, Baudrillard's crucial insight is that the silence of the animals dooms them to a paradoxically vociferous fate: since they will not speak, they are ceaselessly spoken, cast into a variety of discursive registers, endlessly troped. While rationalism turned them into "beasts of burden," and "beasts of consumption," humanism followed up by making them also "beasts of somatization," forced to carry emotional and psychological identities wholly invented by—and projected onto them by—people. As literary symbols and metaphors, as pets, as performers, as signifiers of the wild, as purveyors of wisdom, in fables, in fairy tales, in nature films, in zoos, in circuses, at fairs, rodeos, fox hunts, dog shows, the animals are forced to perform *us*, to ceaselessly serenade us with our own fantasies.[10] "I wanna walk like you, talk like you ..."

In the face of such discursive and ideological closure, how might an ecoperformative project of animal rites proceed? Petroleum, Brecht famously observed, "resists the five-act form," claiming that "today's catastrophes" called for new dramatic structures (30). The catastrophe this time is not economic but ecological, and the formal challenge is not merely one of replacing linear forms with cyclical ones, but of finding forms that might help to reconfigure the current relation between the human and the non-human. Rosenthal's performance piece *The Others* and Churchill's *Far Away* do this in different ways, the former theorizing its project amply and explicitly, the latter employing a modernist minimalism to decidedly postmodern effect. Both share a commitment to articulating the relations among animals, both human and others, in all its difficulty, necessity, horror, and beauty. Like Mayer's *Corvus*, which literally articulates its animal form out of man-made objects, the animal rites of Churchill and Rosenthal variously evoke the mutual implication of human and non-human animals, and characterize their relation as a matter of deep structure, delicate linkages, and complicated connections.

Although the texts of *The Others* and *Far Away* were published within a year of each other, they are not contemporaneous works. *The Others* was created and performed in the early 1980s. It predates *Far Away* by almost two decades, a period of time during which the discourse on animals has grown well beyond the passionate didacticism of the early animal rights movement and, like ecology as a whole, gained in theoretical sophistication through increasing dialogues with philosophy, politics, and cultural studies. This sophistication registers, for example, in the ironic (if not hilarious) horrors described in *Far Away*: "[Deer] burst out of parks and storm down from mountains and terrorize shopping malls ... the fawns get under the feet of shoppers and send them crashing down escalators, the young bucks charge the plate glass windows" (39–40). The self-conscious unsentimentality toward animals in the world of the play is directly lampooned as a side effect of a pathology of representation now so widely recognized as to have its own name: "Disneyfication."

Harper: Take deer.
Todd: You mean sweet little bambis?
Harper: You mean that ironically?
Todd: I mean it sarcastically ... I know to hate deer (39–40).

Todd's reference to that most iconic and paradigmatic of Disney's neotenized animals, Bambi, marks the self-conscious distance between this play and the anthropomorphic and infantilizing mass-cultural discourse on animals ("just like us, only cuter"). Churchill's strategy of animal representation in *Far Away* proceeds from the recognition that the trivializing of the animal in contemporary culture may be harder to combat than overt hatred would be. The play rigorously desentimentalizes animals, even at the risk of feeding the human sense of distance and disregard that has brought so many animals to the brink of extinction.

The risks of *Far Away* become clearer in comparison with the thoroughly unironic, earnest, proanimal discourse of *The Others*. The publication of this piece almost twenty years after it was created attests to the prophetic nature of Rachel Rosenthal's performance art, which consistently tackled issues of ecology long before they were taken up in the other arts.[11] Like many of Rosenthal's works, *The Others* is a lesson on its subject matter as well as a powerfully expressive and moving performance. The piece illustrates both the considerable reach as well as the instructive limitations of the model of ecoperformance as an "un-muting" of the suppressed non-human; indeed it may be that *The Others* is best read as a metacritical inquiry into the possibility and problematics of animal rites: the sheer scope of the piece points to an experimental "trying out" of various strategies. In formal terms as well as in substance and subject, *The Others* is encyclopedic. Every medium and every channel of performance, every element of the theatrical apparatus is pressed into service to deliver a mountain of information and an ocean of feeling on the subject of animals. Using dialogue, monologue, song, music, dance, movement, slides, voice-overs, video, physical movement, stage architecture, technological devices and—yes—forty-two live animals, Rosenthal embarks upon an epic missionary performance on behalf of animals.[12] The range of discourses she manages to incorporate makes the work a solid introduction to the major tenets of the animal rights movement.[13]

Figure 2.2 Rachel Rosenthal, *The Others*, December 1984, Japan America Theater, Los Angeles.

Photo by Basia Kenton.

Early in her piece Rosenthal invokes Descartes, identifying (as many thinkers do) his notorious denigration of animals as one source of present horrors. Cartesian rationalism is, of course, a standard villain of ecological thought, as are its medieval and Renaissance precursors. The locus classicus of the religious betrayal of the natural world is the Genesis story of man's "dominion" over the animals (Rosenthal quotes Milan Kundera's famous remark that "of course Genesis was written by a man, not a horse").[14] The tradition of Christian exegesis further supported this betrayal, as in this often-cited lesson of St. Augustine's: "Christ himself shows that to refrain from the killing of animals and the destroying of plants is the height of superstition, for judging that there are no common rights between us and the beasts and trees, he sent devils into the herd of swine and with a curse withered the tree on which he found no fruit" (qt. in Passmore 29).

The Renaissance achieved a more systematic debasement of animals by means of conceptual hierarchies like the *scala naturae* and the Great Chain of Being, as revealed, for example, in the derogatory animal imagery of Shakespeare's plays.[15] All these discourses and many others lie behind the reality that Rosenthal presents, the horrifying images of animals being tortured in the name of science and consumerism, the appalling statistics of the slaughter of animals for meat, for fur, even for entertainment (fig. 2.2).

As the screen behind her relentlessly presents this terrible "data," Rosenthal creates action-image sequences by bringing the factual material into relation with highly expressive performance, including dance, chanting, screaming, and violent physical movement and struggle. This is one way that she actively destabilizes the simple project of "giving voice" to "the others." Here is one of the several speeches that contain the seeds of that initial project:

> I scream for the broken spirit. I scream for isolation unto madness. I scream for the paw caught in the jaw that only death can loosen. I scream for the jail barely larger than the body. I scream for the hissing skin under the brand, I scream for the eye that burns but cannot close.
>
> (95)

During this speech, a complex stage image develops around Rosenthal and comments on her utterance: she speaks from within the orchestra pit, which is rigged to move up and down, so that she seems to be sinking as she speaks. She has been pushed into the pit and is forcibly kept there by three masked men who hold her down and make bland Cartesian proclamations: "1. Only man is rational. 2. Only man possesses language," and so on. The whole action is watched by a group of people accompanied by animals. Behind all of them—Rosenthal, the masked men, the moving orchestra pit, the animals, their companions—loom the projected images of lab animals in steel contraptions, rabbits in traps, cattle being branded, and so on. This action sequence is followed by others, equally complex, creating a rigorous scenic discourse in which the logic of animal rights is contextualized within and countered by memories of sadism, justifications for cruelty, and elaborate renditions of the "all too human" excuses for inhumanity: "I'm not a sadist for chrissakes, I'm not a bad person! I've got mouths to feed. It's nature! They're animals, don't you see?" (99)

Don't you see? That is the fundamental logic of *The Others*: by whatever means possible, the piece concerns itself "with seeing that which it is not permitted to see, and with getting others to see it" (Baker 1993: 218). *The Others* locates its "animal rites" project on the slippery ground between speaking for animals and recognizing the extent to which they have always been misspoken:

I was content to let sleeping dogs (toot) lie. But along came this cocksman (toot). He was as wolf (toot) in sheep's (toot) clothing. He seemed real looney (toot) about me, and for a while we were lovebirds (toot) and had a whale (toot) of a time. He was a tiger (toot). Woke up my pussy (toot), and although he looked like a fat pig (toot), I lost weight and no longer felt like an old cow (toot). I was proud as a peacock (toot) and looked so foxy (toot).

(96)

In spite of its encyclopedic form and authoritative tone, *The Others* is ultimately an experiment, an attempt to discover a performance protocol that is complicit neither with the nature-aversive hypermimeticism of modern culture nor with the humanist assumptions that have brought it to the ecological brink. For all her commitment and desire, Rosenthal does not—cannot—speak for the animals. In attempting to do so, however, she gives powerful and honest voice to *their* "others," the human animals who so resent them, and the reasons for that resentment:

How dare they be beyond morality? ... Beyond theology? ... Beyond the arduous apprenticeship of good and bad? Beyond the fretful reconciliation of opposites? What, no history? Who gave them permission to be whole? We see in them who we once were. And we deny them, like immigrants who reject the language of their origin. We dress them in people's clothes and force them to imitate people's ways so that, by this caricature, we may laugh at them and better measure the distance that, we hope, separates us from them.

(106)

Animals are the victims, then, of an enforced dualistic ideology of distance and separation, in which "animal" has become the definitional opposite of "human," instead of its larger context. As such, animals have been forced to play a part in the construction of those biologisms and racisms that have naturalized and justified ethnic cleansing from Auschwitz to Bosnia and beyond.[16]

From its title onward, Churchill's *Far Away* challenges the ideology of distance by interrupting the main ideological and rhetorical protocols of animal representation. Her inclusion of animals *alongside* (rather than *instead of*) human beings in the making of apocalypse is unprecedented. It is a departure from the two major traditions of literary "animalizing," each of which is thoroughly rooted in an anthropocentric mimesis. Churchill's animal representation resembles neither the anthropomorphism of animal fables and Disney films nor the theriomorphism of Orwell's *Animal Farm*, Kafka's *Metamorphosis*, or Ionesco's *Rhinoceros*. Churchill's animals are not pawns in a game of human symbolization, nor are they made to stand for an undifferentiated realm of wildness, a definitional opposite to the human. Side by side instead of subordinated to human beings, the animals of *Far Away* invite us to imaginatively inhabit a world of animal agency, and thereby to explore the politics of a new mixed relation of proximity to—yet autonomy from—human beings. Their apparent presence as autonomous agents in the world of the play,[17] and, further, the striking politicization of their agency locates *Far Away* at a decisive distance from the exclusively human world given by modernism.

From the perspective of Baudrillard's insight that in modernism "animals must be made to say that they are not animals," the animals of *Far Away* are remarkably self-nominating (129). They may do unusual things, but they do these things *as animals*, not as human stand-ins. Nor, like most other nonmetaphorized animals (such as the animals in circuses, zoos, bullfights, rodeos), is their behavior intended primarily to prove something flattering about human beings.[18] Rather, they act *along with* yet *independently of*, human beings. It is this dual relation—a relation of both continuity and separation—that constitutes Churchill's major insight and contribution to an ecologically informed, postmodern, and postnational politics. This politics, articulated through the play's final act—its "animal act," as it were—explains and illuminates the mysterious events of the earlier acts, giving them a significance different from the absurdist one that their content might otherwise suggest.

The first two acts of *Far Away* present an insidious dystopia, a Kafkaesque world of a deep structural brutality shrouded in performances of normalcy. Act 1 begins as an innocent conversation, in which a woman seems to want to reassure her young niece, Joan, who is staying with her and having trouble sleeping. "It's the strange bed," she suggests. The girl demurs, and begins to question the older woman about certain inexplicable things she has witnessed from her bedroom window. As the Aunt offers and then retracts a series of increasingly disturbing explanations, a frightening reality emerges. Gradually, our perception of the scene changes from cozy cottage to hostile outpost where truckloads of people arrive secretly, are imprisoned, beaten, and then carted off to an uncertain fate.

In the next act, an older Joan is at work as a hatmaker, as innocuous a profession as can be imagined. But as Joan converses with her co-worker Todd, it slowly emerges that the hats they are making—each unique, handmade, and wildly elaborate—are intended for a terrible purpose: to be worn by prisoners on a kind of "death parade" whose nature and meaning remains obscure. Some hats, we learn, are singled out as especially artistic and honored by being preserved in a museum. The others, shockingly, are "burned with the bodies" (31). Most shocking of all is the characters' conversation: they worry and complain about their working conditions, showing no concern for the barbarity to which they are contributing.

In the early critical reaction to *Far Away*, Kafka was immediately invoked, as were Pinter and Hitchcock. The sense of mystery and menace that pervades the play's first two acts suggests an affinity with mid-century modernist dramas of alienation, stories of the "little man" lost in the vast machinery of the corrupt state. The politics of that drama, because of its exclusive focus on the individual, are largely irrelevant to ecoperformance. By following the "absurdist" first two acts of her play with an "animal act," in which animal equality and agency are imaginatively realized and taken for granted, leaving the human protagonists bewildered and powerless, Churchill reveals the complicity of those dramas of alienation in the dualistic, distanced, and ecologically disastrous ideologies of modernism.

The animal act of *Far Away* is a multiplicitous and potential-filled event in the Deleuzian sense. It is a whole-scale imaginative "becoming-animal" that unleashes untold opportunities for interface and exchange with multiple alterities. By drawing the spectator or reader into a world where animals are no longer mute subordinates, the play raises the fundamental question of animal rites: "How might one interact with another whose difference is recognized as an active event, rather than a failure of plenitude?" (Williams 29). The first answer to that question, *Far Away* suggests, is to abrogate the sentimentalities that mask our disdain for animals. Instead of "fluffy little darling waterbirds," mallards who "commit rape" (38–39). Or, to return to the visionary animal art of Emily Mayer: instead of Mickey Mouse ears, a "rat hat" (fig. 2.3).

Figure 2.3 Emily Mayer, *Rathat*, 2001.

Courtesy of the artist.

On the far side[19] of this vision of animality as a continuum that both includes and exceeds human identity, lies a posthumanist politics of mutuality and respect. There too, far away though it may be, lie animal rites worthy of human performance.

Notes

1 Montgomery 1991: 267.
2 Baker 1993: 174.
3 Quoted in Alan Bleakley, *The Animalizing Imagination* (2000). Bleakley cites Steiner's BBC interview (page 11) and Baudrillard's *Libération* article, "The Revenge of the Cows" (page 10).
4 It is believed that the cattle's immune systems were weakened because they were fed animal protein. Bleakley quotes a newspaper article that asked: "Why did we start feeding animals to animals?" adding: "more specifically, why did we feed animal protein to herbivores?" (4).
5 In her important contextualization of ecology within the philosophical tradition of dualism, Val Plumwood introduces and defines this term as follows: "Backgrounding is a complex feature which results from irresoluble conflicts that the relation of domination creates for the master, for he attempts both to make use of the other, organizing,

relying on and benefiting from the other's services, and to deny the dependency which this creates." Plumwood 1993: 48.

6 "The sense of interconnectedness between nature and culture, between human and animal, social and religious institutions, which Victorian anthropology saw as a fascinating error of primitive man, a view that Lévi-Strauss in turn dismissed as an erroneous misreading of primitive protoscience, has been rehabilitated in Western scholarly thought as an accurate reflection of existential reality: in this view humankind is part of nature and everything in the universe is connected with everything else, or so the physicists assure us. Western culture, it seems, is now in a phase that might be called neototemistic." Willis 1990: introduction, 6.

7 Conley 1997: 52.

8 "The construction of the human is a differential operation that produces the more and less 'human,' the inhuman, the humanly unthinkable. These excluded sites come to bound the 'human' as its constituted outside, and to haunt those boundaries as the persistent possibility of their disruption and rearticulation." Butler 1993: 8.

9 One of the best known and most controversial of these is Lynn White, Jr.'s "The Historical Roots of Our Ecological Crisis," in *Science*, March 10, 1967: 1203–7.

10 Cultural studies writings on animals include Susan Davis, *Spectacular Nature: Corporate Culture and Sea World* (1997); Elizabeth A. Lawrence, "Rodeo Horses: The Wild and the Tame" (1990), 222–35; Gary Marvin, "Natural Instincts and Cultural Passions: Transformations and Performances in Foxhunting" (2000), 108–15; Margaret J. King, "The Audience in the Wilderness: The Disney Nature Films" (1996), 60–68; S. Baker, *Picturing the Beast: Animals, Identity, and Representation* (1993).

11 See Rosenthal 2001.

12 Part of the mission was specific, immediate, and successful: many of the animals featured in the performances were taken from local shelters and were put up for adoption to the audiences of the shows. All were adopted.

13 A prefatory note to the published script recognizes, as the major sources of the play's data, two classics of the animal rights movement, Peter Singer's *Animal Liberation* (1975), and Tom Regan's *The Case for Animal Rights* (1983).

14 Rosenthal, *The Others*, in *Performance Research* (2000), 94. Subsequent citations are given in the text.

15 Most of the more than four thousand allusions to animals in Shakespeare's plays are used to express "sensuality, stupidity, or cruelty." Yoder 1947: 62.

16 There is now a long tradition of thought linking animal abuse with the Holocaust. Among the most quoted formulations are Theodor Adorno's "Auschwitz begins wherever someone looks at a slaughterhouse and thinks: they're only animals," and Isaac Bashevis Singer's chilling phrase "eternal Treblinka" ("In relation to animals, all people are Nazis; for the animals it is an eternal Treblinka." (I.B. Singer, "The Letter Writer", 2004: 750.) See also David Clark, "The Last Kantian in Nazi Germany," 1997: 165–98.

17 The mysterious form of the play leaves open the possibility that the
description of the animals' actions is a fantasy on the part of the human
speakers, or a code, or some other counterfactual discourse.
18 For an illuminating account of how an animal act serves to bolster egoistic
cultural accounts of human beings, see Lawrence, "Rodeo Horses" (1990).
19 The pun is intended. Cartoonist Gary Larson's *Far Side* commentaries on
our relationship to animals are close in spirit to Churchill's vision in *Far
Away*. See Charles D. Minahen, "Humanimals and Antihumans in Gary
Larson's Gallery of the Absurd," in Ham and Senior, *Animal Acts*, 231–51.

Works cited

Baker, S. (1993) *Picturing the Beast: Animals, Identity, and Representation.*
Manchester: Manchester UP.

—— (2000) *The Postmodern Animal.* London: Reaktion.

Baudrillard, J. (1994) *Simulacra and Simulation*, trans. S.F. Glaser. Ann
Arbor: U of Michigan P.

Bleakley, A. (2000) *The Animalizing Imagination.* London: Macmillan.

Brecht, B. (1978) *Brecht on Theatre: The Development of an Aesthetic*, ed.
and trans. J. Willett. New York: Hill and Wang.

Butler, J. (1993) *Bodies That Matter: On the Discursive Limits of "Sex."*
New York: Routledge.

Chaudhuri, U. (2002) "'AWK!': Extremity, Animality, and the Aesthetic of
Awkwardness in Tennessee Williams's *The Gnädiges Fräulein*," in P.
Kolin (ed.) *The Undiscovered Country: The Later Plays of Tennessee
Williams.* New York: Peter Lang.

Churchill, C. (2001) *Far Away.* New York: Theatre Communications Group.

Clark, D. (1997) "The Last Kantian in Nazi Germany: Dwelling with
Animals after Levinas," in J. Ham and M. Senior (eds) *Animal Acts:
Configuring the Human in Western History.* London: Routledge.

Conley, T. (1997) "Pantagruel-Animal," in J. Ham and M. Senior (eds.)
Animal Acts: Configuring the Human in Western History. London:
Routledge, 34–60.

Davis, S. (1997) *Spectacular Nature: Corporate Culture and Sea World.*
Berkeley and Los Angeles: U of California P.

Ham, J. and Senior, M. (eds) (1997) *Animal Acts: Configuring the Human
in Western History.* London: Routledge.

Haraway, D. (1985) "A Cyborg Manifesto: Science, Technology, and Socialist
Feminism in the Late Twentieth Century." *Socialist Review* 80: 65–108.

Huysmans, J.-K. (2003) *Against Nature* [*À Rebours* 1998], trans. R.
Baldick. London: Penguin.

King, M.J. (1996) "The Audience in the Wilderness: The Disney Nature
Films." *Journal of Popular Film and Television* 24: 60–68.

Lawrence, E.A. (1990) "Rodeo Horses: The Wild and the Tame," in R.
Willis (ed.) *Signifying Animals.* London: Unwin Hyman, 222–35.

Mannes, C. (1996) "Nature and Silence," in C. Glotfelty and H. Fromm (eds) *The Ecocriticism Reader: Landmarks in Literary Ecology*. Athens, GA: U of Georgia P.

Marvin, G. (2000) "Natural Instincts and Cultural Passions: Transformations and Performances in Foxhunting." *Performance Research* 5 no. 2: 108–15.

Minahen, C.D. (1997) "Humanimals and Antihumans in Gary Larson's *Gallery of the Absurd*," in J. Ham and M. Senior (eds) *Animal Acts: Configuring the Human in Western History*. London: Routledge, 231–51.

Montgomery, S. (1991) *Walking with the Great Apes: Jane Goodall, Dian Fossey, Biruté Galdikas*. Boston: Houghton Mifflin.

Passmore, J. (1971) *Man's Responsibility for Nature*. London: Duckworth.

Plumwood, V. (1993) *Feminism and the Mastery of Nature*. London: Routledge.

Read, A. (2000) "Editorial: On Animals," in *Performance Research* 5 no. 2: iii-iv.

Regan, T. (1983) *The Case for Animal Rights*. Berkeley and Los Angeles: U of California P.

Rosenthal, R. (2000) *The Others*, in *Performance Research* 5 no. 2: 92–107.

—— (2001) *Rachel's Brain and Other Storms: The Performance Scripts of Rachel Rosenthal*, with introduction and commentaries by U. Chaudhuri. London: Continuum.

Singer, I.B. (2004) *Collected Stories: "Gimpel the Fool" to "The Letter Writer."* New York: Library of America.

Singer, P. (1975) *Animal Liberation*. New York: New York Review/ Random House.

Wheeler, W. (1999) *A New Modernity? Change in Science, Literature, and Politics*. London: Lawrence and Wishart.

White, L., Jr. (1967) "The Historical Roots of Our Ecological Crisis." *Science*, March 10: 1203–7.

Williams, D. (2000) "The Right Horse, the Animal Eye—Bartabas and Théâtre Zingaro." *Performance Research* 5 no. 2: 29–40.

Willis, R. (ed.) (1990) *Signifying Animals*. London: Unwin Hyman.

Yoder, A.E. (1947) *Animal Analogy in Shakespeare's Character Portrayal*, reprint. New York: AMS.

Chapter 3

Animal Geographies
Zooësis and the Space of Modern Drama

All sites of marginalization—ghettoes, shanty towns, prisons, madhouses, concentration camps—have something in common with zoos. But it is too easy and too evasive to use the zoo as a symbol; the zoo is a demonstration of the relations between man and animals: nothing else.

Berger (1980: 23)

When we go to the zoo, we take with us all our worries and joys, our heroes and villains, and we dole them out to the various species, casting each one in the role best equipped for it on the basis of accidental human resemblances.

Morris and Morris (1981: 172)

Confined within this catch-all concept [...] within this strict enclosure of this definite article ("the Animal" and not "animals") as in a virgin forest, a zoo, a hunting or fishing ground, a paddock or an abattoir, a space of domestication, are *all the living things* that man does not recognize as his fellows, his neighbors, or his brothers.

Derrida (2002: 402, original emphasis)

The field of animal studies offers a new perspective on that overlap of cultural and performance space that we call mimesis. In proposing the neologism "zooësis" for this new perspective, I want to invoke, as a foundation for my exploration of animal discourses in modern drama, the path-breaking work of Cary Wolfe, whose term "zoontologies" recognizes the central role played by the figure of the animal and the category of animality in all those "seminal reroutings of contemporary theory away from the constitutive figure of the human" (2003b: xi). Zooësis, as I conceive it, includes the myriad performative and semiotic elements involved in the vast range of cultural animal practices. Comprising both our actual and imaginative interactions with nonhuman animals, zooësis is the *discourse of animality* in human life, and its effects permeate our social, psychological, and material existence.

From its shifting locations on the margins of human life, the nonhuman animal participates in the construction of such human categories as the body, race, gender, sexuality, morality, and ethics. It also intervenes decisively in the social construction and cultural meaning of space. Animal practices shape not only the specific and actual spaces in which they occur, but parallel and opposite spaces as well, spaces to which they are related through the logic of the nature–culture divide that enables so much cultural meaning. Thus zooësis pertains not only to, for instance, the zoo, the dog run, the slaughterhouse, but also the nursery, the playground, the dining room.

As a complex ideological discourse of space and place, zooësis offers a new perspective on that privileged space of modem drama, the family "home." In the plays I shall discuss here—Edward Albee's *The Goat* (2000) and *The Zoo Story* (1959), and Terry Johnson's *Cries from the Mammal House* (1993)—zooësis rewrites the dramatic discourse of home from the point of view of the animal, figured either as the radically excluded Other, the very exemplar of homelessness (*The Goat*), or as the radically contained Other, exemplar of repression and imprisonment (*Zoo Story* and *Mammal House*). These plays differ, however, in their relation to a central issue of animal studies, the two poles of which are captured by the first two epigraphs of this essay. Berger's insistence on the literalism of the zoo, and hence on the actual relation between human beings and animals, is in fact an enormous challenge to the tradition of literary animal discourse. His "nothing else" is nothing like the simple limit which that brief phrase implies. It is an injunction to resist the anthropocentric and metaphoric logic of most "zoo stories," which invariably "cast" animals, as Morris and Morris say, in anthropomorphic dramas (172). This anthropocentric zooësis, Jean Baudrillard has provocatively argued, is the foundation of modernity. In modernism, writes Baudrillard, "animals must be made to say that they are not animals" (129). They must join the group of discursively colonized "others"—the insane, children, "savages"—upon whom rationalism imposes its hegemony, forcing them to speak in its terms. Not only do we exploit animals as beasts of burden and subjects of scientific experimentation, says Baudrillard, we have also made them creatures of somatization, forcing them to carry our symbolic and psychological baggage. As pets, as performers, and as literary symbols, animals are forced to perform *us*—our fantasies and fears, our questions and quarrels, our hopes and horrors. Refusing the animal its radical otherness by ceaselessly troping it and rendering it a metaphor for humanity, modernity erases the animal even as it makes it discursively ubiquitous.

Casting the Animals

The program for the Broadway production of *The Goat* exemplifies the tendency to transform the animal into a sign, and does so in a way that reminds us of a specifically theatrical version of this practice: "The he-goat (see also SCAPEGOAT) symbolizes the powers of procreation, the life force, the libido, and fertility" ("What's the word?"). The note goes on to say that the word "tragedy" comes from a Greek word meaning "goat-song." Thus, in one short note—invoking one long history—is the whole mystery of the play apparently solved: the shocking story of Martin, a successful, happily married architect who falls in love with a goat, is quickly translated into the latest in the American theater's long quest for a dramatic formula that could bestow tragic grandeur on the "common man." From this perspective, Martin would seem to be just a higher-class Willy Loman, yearning for the one thing materialist success cannot deliver: an experience of transcendence.

But surely this is much too neat a parcel for the whole shame-filled, guilt-ridden mess of bestiality that spills out on stage in Albee's play, shattering the attractive lives that have been holding a flattering mirror up to the audience. This shattering is astonishingly literal: Martin's wife reacts to every new revelation about his love affair by grabbing some decorative item off the shelves of the tastefully decorated living room and violently smashing it on the floor. Her repeated (and increasingly deliberate) action clearly establishes physical destruction as an alternative strategy to the one that these people have hitherto favored in their dealings with the world: a conspicuously *literary* strategy composed of word play and witty repartee. Martin, especially, is a stickler for correct usage and a sucker for verbal cleverness. Early in the play, a self-conscious quotation from Noël Coward both acknowledges the dramatic lineage that Albee's couple has inherited, and begins the process of disavowing it.

The disavowal involves exposing the foundation of that tradition in a particular co-articulation of animality with language to which Jacques Derrida has given the name "carno-phallogocentrism" (1991: 113). This portmanteau term designates a discourse in which the threatening multiplicity of animal lives is contained by language, reduced and singularized. The countless species of non-human creatures, and the countless members of those species, all captured in a single word: "the animal," says Derrida, "what a word!" (2002: 392). Cary Wolfe summarizes Derrida's argument as follows:

> The Word, *logos*, does violence to the heterogeneous multiplicity of the living world by reconstituting it under the sign of identity, the *as such* and *in general*—not "animals" but "the animal." And as such, it enacts what Derrida calls the "sacrificial structure" that opens a space for the "non-criminal putting to death" of the animal—a sacrifice that (so the story of Western philosophy goes) allows the transcendence of the human, of what Heidegger calls "spirit," by the killing off and the disavowal of the animal, the bodily, the materially heterogeneous, the contingent—in short, *différance*.
>
> (2003a: 66)

Albee's play traces an unraveling of the sacrificial logic Derrida describes, for here the animal that has been sacrificed to—and for—the power of language creeps back into view. While the opening of the play shows us a lifestyle dominated—even defined—by language, the body of the play takes us as far into non-verbal territory as textual drama can go. The final moments complete the play's endorsement of *breakage*, for the "solution" to the hero's dilemma entails smashing the rules of realistic drawing-room drama by displaying the everyday brutality of animal slaughter in a space that programmatically excludes (to use Hamlet's phrase) such "country matters" (3.2.119). It goes one long literal step beyond Harold Pinter's famous formula for menacing realism—"the weasel under the cocktail cabinet" (qt. in Taylor 285)—by dragging animality out of hiding and into plain view: exposed, center-stage, *there* for all to see.

What does it mean to see the animal? In the title of a 1980 essay that has become a classic of modern animal studies, John Berger asked the question, "Why Look at Animals?". Like Baudrillard later, Berger addresses the place (or rather non-place) of animals in modernity, and comes to the chilling conclusion that we are currently living through their final vanishing: "a historic loss," as he puts it, "irredeemable for the culture of capitalism" (26). Animals are commercialized as images, reduced as ever-more realistic toys, infantilized as Disney characters, denatured as pets, and—most significantly for Berger—monumentalized in zoos. "In zoos," he says, "they constitute the living monument to their own disappearance" (24). Animals can no longer perform the vital function for which human beings had long prized them: their ability to foster in us a kind of self-consciousness that is impossible to attain within the human species itself. The look between man and animal, says Berger, is a recognition across the abyss of sameness and difference by which animals are related to us: "With their parallel lives, animals offer man a companionship which is different from any offered by human exchange. Different because it is a companionship offered to the loneliness of man as a species" (4).

For Berger, the "loneliness of man as a species"—which had for centuries been affirmed in the look between man and animal—has in modern times been bartered for a false sense of mastery, to which animals are regularly sacrificed: spectacularly in zoos, but also psychologically and imaginatively, as fantasy images, as nostalgic markers of a lost rural idyll, and, of course, as pets. In an analysis that anticipates Deleuze and Guattari's more famous critique of the pet as an "oedipal" animal, Berger regards the pet as a key element in "that universal but personal withdrawal into the private small family unit, decorated or furnished with mementoes from the outside world, which is such a distinguishing feature of consumer societies" (Deleuze and Guattari 240; Berger 12). Berger's description of the modern home perfectly describes the set of the Broadway production of *The Goat*, which exemplified the commodification and domestication of the alien, the exotic, and the natural.

Interestingly, this model modern home of the play does not include a pet, except perhaps discursively, through Albee's subtitle—"Who Is Sylvia?" By naming his goat Sylvia, Albee's hyper-literate Martin may be unconsciously channeling Shakespeare's *Love's Labor's Lost*, but audience members might also be reminded of A.R. Gurney's 1995 play, *Sylvia*, whose eponymous character is a dog. Gurney's play is a rueful meditation on the pet as oedipalized animal, for the dog Sylvia (like Albee's goat Sylvia, only platonically) also triangulates a married couple, almost to the breaking point. By replacing the dog with a goat, Albee exposes to view (much more violently than Gurney) the usually occluded signifying structure of the modern animal, which balances separation and longing, disdain and desire. Interestingly, Derrida's recent philosophical explorations of the figure of the animal also center upon the pet—in fact his own pet, a cat. Derrida essentially reverses Berger's question, "Why look at animals?," asking rather why animals look at us, or at least what it might mean to entertain the possibility that they actively regard us instead of simply receiving our gaze, passively or at best reactively.

To breach the modern world's systematic occlusion of animality is also to disturb the delicate ecology of animal symbolism. By bringing a real goat into his story, Albee both invokes and disavows the entire symbology of the scapegoat. In the same way, he challenges the tragic formula of a heroic longing for transcendence by bringing in the coarse subject of bestiality. Although Martin insists on calling his experience an "epiphany" and identifying the object of his adoration as Sylvia's "soul," none of the other characters can resist describing it—repeatedly and hilariously—as "goat-fucking" (48). It is not Martin's love for the animal that violates taboos and threatens to "bring down" the family—it is the fact that this love is physical, sexual (heterosexual!), corporeal. The presence of this most transgressive of sexualities strains the tragic formula to the limit.

Animality also breaks the frame of drawing-room drama by recontextualizing its inhabitants in a wider world. Animal plays often contextualize their inter-species encounters within "eco-sites," heterotopias of "nature" in culture. Others stage literal destructions of the traditional stage spaces of realism: Ionesco's herds of rhinoceroses famously thunder in the wings, reducing bourgeois spaces to rubble, Alan Strang, the young protagonist of Peter Shaffer's *Equus*, attacks the *theatron's* privileged organ, the eye, by blinding the horses he loves: animality and theatricality cancel each other out. Elizabeth Egloff's 1994 play, *The Swan*, in which one of the three main characters is the eponymous bird, ends with the following stage direction: "There is a huge noise: glass breaking, the world breaking, a tree cracking" (54). In Albee's play, the recontexualization is less cosmological and more sociological. The move from dog (as in Gurney) or cat (as in Derrida) to *goat* is also a move out of the urban domestic sphere of modernity, a move toward, to use Hamlet's phrase again, "country matters" (the salacious pun is perhaps even more apt here than in Shakespeare). For indeed it is the country—that most paradigmatic of all eco-sites—that unleashed all the chaos to begin with: we learn that Martin fell in love with Sylvia, the goat, while he was country-househunting, or, as he says "barn-hunting" (40). The circumstances, as he reveals them, point to the cultural codes within which "the country" is embedded: "Actually, Stevie and I had decided it was time to have a real country place—a farm, maybe—we deserved it." "Beyond the suburbs," says his friend Ross, and Martin agrees: "Yes: beyond the suburbs" (40).

Almost four decades before *The Goat*, Albee had given more straightforwardly tragic expression to the cultural geography that increasingly separates human beings from other animals. In *The Zoo Story*, Albee pointedly contextualizes alienation within another paradigmatic eco-site: the city park. The play is set, famously, in Central Park, and its action suggests that the park is not just any space; rather it is so complicated a response to the increasing dichotomization of city and country as to be something of a geopathological syndrome. Both the characters approach it desperately, as a potential solution to the problem of city life, though Jerry is more conscious of this project than Peter, who is content to use the park as per the culture's instructions, as a brief respite from bourgeois pressures and domestic oppression. In the course of the play, Jerry manages to turn the park into a weapon, effectively reversing the planners' intention for the space: instead of a safe outlet for the aggression engendered by (unnatural?) urban life, the park turns into a stage for a quiet modern *agon* which pits humans against animals, men against women, "the upper-middle-middle-class" against the "lower-upper-middle-class," and individuals against themselves (20).

The Zoo Story might have been more accurately called *The Park Story*. There is actually no zoo in it (nor, for that matter, a zoo story, although one is repeatedly promised by Jerry). But the displacement of the zoo by the park in the play (and *vice versa* in the play's title) is a key to its account of modern metropolitan experience. The role of animality in characterizing the space and action of the play makes that account classically modernist, with the animal standing in, as so often in modernism, for the descent into primitive emotionality. The descent begins, in this case, by establishing space as a deterministic force. There may be no zoo in *The Zoo Story*, but the one Jerry keeps mentioning is real enough, and the play is at pains to locate it quite specifically, with numerical coordinates like street numbers. Jerry's insistence on distances and directions ("I've been walking north. [...] But not due north") sets the stage, as it were, for a distinctly *territorial* encounter, with both characters making significant cultural assumptions about each other based on the city's cultural geography of East Side, West Side, Greenwich Village, and so on (12–13). The cumulative effect is to frame the action of the play within a deterministic spatial logic. The park becomes a kind of vortex of tragic self-discovery. It is a "heart of darkness" where (like all such sites in modernism) the human descent into primitive emotionality is figured as *animality*.

Just as the zoo is displaced here, so is the zoo *story*. In its place we get a dog story. Not, one might say, a shaggy dog story, for "The Story of Jerry and the Dog" is anything but pointless. Rather, it is a kind of modern beast fable, packed with ethical implications. The dog Jerry first tried to tame and then tries to kill, is a grotesque version of the household pet as oedipalized animal. It belongs to Jerry's hideously amorous landlady, and resembles the hell hound to which Jerry explicitly compares it: "a black monster of a beast: an oversized head, tiny, tiny ears, and eyes [...] bloodshot, infected, maybe" (30).

The landlady's horror-cartoon of a pet is contrasted with the pets in Peter's house. These Disneyfied animals, benign enough at first, become disturbingly humanized during Peter's hysterical giggling fit: "Hee hee hee. I must go. After all, stop, stop, hee, hee, hee, after all, the parakeets will be getting dinner ready soon. Hee, hee, hee. And the cats are setting the table" (38). His fantasy turns his home, as Peter himself says, into a *zoo*, just as Jerry's description of the inhabitants of his rooming-house—each as distinctive as a species, and each locked into his or her tiny enclosure—recalls nothing so much as the zoo that he has recently visited, where everyone is "separated by bars from everyone else, the animals for the most part from each other, and always the people from the animals" (40). Thus the zoo that fails to appear in a story nevertheless saturates the symbolic space of the play, redefining modern metropolitan life as bestialized, partitioned, and brutally confined. The zoo story turns out to be only a park story, its zoo displaced and "used," as John Berger puts it, "as a symbol" (Berger 23). In the end, the only animals we see in the play turn out to be Peter and Jerry themselves: Jerry's death cry is that of "an infuriated and fatally wounded animal," and Peter learns that "it's all right, you're an animal. You're an animal too" (Albee 47, 49).

Ultimately, then, *The Zoo Story* remains captivated by the figure of the human, sacrificing the animal to that figure by turning it into a metaphor. The actual animal returns, with a vengeance, in *The Goat*, where its presence is stunningly literal. It is also, however, utterly beyond dramatic resolution. The appearance of the animal, in all its fleshly embodiment, brings the human story to a screeching halt. The family stands paralyzed. There is nowhere to go: neither city nor country, neither apartment nor zoo. The animal is understood quite literally as a defeat of meaning, a black hole in the family's comfortable universe: "one of them has been underneath the house, down in the cellar, digging a pit so deep, so wide!, so ... HUGE! ... we'll all fall in and never ... be ... able ... to climb out again—no matter how much we want to, how hard we try" (101–2).

Between the unmeaning (or resistance to meaning) of the literal animal and the unmeaning (or surfeit of meaning) of the animal as metaphor lies another kind of zooësis, which I now propose to explore in Terry Johnson's extraordinary zoo story, *Cries from the Mammal House*. A crucial characteristic of this kind of zooësis is the fact that it begins with—and returns us to—an understanding that animals are themselves, not us: not metaphors, not convenient codes for our prejudices. It is a salutary reminder, this "nothing else" of the animal, even if it is one we humans can sustain only fleetingly. For, as Wolfe puts it, "even though the *discourse* of animality and species may theoretically be applied to an other of whatever type, the consequences of that discourse, in *institutional* terms, fall overwhelmingly on nonhuman animals, in our taken-for-granted practices of using and exploiting them" (2003b: xx). For non-human animals, at any rate, a more literalistic zooësis is a matter of life over death.

Nothing Else

Cries from the Mammal House is a veritable compendium of animal practices, including zoo-keeping, veterinary medicine, animal-behavior-based psychology, repopulation of endangered species, euthanasia, animal worship, bestiality, taxidermy, trafficking in exotic animals, slaughtering, butchering, and meat-eating. The play's cataloguing of the many ways in which humans relate to animals is a principal strategy of its remarkably non-reductive zooësis. Its highly differentiated and pluralistic view of animality is also reflected in its title. I called the play a zoo story, and indeed it is set in a zoo, but the play's title is the first of its many interventions into the homogenized and impacted view of animals that Derrida identifies as the key strategy of carno-phallogocentrism. In using the less familiar, more archaic term "mammal house" in the title of the play, Johnson disturbs that comfortable dissociation we have achieved between the words "human" and "animal," and forces us back into the biological field we prefer to distance ourselves from.

From its title onwards, the logic of Johnson's play fosters the re-recognition of animals as humankind's "neighbors"—to use Derrida's term (2002: 402)—but does so within a tragic view of eco-history, asking whether this recognition comes too late. In an instance of inspired zooësis, the play opens with a direct address to the audience that is cleverly doubled as a dialogue with an animal. Staring "straight ahead of her," Anne speaks "directly to the audience":

> Listen! This isn't the real world. This is a zoo. You think you'd prefer the real world? Foraging for yourself instead of opening that mouth for whatever we chose to drop into it? Nothing but nature between you and the horizon? You dream of it as a sort of freedom, the real word? Elephants might fly? Let me tell you, when we stole it from you, this dream of yours, the weapon we used was our intelligence. And now the world's been stolen from us by a small elite of our own species and the weapon they used was money. So we sit in our enclosures, our horizons painted on glass, our mouths wide open.
>
> (141)

By explicitly articulating the "modern-life-as-zoo" metaphor *within a zoo*, and especially by embedding it within a surprising instance of cross-species address, Anne's speech exposes to critical view the kind of metaphoric zooësis that, in Albee's *Zoo Story* as in so much other animal discourse, effectively displaces the animal.

As the play opens, Alan is reluctantly taking possession of a small-town zoo he has just inherited from his father. As his first act of ownership, he must kill the zoo's most popular exhibit, an elephant, which was, in a manner of speaking, "responsible" for his father's death. At the very outset, then, zooësis is at work: the merging of the issue of the animal's criminal culpability with the more familiar family plot provides a brilliant twist on the old theme of the revenge of a father's murder. Instead of a murderous human "beast," this play's reluctant Hamlet or Orestes, Alan, must dispatch a real animal.

Alan must not only kill the elephant but will spend much of the play euthanizing many other animals, once it is learned that the zoo is bankrupt and has to be closed down. Thus one major line of the play's action is a kind of reversal of the Noah story, with animals being systematically destroyed instead of systematically saved by human beings. Creature by creature, species by species, Alan administers the right dose of poison needed to extinguish each one. The last syringe is for himself, making him an inverse Adam, with no animals left to name, and no reason to live.

This animal extinction plot is countered by the story of David, Alan's brother, a biologist specializing in the rescue and rebreeding of endangered species. His current project takes him (and, surprisingly, the play itself) to Mauritius, where, in addition to the pink pigeons he is seeking to rebreed, he also finds a secluded tribe which worships a group of dodo birds that have survived the famed extinction of their species. On the island he also encounters a rich mixture of human cultures, from which he acquires a kind of new family to replace the decimated one back in England. Significantly, the human diversity is characterized (by the ludicrously conservative colonial wife Lady Palmer) as "a sort of religious zoo" (173). Her disquisition neatly demonstrates the complex and contradictory use of the animal in constructing ideologies of difference: "I draw the line at black magic. [...] It's a silly game that requires the slaughter of innocent creatures. Its perpetrators deserve the wrath of the Lamb" (173).

The play's animal-centered exploration of cultural geographies involves a dialectic between two spaces: the "home-world" of late twentieth-century England and the distant "other-world" of Mauritius. The contrasts between the two—the dying Mammal House and the teeming island, systematic extinction and uncontrollable evolution—eventually produce, in the play's final act, a wholly unexpected new social configuration, a new world, as it were. "Paradise"—as David calls Mauritius—is regained by the family: the zoo is saved (161). Not surprisingly, the agent of this rescue is an animal. Johnson's choice of animal for the role of ecological messiah is inspired. At the center of his play's ironic apotheosis he places the creature who, more than any other, signifies all the grim strangeness of the human relation to non-human animals: the dodo.

The extravagant and unexpected "happy ending" the play affords all its characters—all happily united in England—reads like an ecological parable: David makes the biological find of the century (that the dodo, poster-animal of extinction, is in fact not extinct) because he had in his possession, when he arrived in Mauritius, a stuffed dodo. This moldy specimen of taxidermy is from the old zoo-keeper's collection—"anything died, he'd have it stuffed. And the meat roasted for his gourmet's circle"—and David has brought it to Mauritius to barter with the local museum for museum facilities (152). But for David's creole assistant, Victor, the dodo is a sign that David is the fulfillment of a prophecy, and he leads David to his village, where David is "introduced" to the mythically stupid birds in a suitably outlandish fashion:

> They lifted up this gigantic lid, and there was the pit. I was scared out of my wits. They picked me up and threw me in it. I couldn't see a thing [...] Something was moving. I presumed it was there to eat me. Then someone lowered down a torch; the pit filled with that lovely flaming torchlight [...] and there was something there. In the middle of the light it stood, blinking its eyes and wondering why on earth it had been woken up at this ungodly hour. It was a dodo. It looked at me, I swear to God, and it opened its beak and it made the daftest sound I've ever heard. And there were females roosting and younguns being sat on, and all around me these grinning bloody conservationists showing off their handful of gods for the very first time.
>
> (208)

David himself gives the meaning of the play's ecological parable: "I was just in the right place at the right time" (208). By this time, however, the notion of place—and further the question of what makes a place "right"—is anything but simple. The play has deployed the figure of the animal—or rather, remembering Derrida's warning about that singular—the figure of *animals*, to remap the cultural geography of late century Europe as a rapidly emptying "mammal house," its inhabitants engaged in an ecocide that will eventually ensure their own extinction. "What is wrong with all of you?" David asks his niece when he first arrives on the scene. "We're related," she answers (162).

But the fact is that they are *not* adequately—that is meaningfully— related. The last act includes a lengthy scene of introductions, in which the conditions of a more creative, more sustaining relation, are enacted. Not surprisingly, this new relation is one that centrally involves both human and non-human animals. Once introduced to each other, all the characters gather around a crate that David opens: "From the crate there issues an absurd cry which echoes around the mammal house" (209). The cry of the dodo, absurd in itself but more absurd in its absence, invites an imaginative rethinking—beyond the human—of the figures of home, family, relationship. Like *The Zoo Story*, *Cries from the Mammal House* reads the zoo as a site of modern culture's anxieties about alienation from nature and from our animal selves. Unlike Albee's play, however, this one does not abandon the zoo to its metaphoric fate. Instead it undertakes a complex and differentiated zooësis, engaging a wide range of actual animal practices. This zooësis explores the possibility and argues the necessity of reintegrating the animal into modern consciousness.

That this is a difficult, perhaps even futile, project is signaled by the play's ironic ending, its "dodo *ex machina*." An additional, theatrical acknowledgment of the animal's vexed relationship to cultural meaning is made through the mimetic strategies explicitly called for in a note at the start of the play: "all live animals should be invisible, and mimed by the actors. All dead animals, in whatever condition, should be present" (140). Thus the play's dialectic of spaces is overlaid with a performance dialectic which enacts the tragic contingency of the animal in the modern world. Flickering in and out of mimesis, the animal shapes and reshapes the spaces of human culture. In the same way, various modes of zooësis—from the troping of the animal to the reflexive and critical interrogation of its place among us—either reproduce or excavate the humanist assumptions that determine the geography of modern drama.

Works cited

Albee, E. (1959) *The Zoo Story*. New York: Signet.
—— (2000) *The Goat, or Who Is Sylvia?* New York: Overlook.
Berger, J. (1980) *About Looking*. New York: Pantheon.
Baudrillard, J. (1994) *Simulacra and Simulation*, trans. S.F. Glaser. Ann Arbor: U of Michigan P.
Deleuze, G. and Guattari, F. (1988) *A Thousand Plateaus: Capitalism and Schizophrenia*, trans. B. Massumi. London: Routledge.
Derrida, J. (1991) "'Eating Well' or the Calculation of the Subject" in E. Cadava, P. Connor, and J.-L. Nancy (eds) *Who Comes after the Subject?* New York: Routledge, 96–119.
—— (2002) "The Animal That Therefore I Am (More to Follow)." *Critical Inquiry* 28 no. 2: 369–418.
Egloff, E. (1994) *The Swan*. New York: Dramatists Play Service.
Gurney, A.R. (1995) *Sylvia*. New York: Dramatists Play Service.
Johnson, T. (1993) *Cries from the Mammal House*. Plays, Selections. London: Methuen.

Morris, R. and Morris, D. (1981) *The Giant Panda,* revised edn., rev. J. Barzdo. London: Kogan Page.

Shakespeare, W. (1997) *Hamlet,* in G.B. Evans and J.J.M. Tobin (eds) *The Riverside Shakespeare,* 2nd edn. Boston: Houghton Mifflin.

Taylor, J.R. (1966) *Anger and After.* Harmondsworth: Penguin.

"What's the word?" (2002) in *"The Goat Gazette"* 1 no. 4: 1–2, *Playbill.* New York: Playbill Inc.

Wolfe, C. (2003a) *Animal Rites: American Culture, the Discourse of Species, and Posthumanist Theory.* Chicago: U of Chicago P.

—— (ed.) (2003b) "Introduction." Zoontologies: The Question of the Animal. Minneapolis: U of Minnesota P, ix–xxiii.

Chapter 4

"AWK!"

Extremity, Animality, and the Aesthetic of Awkwardness in Tennessee Williams's *The Gnädiges Fräulein*

> Is there a more mysterious idea for an artist than to imagine how nature is reflected in the eyes of an animal? ... It is a poverty-stricken convention to place animals into landscapes as seen by men; instead we should contemplate the soul of the animal to divine its way of sight.
>
> (Franz Marc)[1]

> We believe in the existence of very special becomings-animal traversing human beings and sweeping them away, affecting the animal no less than the human.
>
> (Gilles Deleuze and Félix Guattari)[2]

The subject of this essay lies somewhere between the meaningless monosyllable of my title and the possibly utopian program of my epigraphs.[3] This "AWK!" encapsulates the questions raised by the encounter between art and animality that frames my inquiry. In both its significations, as animal yelp, or, more familiarly, as marginal notation in red ink, this "AWK!" helps me to ask if that encounter is always—by definition—*awkward*? And if it is, can something be made of that awkwardness: a new aesthetic, perhaps, with which to undertake such visits to the non-human as are envisioned in my epigraphs and which have traditionally remained out of artistic bounds?

Those seeking to rescue the late plays of Tennessee Williams from critical and commercial oblivion generally contest the earlier verdicts on these plays as aesthetically limited and insufficiently realized. The idea of awkwardness leads me to propose a different possibility: that what is important and valuable about these plays is precisely their apparent failure. My claim rests on a new conceptualization of failure itself, drawn from an extreme margin of postmodern theory. Reading failure as a productive *crisis of expertise*, a *creative refusal* of mastery and authority, theorists of postmodernism have urged a renewed interest in the values of *not knowing* and *not succeeding*. In *Terror and Experts*, Adam Phillips opposes "curiosity," which is endless and creative, to "answers," which seduce us with their airs of authority while also entrapping us in their false finalities. From this radically altered perspective on artistic accomplishment, the challenge for serious practitioners in any field, artistic or otherwise, is how "to learn how not to know what [one] is doing" (104).

Williams's experimentalism, while it may have stopped far short of not knowing what he was doing, certainly opened him up to margins and transgressions of all kinds: cultural, aesthetic, sexual, generic. Did it also open him up to that ultimate artistic transgression, failure? One of his plays in particular, *The Gnädiges Fräulein*, suggests an experimentalism pursued beyond the usual motivation of new discoveries en route to new successes. The imagistic, linguistic, and psychological excesses and attenuations of this play could signal an anti-aesthetic that might shed light on other late plays as well. Of all Williams's failed human beings (and these were, of course, his stock in trade: failed artists, priests, lovers, mothers, sons), few are more abject than the eponymous protagonist of this play. Her abjection, moreover, is precise, placing her in another extreme margin of postmodernism: the rethinking of the animal.

Postmodernism comes to the animal as to a figure capable of inspiring and guiding a new journey across the ideological borders with which modernism has kept the human separate from its many "others." While traditional shamans undertook their spirit travels in the company of animal "familiars," postmodern travelers favor odd and ungainly beasts, "unfamiliars" with strange—and strangely powerful—forms. One recent sculpture that exemplifies this kind of "postmodern animal" is John Isaacs's *Untitled (Dodo)* (1994) (fig. 4.1), courting awkwardness as a strategy, a discourse, and a revisioning of aesthetic values. It belongs to the genre that Steven Baker memorably dubs "botched taxidermies" (55), deliberately messy animal representations that register modernity's alienation from the non-human. Isaacs's dodo strikes me as a particularly appropriate "animal unfamiliar" to invite along as I venture into the awkward world of Tennessee Williams's late plays.

Figure 4.1 John Isaacs, *Untitled (Dodo)*, 1994, fiberglass, oil paint, steel, glass, silicone rubber, wood, electric motor and kinetic mechanism, 81 x 72 x 41 cm.

© John Isaacs. Courtesy Arts Council Collection, Hayward Gallery, London.

Though little-known and rarely produced, *The Gnädiges Fräulein* encapsulates paradigmatic elements of Tennessee Williams's late plays and extends them to their signifying limits. The play's set— and its setting—are a case in point. Like so many of the late plays, this one performs Williams's drift away from classical dramatic modernism by eschewing the normative domestic interior of dramatic realism. The "big dormitory" of this play is surely the extreme version of the transient spaces in which Williams increasingly located his attempts to stage the kinds of "limit-experiences" which increasingly interested him—and which Raymond Williams calls those "crucial areas of experience [which] the language and behavior of the living room could not articulate or fully interpret" (85). The civic values and kinship relationships once articulated by the stage living room are nowhere to be found in the nightmarish boardinghouse of *The Gnädiges Fräulein*, where shelter itself has become a grotesque balancing act: in this hotel, those who cannot afford a bed can rent a "standing room" for the night and try to sleep on their feet like (as one character notes) flamingos! The play's set is as fractured as its setting. Williams explicitly requires "a totally unrealistic arrangement of assorted props, porch steps, yard, and picket fence . . . as if Picasso had designed it" (217). This literal displacement reflects the play's thematics, which push notions of social slippage and psychological dislocation to their human limits. The characters of *The Gnädiges Fräulein* are so radically transient that they are sliding off the map, barely clinging to the "southernmost tip of terra firma" (219). The long opening monologue riffs on this geographical extremity, quickly thrusting us into the surreal enactment of the play's most original and extreme realization of human extremity: namely, the slide into animality.

The Gnädiges Fräulein tells the story of a former European showgirl now fallen on hard times and struggling to survive in a poverty-stricken town on the Florida shore. Her fate is in the hands of a sadistic boardinghouse keeper named Molly, who gives the Fräulein (we never learn her real name) a roof over her head in exchange for a daily payment of three fish, which the Fräulein scavenges from the rejected catch of passing fishing boats. This grim arrangement is described by Molly for the benefit of Polly, a reporter from the local paper, whom the landlady hopes to persuade into giving her some free publicity for her boardinghouse. In the course of the narration, the Fräulein makes several scavenging forays to the offstage docks, each time returning more damaged and debilitated. In her quest for fish she is, it turns out, in competition with the vicious cocaloony birds, who do not take kindly to having a human rival. They violently attack her every time she ventures out, leaving her, by the play's end, horribly tattered, bloodied, and blinded in both eyes. The main action of the play, then, is the cruel disintegration of the Fräulein at the hands of the brutal birds.

With two notable exceptions, critical discussions of *The Gnädiges Fräulein* have focused on this action, reading it as a bitter but unsuccessful satire on the fate of the artist in modern society. A discussion by Linda Dorff brings enormous texture and renewed interest to this reading, arguing that Williams's use of cartoonish characters and actions extends his satire far beyond the autobiographical into the generic and institutional. According to Dorff, Williams used "the two-dimensional aesthetics of the cartoon" not only to construct a parable for "the grotesquely disfigured position of the artist within the frames of the theater and of the larger American society" but also to parody—in a distinctly *meta*-mimetic mode—the tradition of psychological tragic realism to which he had always had an ambivalent relationship (16). An even more recent discussion of *The Gnädiges Fräulein*, by Philip Kolin, furthers Dorff's method by reading Williams intertextually with other cultural and pop-cultural forms. Exploring the connections between *The Gnädiges Fräulein* and Alfred Hitchcock's roughly contemporaneous film *The Birds*, Kolin locates *The Gnädiges Fräulein* in relation to an apocalyptic streak in Cold War American culture. Both *The Birds* and *The Gnädiges Fräulein* are, writes Kolin, "cultural scripts of fear," which evoke the "lunacy and dread of nuclear attack in the mid 1960s" (6). As the only article to pay sustained attention to what is surely the most unusual feature of this play—the role played in it by other-than-human figures—Kolin's article opens the door for my "animalized" reading. I submit that by "taking [the] animals seriously" (DeGrazia, title), we can discover a transgressive animalizing imagination that complements the pop-cultural imagery and political resonance which critics like Dorff and Kolin have already uncovered in this supposed "failure" of a play.[4]

The Gnädiges Fräulein is, of course, hardly unique among Williams's plays in using animal and bird imagery: such imagery appears in the titles of several of his plays—*Not About Nightingales, Sweet Bird of Youth, I Rise in Flames Cried the Phoenix, A Perfect Analysis Given by a Parrot*—as well as in key symbolic elements, such as Val's snakeskin jacket and peacock sleeping curtain in *Orpheus Descending*. Actual animals—represented either diegetically or mimetically—are also memorably troped in several plays, most famously in Sebastian's soul-shattering vision of the carnage wrought by predatory birds in the Galapagos *(Suddenly Last Summer)*. In two other important plays mimetically represented animals provide powerful theatrical (acoustic) imagery as well as central dramatic symbolism: the howling dogs that chase Val at the end of *Orpheus* and the trapped reptile that gives its name to *The Night of the Iguana*. The animals in these two cases occupy a potent dramatic margin, an unseen but hyper-audible space resounding with danger, cruelty, and violence. This is precisely the space that *The Gnädiges Fräulein* attempts to enter and inhabit.

While animals and animal imagery are pervasive in Williams's drama, *The Gnädiges Fräulein* is unique in the Williams canon for its attempt to confront animality on the far side of metaphor. Literalism is one crucial characteristic of postmodern animalizing, the mark of its refusal of modernism's various (and, as we shall see below, constitutive) tropings of the non-human. Another characteristic of the "postmodern animal," writes the author of a book by that name, is its look: the animal that escapes modernism's metaphorizing power is often "a fractured, awkward, 'wrong,' or wronged thing" (Baker 54). There could hardly be a better description of Williams's Fräulein, whose miserable condition, grotesque appearance, and bizarre history put her almost beyond the human pale. Almost, but not quite. The Fräulein is saved from actually embodying animality by the presence in the play—on stage—of an actual (though neither real nor realistic) animal. *The Gnädiges Fräulein* is one of surprisingly few plays to include an actual animal in its list of active characters. This is not to say that *The Gnädiges Fräulein* is a play "about animals." Actually, Williams explicitly contested (and bemoaned) the reading of *The Gnädiges Fräulein* as "a play about terrible birds," insisting that the real subject was "the tragicomic subject of human existence on this risky planet" (Preface 95). Moreover, the animals in it, though literal, are not real. They are an extravagant and preposterous invention: "vicious, over-grown sea birds" who give their cartoonish name to the Key where the action takes place, Cocaloony Key (220).

In a production note to the play, Williams says that he thinks of the cocaloony "as a sort of giant pelican." He then goes on—puzzlingly—to share the following information about his compositional process: "in fact, all through the first draft of the play I have typed the word 'pelican,' scratched it out and written over it 'cocaloony'" (218). What, one wonders, is the significance of this detail? Might it inflect our understanding of the play's central fiction to know that it had its origins in reality? Does the pelican's metamorphosis into a creature of imagination signal other transformations, possibly in the realm of the human, where something might also be getting "scratched out" and "written over"? It is worth remembering, too, that Williams explicitly connects the monstrous pelican of *The Gnädiges Fräulein* to its counterpart in *The Mutilated*, the play with which William paired this one for a double bill he called *Slapstick Tragedy*. In both plays, it would seem, a figure of grotesque animality is needed to fully explicate Williams's genre-bending vision of human extremity "on this risky planet" (Preface 95).

At the limits of their resources, Williams's protagonists are at risk of devolving into non-human creatures. But the social margin they inhabit, like the little planet to which it clings, is also at risk. The play's vision of extremity extends beyond the human, situating human risk on a continuum that traverses (to use Deleuze and Guattari's term) traditional taxonomies just as readily as his set transgresses the boundaries of realism's living room. The play's challenge to modernism lies in this "traversing," directly challenging modernism's "process of purification" (Lykke 16). Modernism rejected anything that unsettled boundaries, rendering "the world intelligible by eliminating and suppressing inconsistencies, impurities, and dissimilarities" (Baker 99). Modernism assigned all beings to one of two camps, the human and the non-human, denying the continuity between humans and others, be they machines, monsters, or animals. In the rhetoric of modernism "animal" became the *opposite* of human rather than its larger context. In this process, the animal turned into a powerful rhetorical device, a figure of *lack* in relation to the plenitude of human identity. This rigidly oppositional construction makes the animal a potent figure for postmodernism's attack on all binarisms. If modernism insisted on using animals to construct its "humanist politics of norms and identities," the animal now offers itself as a powerful tool for postmodernism's challenge to identity-thinking (Shildrick 2).

In modernism, as an important theorist of postmodernism puts it, "animals must be made to say they are not animals" (Baudrillard 129). Noting that animals were only "demoted to the status of inhumanity" with the triumph of rationalism and humanism, Baudrillard lists the various new roles in which this progress cast animals. Among these is their role as "beasts of somatization": forced to carry a psychological life entirely invented by—and projected onto them by—humans (133). Humanism constructs itself by denying that humans are animals too, and modernism follows up by *troping* the animal, putting it to work as a metaphor for the human, and denying it its difference. Modernism's constitutive dualisms rest on a compulsive silencing of the animality around us and within us, wresting preeminence for culture by making nature mute. Lurking beneath all the great narratives of modernism is a great animal silence, born of a programmatic misrecognition.

The supposed "failure" of *The Gnädiges Fräulein* is a function of and a thematization of this very misrecognition. The voices raised in this play are precisely the ones which are excluded by the standards of cultural value on which theatrical success has traditionally rested. To scour the play for the latter values—to read it, for instance, as yet another (autobiographical) portrait of the alienated artist—turns up a judgment of clumsiness, or worse.[5] To refuse such metaphorical readings, however, is to find here an altogether different register of expression, another set of voices.

The voices I hear in *The Gnädiges Fräulein* are not animal voices but rather human voices in search of and in expression of what Alan Bleakley, following and expanding upon Deleuze and Guattari's notion of "becoming animal," has named, in the title of his book, "the animalizing imagination." The animalizing imagination is emphatically not a matter of giving animals human form, either physical or psychological. Rather, it is the consequence—and bringing to consciousness—of our own animality, and its forms are not actual animals but psychological animals, of great importance to our sanity and our life in the world.

Besides Deleuze and Guattari, Bleakley is inspired in his formulations by Gaston Bachelard, who proffered the "surprising but delightful notion that imagination creates the natural, as a 'biological dream'" (104). In his reading of Lautréamont's animalized text *Maldoror*, Bachelard discovered evidence that, contrary to common belief, it is not animals who give their shapes to human visions of the marvelous and the monstrous but just the opposite: when human imagination conjures wonders and marvels, they naturally take the form of animals. "The first function of imagination," says Bachelard, "is to create animal forms" (27). The imagination animalizes. The animalizing imagination, then, is a fundamental aesthetic register, furnished with animal forms, shapes, sounds, smells, sensations, and experiences. It allows and invites a mode of expression in which the human animal can acknowledge its participation in animality, can manifest its own animal nature.

As powerful as it is both prohibited and hence transgressive, this imagination furnishes one of the more progressive and promising resources of postmodernism. The animalizing imagination, like the cyborgian imagination theorized by Donna Haraway, belongs to a consciously post*humanist* and ecologically invested postmodernism. This, in turn, belongs to a "second moment" or "late stage" of postmodernism, in which, as Hal Foster says, the "highs of the simulacral image" are sacrificed for the "lows of the depressive object" (165). Leaving the surface aesthetics of parody and pastiche, this postmodernism replaces early postmodernism's ironic "fragmenting of bodies and texts" and attempts instead to "imagine differently reconstituted communities and selves" (Wheeler 74). Among the categories with which the new selves and communities are reconstituted are (non-human) animals and species. It is as a manifestation of this discourse that I propose to read *The Gnädiges Fräulein*, arguing also that this "biocentric," posthumanist stream of postmodernism might provide an as good if not better aesthetic framework for re-evaluating Williams's late plays than even those counter-realisms—expressionism, absurdism, surrealism, etc.—to which these plays resonate so powerfully.

If such a thing as an aesthetic of awkwardness could be said to exist, *The Gnädiges Fräulein* would be its exemplar. Awkwardness permeates the play, systematically distancing it from the accomplished aesthetics of modernism and the purist norms of humanism. This awkwardness is given its fullest representation in the figure of the cocaloony bird, "stalking jerkily about, poking its gruesome head this way and that with spastic motions" (234). In both appearance (fig. 4.2) and expression, the cocaloony is awkward, in expression literally so, since its "discourse" (no other

Figure 4.2 Broadway premiere of *The Gnädiges Fräulein* at the Longacre Theater, February 22, 1966, with Zoe Caldwell as Polly, Kate Reid as Molly, and Art Ostrin as the cocaloony.

Photo by Friedman-Abeles. Courtesy of the New York Public Library.

word will do, yet no other word is more ironic in this context) consists of the single word "AWK!" Taken up and repeated in various tones by the human characters, this "word" is the play's hymn to the animal. Why this animal needs to be so ugly and its hymn so dissonant[6] has to do with its postmodernity.

Williams's bird belongs to that category of postmodern animal art that Baker calls "botched taxidermies"— works like John Isaacs's dodo, which use effects of tattiness, messiness, bungling, and deliberate imperfection to draw attention to modernity's "botched" relationship to the non-human world. Like the grotesque bird Williams invented for his play, Isaacs's dodo captures the final moments of a long misapprehension of animals by human beings. At the extreme point of its relationship to human beings, at the point, indeed, of giving up on the thankless task of trying to engage human beings in a genuine sharing of the world, these animals attain their most vivid, most powerful, and most tragic expressivity. Like the cocaloony's tragedy, the dodo's is "slapstick" as well, a matter of jerky movements and ineffective flappings (Isaacs's sculpture incorporates a motor scavenged from a washing machine) that allows movement but no flight. In these works, awkwardness becomes a strategy for lifting the modernist repression of animality: "tattiness, imperfection, and botched form ... render the animals *abrasively visible*, and they do so regardless of how the artist thinks about animals" (Baker 62). The last point is especially important. The expression of animality requires strategies that circumvent the artist's unwitting participation in modernity's repression. The postmodern animal must emerge *"regardless of how the artist thinks about animals,"* and awkwardness marks the independence of the postmodern animal from its human frames, its ideological "cages." Thus the cocaloony's "AWK!" has something of the *negative communicative power* that Jacques Derrida seeks in his recent "zoo-auto-bio-biblio-graphy," *L'animal que donc je suis*. To invoke animals without falling prey to the rhetorical abuses with which animals have been entrapped within human discourse, Derrida invents the punning neologism *"animot."* This "awkward living word-thing" is needed to escape from modernism's trap of subjectivity, yet that same trap prevents one from defining the term other than negatively: the *animot* is *"ni une espèce, ni un genre, ni un individu"* (Baker 74; Derrida 292).

Neither species, nor genre, nor individual, the Derridean *animot* relates to the Deleuzian notion of "becoming-animal" (*"devenir-animal"*). Originally formulated by French philosophers Deleuze and Guattari in a study of Kafka (1975), the concept was later elaborated as part of a vast program of "anti-oedipal" "becomings" (including "becoming-minoritarian, becoming-woman, becoming-molecular and becoming-imperceptible" [Baker 103]). The Deleuzian becoming-animal consists of a "deterritorialization," an escape from the human which is "proposed" by the animal and which can defeat the tyrannies of individual subjectivity and exclusivist human identity upon which modernism stakes its claims. The state of becoming-animal is a state of flux, uncertainty, openness, and experimentation. It counters the forces that Deleuze and Guattari call "Oedipalization": the forces of control, conformity, meaning, interpretation. Becoming-animal occurs outside of metaphor, allegory, imitation, or fantasy: it is "a human being's creative opportunity to think themselves other-than-in-identity" (Baker 125).

The first description of the cocaloonies makes it clear not only that they are inventions, but that they will not escape the fate that Baudrillard diagnosed for animals in modernism—to be captured for symbolization: "they flap and waddle out to the boat with their beaks wide open on their elastic gullets to catch the throwaway fish, the discards, the re-jecks, because, y'see—tell it not in Gath!—the once-self-reliant-and-self-sufficient character of this southernmost sea-bird has degenerated to where it could be justly described as a parasitical creature, yes, gone are the days it would condescend to fish for itself …" (Williams 220). Parasitical and nearly paralytic, the cocaloonies are a grotesque version of the romantic denizens of many modernist bohemias, best exemplified perhaps in O'Neill's *Iceman*. In this play, however, that kind of milieu, represented by "the big dormitory," is utterly transformed in effect and in meaning by the *actual* presence within it of actual animals. The animal clamor that fills the skies above Cocaloony Key, and the animal forms and features that increasingly appear among and upon its human inhabitants, suggest a new framework for understanding human life "on the edge." This framework depends on acknowledging the *continuity* between animal and human nature, of thinking of humans as animals, and of animals (as some recent ecologists have insisted) not with the discounting phrase "non-human" but as "*other-than-human.*"

The other-than-human (and, for that matter, the "other-than-pelican"!) makes *The Gnädiges Fräulein* not a play "about animals" but rather an "animalized" play, a play that has anticipated Deleuze and Guattari's notion of "becoming-animal" as a mode of aesthetic expression. In *The Gnädiges Fräulein*, Williams manages to clear a rare dramatic space within which to explore and express the human experience of animality *in and of itself*, not as a metaphor for something else but as an extreme condition of humanity. This level of the play—always ignored—is to be found not only in the miserable present condition of the Fräulein, but also in her remarkable history. The unusual skill she displays in competing with the cocaloonies in their scavenging for fish has an amazing origin. The Fräulein, it appears, once worked as the stage assistant to an animal trainer, helping him show off his trained seal. Then, one day, the Fräulein did something extraordinary. As told to Polly by Molly, drum rolls and all, it is worth quoting in full:

> [*Drum.*] Scene: a matinee at the Royal Haymarket in London? Benefit performance? Before crowned heads of Europe? ... *The Gnädiges Fräulein*!—The splendor, the glory of the occasion, turned her head just a bit. She overextended herself, she wasn't content that day just to do a toe dance to music while bearing the paraphernalia back and forth between the seal and the trainer, the various props, the silver batons and medicine ball that the seal balanced on the tip of his schnozzola. Oh, no, that didn't content her. She had to build up her bit. She suddenly felt a need to compete for attention with the trained seal and trained seal's trainer... . Now then ... the climax of the performance. [*Drum.*] The seal has just performed his most famous trick, and is balancing two silver batons and two gilded medicine balls on the tip of his whiskery schnozzle while applauding himself. [*Drum.*] Now, then. The big switcheroo, the surprising gimmick. The trained seal trainer throws the trained seal a fish. What happens? It's intercepted. Who by? *The Gnädiges Fräulein*. NO HANDS. [She imitates the seal.] She catches the fish in her choppers! [*Drum.*] Polly, it brought down the house!

(256)

Perhaps this play merits its putative genre of "slapstick tragedy"; there is a destiny at work here, however grotesque. Things do come full circle, however absurdly. The Fräulein's current method of survival—*acting the animal*—is actually the final stage of a process that began during *an animal act*.

Animal acts occupy a particularly overdetermined position in the human relationship to animals and, in particular, to the kind of rethinking of that relationship initiated by Deleuze and Guattari and now taken up by others. The animal act appears at first glance to be an instance of human beings *appreciating* animals, gathering to marvel at and celebrate their powers. On closer inspection, however, the occasion seems rather to be one of human beings gathering to collectively mark animals *as inferiors*—that is, as creatures capable only of the most superficial mimicry of human skills. Though individual animal acts encode specific attitudes from the vast array of attitudes through which human beings manage their relationships with animals,[7] the fundamental principle of all animal acts is a performance of the superiority of culture over nature. The animal act, in short, is one of the (paradoxical) ways in which human beings distinguish themselves as uniquely creative creatures, capable of play and display of a kind that animals can only imitate, clumsily and hilariously. By forcing animals to perform as quasi-humans, the animal act actually stages the animal's otherness, its "bestiality." In the animal act, the work of mimesis is to mark the animal's ontological distance from the human. As such, the animal act is an ideal site for performing the constitutive fiction of humanism, the fiction that humans are not animals.

When the Fräulein disrupted the animal act (a disruption already prepared by Williams, I think, in the unlikely claim that such an act was being presented to the "crowned heads of Europe"), she was intervening in something rather more significant than a successful sideshow. She was initiating a transgression to protest against the injustice of her decline from success, youth, and beauty. Shorn of dignity and hope within the established social terms of her milieu, she resorted to animalizing. The Fräulein's impulsive and outrageous reaction to her social marginalization was, we learn, the first step in a process—an alarmingly logical process—that has ended up in a life on the very margins of humanity. When the Fräulein disrupted the animal act, she was pointing to the transgressive awkwardness that she now inhabits.

For all its bizarre inventions and grotesque images, nothing makes this play more original than the fact that its exploration of "becoming-animal" is narrativized, recognized, and explored *as an autonomous process*. The point I want to make here can perhaps be clarified by comparing *The Gnädiges Fräulein* to another well-known modern play, Peter Shaffer's *Equus*. Both plays centrally involve what we might call (invoking Bottom, that early figure of animal-becoming in drama) a "translation." Both offer a "biocentric" perspective: the animal nature of the animals is more important than their human qualities, and the human characters discover and confront this otherness in the course of a long and painful process. In *Equus*, however, the animalizing potential of the horse, although it is experienced by the boy, is, for the audience, contained and limited by the authoritative discourse of the psychiatrist, Dr. Dysart. While he does not reduce the animal to a small set of human meanings, Shaffer nevertheless does not allow the meaning of the horse to appear (or not appear) from the act of becoming-animal itself. The psychiatrist, true to his trade, supplies symbols and interpretations, thereby curtailing that full-scale "traversing" and "sweeping away" of human beings that distinguishes the Deleuzian "becoming-animal."

The world of *The Gnädiges Fräulein* is conspicuously devoid of any authoritative discourse. Indeed, the play's characters all suffer various degrees of grotesque discursive failure: Molly and Polly frequently lose their "concentration," breaking off many topics in mid-sentence. The Fräulein herself communicates only by reciting memorized program notes and song titles from her soubrette days, and her most memorable utterance is an elongated "AHHHHHHHHHH!"— "expressing," Molly explains oxymoronically, "the inexpressible regret of all her regrets" (248). The play's only other "speaking characters" are Indian Joe and the Cocaloony Bird, both of whom restrict themselves to monosyllables like "How," "Pow," "Wow," "Ugh," and "Awk." Of course Molly and Polly, as their twinned names suggest, are loquacious, parrotty creatures, but their theories about the strange goings on of the humans and animals around them lack authority or eloquence (asked why the Fräulein uses a lorgnon even after the cocaloonies have gouged out both her eyes, Molly proclaims: "Habit! Habit! Now do you get the point?" [247]).

With no one in the play capable of successfully capturing the animal for symbolization (as Dysart, in *Equus*, captures the horse), a space is cleared for a different kind of literary animalizing, "affecting the animal" as Deleuze and Guattari say, "no less than the human" (237). *The Gnädiges Fräulein* is "traversed" by animality, as is the Fräulein herself. Having allowed herself that one desperate act of animality in the past, the Fräulein now performs it routinely, as a very means of survival. While once it was impulsive, extraordinary, and spectacular, her becoming-animal is now necessary and quotidian. Flapping her arms like wings as she dashes off stage to battle the cocaloonies, the Fräulein is a figure of the animalizing imagination, journeying into otherness. She returns, shaman-like, from the wilderness, bringing nourishment for all. The play ends, astonishingly, with a feast, a ritual incorporation that "invites a participatory animality as emotional response" (Bleakley xii). The invitation is accepted: the other characters are "swept away," as Deleuze and Guattari say: Molly moos like a cow, Polly awks, and Indian Joe struts like a cocaloony. The slapstick tragedy ends not with death or defeat but with perseverance. Though blood-soaked and blinded, the Fräulein keeps flapping her skinny arms like wings, awkwardly performing the awkwardness of survival on "this risky planet."

Notes

1 Marc 1968: 178.
2 Deleuze and Guattari 1987: 217.
3 This essay is dedicated to the memory of Linda Dorff, passionate Williams scholar and treasured friend, and to her beloved bird, Popcorn.
4 The original production closed after seven performances to terrible reviews and hostile audience response (Schneider 1986: 370). Martin Denton estimates that the play has received no more than twenty New York performances since it was written (qt. in Kolin 2001: 2).
5 Richard Gilman called the play a "witless arbitrary farce," and John McCarten said it was "spectacularly undisciplined" and "too outlandishly horrible to be tolerated" (qt. in Kolin 2).
6 The play begins with the sound of "a loud swoosh above …" after which a character says: "Was that two cocaloony birds that flew over or was it just one cocaloony bird that made a U-turn and flew back over again? OOPS! Birdwatchers, watch those birds! They're very dangerous birds if agitated and they sure do seem agitated today!" Throughout the play, characters have to periodically crouch down as the birds "swoosh" overhead, and the Fräulein's many entrances from the direction of the docks are accompanied by "terrific flapping and whistling noises" (243). A reviewer of the first production wrote that the "whistling, whooshing, cackling flight" of the cocaloony birds sounded "like a half-spent rocket dragging a loosely screwed wooden caboose along neglected tracks" (Nadel 1966).
7 For an illuminating analysis of the complex ideological agendas underlying animal acts, see, for example, Elizabeth A. Lawrence's essay on rodeo (1990).

Works cited

Baker, S. (2000) *The Postmodern Animal*. London: Reaktion Books.
Bachelard, G. (1986) *Lautréamont*. Dallas: The Dallas Institute Publications.
Baudrillard, J. (1994) *Simulacra and Simulation*. Michigan: U of Michigan P.
Bleakley, A. (2000) *The Animalizing Imagination*. London and New York: Macmillan and St. Martin's Press.

DeGrazia, D. (1996) *Taking Animals Seriously: Mental Life and Moral Status*. Cambridge: Cambridge UP.

Deleuze, G. and Guattari, F. (1987) *A Thousand Plateaus: Capitalism and Schizophrenia*, trans. B. Massumi. Minneapolis: U of Minnesota P.

Derrida, J. (1999) "L'Animal que donc je suis (à suivre)." *L'Animal autobiographique: Autour de Jacques Derrida*, ed. M.-L. Mallet. Paris: Galilée.

Dorff, L. (1999) "Theatricalist Cartoons: Tennessee Williams's Late 'Outrageous' Plays." *The Tennessee Williams Annual Review* 2: 13–34.

Foster, H. (1996) *The Return of the Real: The Avant-Garde at the End of the Century*. Cambridge, MA: MIT Press.

Kolin, P. (2001) "A play about terrible birds: Tennessee Williams's *The Gnädiges Fräulein* and Alfred Hitchcock's *The Birds*." *South Atlantic Review*, Winter: 1–22.

Lawrence, E.A. (1990) "Rodeo Horses: The Wild and the Tame," in R. Willis (ed.) *Signifying Animals*. London: Unwin Hyman.

Lykke, N. (1996) "Between Monsters, Goddesses, and Cyborgs: Feminist Confrontations with Science," in N. Lykke and R. Braidotti (eds), *Between Monsters, Goddesses, and Cyborgs: Feminist Confrontations with Science, Medicine, and Cyberspace*. London: Zed Books.

Marc, F. (1968) "How Does a Horse See the World?" in H. B. Chip (ed.), *Theories of Modern Art: A Source Book by Artists and Critics*, contributions by P. Selz and J.C. Taylor. Berkeley and Los Angeles: U of California P.

Nadel, N. (1966) "Bizarre, Grim 'Slapstick Tragedy.'" *New York World Telegram*, February 23: 30.

Phillips, A. (1996) *Terrors and Experts*. Cambridge, MA: Harvard UP.

Schneider, A. (1986) *Entrances: An American Director's Journey*. New York: Viking.

Shildrick, M. (1996) "Posthumanism and the Monstrous Body." *Body and Society* 11 no. 1.

Wheeler, W. (1999) *A New Modernity? Change in Science, Literature, and Politics*. London: Lawrence and Wishart.

Williams, R. (1989) *The Politics of Modernism*. London: Verso.

Williams, T. (1970) *The Gnädiges Fräulein* in *Dragon Country: A Book of Plays*. New York: New Directions, 215–62.

Chapter 5

Zoo Stories

"Boundary Work" in Theater History

> Zoos ultimately tell us stories about boundary-making activities on the part of humans ... Western metropolitan zoos are spaces where humans engage in cultural self-definition against a variably constructed and opposed nature. With animals as the medium, they inscribe a cultural sense of distance from that loosely defined realm that has come to be called "nature."
>
> (Kay Anderson)[1]

> You don't go to a zoo to see a lion or a tiger, but rather to see a *mise en promiscuité* of African lions, polar bears, Bengal tigers, Australian kangaroos.
>
> (Alain Fleischer)[2]

My point of departure is an improbable one for a project in theater ecology: a formulation by F.T. Marinetti, founder of the modernist theatrical movement that was arguably the least interested in, if not most hostile to, the claims of the natural world. The Futurists' unabashed technophilia was the cutting edge of that programmatic suppression of the non-human upon which modernity's ideal of progress increasingly depended. That suppression returned, as often happens, in metaphor, and among the many metaphors with which Marinetti, like other modernists, theorized the emerging theater are two that interest me especially: the zoo and the circus. Marinetti compared the zoo to the conventional psychological theater, which he despised, and the circus to his Futuristic ideal of a theater of action and energy:

> The conventional theater exalts the inner life, professorial meditation, libraries, museums, zoos, monotonous crises of

conscience, stupid analyses of feelings, in other words, psychology, whereas on the other hand the circus and variety theater exalt action, heroism, life in the open air.

(120)

Like other theatrical modernists, notably Frank Wedekind[3] and Max Reinhardt,[4] Marinetti was drawn to what he saw as the freedom, dynamism, danger, and passion of the circus. With its (apparently) novel configurations of animal and human behavior, the circus represented transformation and transcendence, principles that the modernists valued so highly. The circus offered the spectacle of nature overcome, set aside, or remade by the imagination and ingenuity of humankind. From this perspective, the zoo appeared, by contrast, as a space of rationalistic analysis and static observation.

Though he did not know it, Marinetti's formulation mirrored a new animal discourse that was arduously installed in Western culture from the eighteenth century onward, within which the zoo eventually emerged as an exemplary site of serious, even scientific public knowledge about the natural world. The main themes of this evolving discourse were observation and education; its main ideological purpose was to justify the cruelty involved in the age-old practice of removing animals from their natural habitats and forcing them to endure lifetimes of loneliness and captivity for the entertainment of human beings. In the rhetoric of this discourse, the circus was often invoked, as were other animal acts and animal sports, as examples of an opposite relation to animals—a barbaric and unethical relation—utterly different from the enlightened one supposedly represented by the zoo. The contrast conveniently masked the fact that the origins of the zoo lay in impulses and practices that were virtually indistinguishable from those underlying the use of animals in circuses: namely, acquisitiveness, exoticism, sensationalism, and cruelty. Marinetti's contrast, then, was as bogus as it was common.

But it is not my purpose here to contest Marinetti's formulations, nor to test the value of his metaphors as descriptors of modernist theater. Rather, I want to propose that his models be understood not as metaphors at all, but instead as cultural and institutional contexts within an expanded scene of theater history. It is not only metaphorically that the zoo and the circus can illuminate theater history: their relation to theater is not only the *paradigmatic* one that Marinetti intended; it is also a syntagmatic one, a relation of contiguity and continuity, of cultural co-presence. Like all those other metaphors with which the modernist theater attempted to theorize itself—the theater as laboratory, as temple, as fairground booth, lecture hall, street accident, court of law, sports arena—the circus and the zoo were not only cultural institutions *like* theater; they were also cultural institutions existing *alongside* theater. As such they deployed contemporaneous ideological discourses in ways that paralleled but also significantly differed from their use in theater. To explore the relationships—formal, taxonomic, and material—between the theater and these institutions is to link the projects of theater history and cultural studies. In what follows, I initiate one such linkage: by enquiring into the relationship between theater and animals, I propose to relate theater history to that branch of cultural studies that, in the last decade of the twentieth century, began "to bring 'nature' 'back into' social theory by contesting its abstraction from society" (Fitzsimmons and Goodman 194).

Cultural studies turns to the animal as it has previously turned to other marginalized groups (like the insane, the disabled, the "primitive"), with a recognition of the constituent power of the margin. It turns to the animal with the recognition that it is often the most active ideological categories that are hardest to see, since ideology works by naturalizing its terms and veiling its taxonomies. As the editors of an important recent collection on animals put it: "animals have been so indispensable to the structure of human affairs and so tied up with our visions of progress and the good life that we have been unable to (even try to) fully see them. Their very centrality prompted us to simply look away and ignore their fates" (Wolch and Emel xi). In recent decades, however, many disciplines have begun to "take animals seriously,"[5] looking at them through disciplinary lenses that include the geographical, the literary, the philosophical, the art-historical, the psychoanalytical[6] and the performative (the latter initiated by an issue of the journal *Performance Research* focusing on animals).[7] What might it mean to turn a specifically theatrical lens on animals? What light might be shed on cultural constructions of animality by framing them in terms of dramatic movements, genres, and structures, or in terms of theatrical protocols, conventions, and aesthetics?

Conversely, what might be revealed by turning an animal lens on theater, or—to use Alan Bleakley's suggestive phrase—by "animalizing" performance? Two possibilities immediately present themselves. First, the ambiguous politics of animal studies might help to illuminate the equally ambiguous politics of theater. Like theater, animals have never secured a clear and strong position on either the right or the left in the ideology of progress. Even today, decades after that ideology has been under attack from the left, only a few branches of feminism and postmodernism have embraced the animal. Most progressive movements tend to associate animal movements with premodern or New Age stances, and, accordingly, to dismiss them politically. Thus the animal, like the theater, is a politically ambiguous site, with a potential for generating perspectives and practices beyond the hardened binaries of the past. This politically deconstructive potential of the animal has, in recent years, drawn postmodern artists and philosophers[8] to it as to "a reminder of the limits of human understanding, and also of the value of working *at those limits*" (Baker 2000: 16).

Second: theater history might also find in the animal a useful site for understanding the historical role of performance in what social scientists call "boundary work": the drawing and blurring of lines of demarcation between and within groups, by means of which social relationships are configured and reconfigured over time. The boundary work that goes on around animals involves the configuration of the human itself, and animal acts are a principal site of this configuration. As the editors of a recent book on the subject write: "The animal act configures the human in the company, in the obscure language and thought of the animal. Animal vitality and consciousness are vicariously restored to the human being, allowing for conceptual breakthroughs and flights of fancy" (Ham and Senior 1). Animal performance, then—especially animal performance alongside or within contexts of human performance— is ideologically fraught. That old piece of advice to actors to avoid being on stage with a live animal may be more than the phenomenological common sense it is usually taken to be; it may be, as the same writers say, that "the spectacle of animals and humans performing together calls the spectator to other self-recognitions than that of the responsible citizen of the polis or the autonomous subject of philosophy and ethics" (1). The performing animal, in short, is the exemplary actor on that conceptual stage that is "the nature-culture borderlands" (Wolch and Emel).

The history of theater offers many points of entry for an enquiry into the theatrical animal. Long before the modernist romanticization of circus, theatrical activity unfolded in the vicinity of spectacular and usually violent animal acts, most famously in ancient Rome and Elizabethan England. In both theater cultures, the syntagmatic relationship between animal acts and theatrical presentation was rendered literal by geographical proximity, as is so graphically seen, for example, in the maps of the South Bank, reproduced in many a theater history textbook, which shows the bear- and bull-baiting rings right next to the Globe. The syntagmatic relationship might also have been actualized in a certain amount of performative overlap, as for example in the possibility that the bear called for in *The Winter's Tale* may not have been an actor in an animal suit but rather an actual bear borrowed from the neighboring Bear Gardens, owned and operated by Philip Henslowe.[9] As for the paradigmatic relation between animal and human entertainment, it is perhaps reflected in the agonistic form of Greek tragedy, and certainly has appeared throughout theater history in imagery and action, ranging from Macbeth's remark about being "tied to a stake" and having "bear-like" to "fight the course,"[10] to Lucky's animal act in *Godot*: "Think, pig!" The paradigmatic use of another and extremely popular form of animal entertainment is the subject of a fascinating study by Edward Berry, entitled *Shakespeare and the Hunt*.

The sharing of architectural forms between animal spectacles and theatrical representation also has a long history, and a strangely inverted moment in that history gives me a point of entry into the theatrical "zoo story" I want to tell here. In 1960, the Bronx Zoo became the first zoo in history to have an in-house multidisciplinary design team. Appointed to the head of the team was Jerry Johnson, a theater designer. His mandate was to infuse the exhibits with visual drama. By "contriving zoo exhibits as stage sets, like gigantic dioramas," Johnson set a new aesthetic standard in zoo design, making exhibits that were "beautifully convincing and almost mystical in their visual appeal" (Hancocks 106).

The Bronx Zoo is at the center of my zoo story, but, as another famous zoo story puts it: "sometimes a person has to go a very long distance out of his way to come back a short distance correctly" (Albee 21). The quotation, of course, is from the most famous zoo story in modern theater, Edward Albee's, which had its New York premiere at the Provincetown Playhouse in 1960. Ironically, there is no zoo in *The Zoo Story*, at least no zoo is *seen* in it, and in fact there is no zoo story either. Although Jerry keeps promising a zoo story, he never actually gets to it. His zoo story is first displaced by another animal story—"the story of Jerry and the dog"—and later by his murder-suicide, in which his death cry (according to the stage direction) is the "sound of an infuriated and fatally wounded animal" (47). In his book *Reading Zoos*, Randy Malamud characterizes this displacement as typical, saying that most zoo stories situate themselves "*against* the zoo—resisting it, subverting it, deconstructing it ... The zoo alleges that it can tell a story, its own story, roughly along the lines of 'Here is a zebra.' The zoo story instead more routinely tells something like 'Here is a voyeur'; 'Here is a victim'; 'Here is a sadist'; 'Here is a corpse'" (55).

Approximately four decades before Albee's play opened, another zoo story had premiered at the same historic New York theater in 1922: Eugene O'Neill's *The Hairy Ape*. This zoo story did not displace the zoo: on the contrary, it made the zoo the scene of its climactic and tragic final act, in which the protagonist, Yank, engineers something resembling Jerry's murder-suicide, but this time at the hands of an animal rather than a fellow human. Yank's encounter with the gorilla in the play's final scene is a rare instance (outside children's theater) of human and wild animal sharing the stage, a rare *live* performance of interspecies interaction, which is the stock in trade of so much popular cinema and television, from *Dr. Doolittle* to *The Silence of the Lambs*.[11] It is, in fact, a classic piece of "boundary work," the use of animality to configure human subjectivity in performance. The explicit target of O'Neill's reconfiguration is the injustice of the class system, but his use of this particular animal, a gorilla, in this particular venue, complicates and obfuscates his class analysis by unconsciously linking it to *racial* difference.

Both Albee's zoo and O'Neill's are, explicitly, New York zoos, the former quite specifically the Central Park Zoo. In both plays, as the critical literature has amply explicated, zoos are troped as exemplars of the alienation and brutality of modern metropolitan civilization, the caged animal standing in for the disempowered and mystified subject of industrial capitalism. In both plays, too, zoos function as ambiguous sites for the fantasy of erasing or overcoming the class differences that American ideology programmatically obscures.[12] Albee's play is set in that paradigm of the carefully constructed public space, Central Park, within which different classes are supposed to be able to safely engage in certain performances of democracy. The class encounter here—between the upper-class Peter and the *lumpen* Jerry—goes horribly wrong. The territorial battle over the park bench turns lethal, turning this zone of supposedly safe civic interaction into a dangerous wilderness where brutish members of society can prey on their social superiors. Three decades after Albee's play, the word "wilding" was used to describe an actual crime in the same park, this time with race added to class in the encounter of difference.[13]

Both the Central Park and its zoo have, of course, played significant roles in the city's geography of class and race. Class was a consideration in the decision to put the new New York zoo, when it opened in 1899, up in the Bronx. The Central Park Menagerie was by then attracting increasingly large numbers of visitors, most of them coming up from the ghettoes of the lower East Side. The rowdy presence of these fervent animal-watchers had begun to represent a threat to Fifth Avenue real-estate prices; if many of them could be deflected north, it was suggested in the fund-raising process, that threat would be reduced. Just as Central Park itself had originally been conceived partly as a buffer between classes—masquerading as a place of communion between them—the Bronx Zoo was part of an effort to redeploy the principle of distance in the service of a new, more proxemous notion of animals. The history of this new notion provides interesting parallels with the history of modern theater, with which it shared the pursuit of verisimilitude and authenticity.

The appointment of Jerry Johnson and the Bronx Zoo design team institutionalized a practice that had been launched with much fanfare in the early years of the twentieth century by one of the greatest zoo innovators of all time, Carl Hagenbeck, whose own peculiar history and interests made him particularly receptive to and reflective of the characteristic ambivalences of the modern zoo. Hagenbeck's project encapsulates many of the very agendas, problematics, and tensions that make the zoo an illuminating context for theater history. Like the second generation of theatrical modernists, Hagenbeck was a passionate innovator who found himself challenging the hard-fought victories of a recent and equally passionate revolution, that of nineteenth-century empirical science. His innovation, like that of all the anti-naturalist modernisms, occupied the slippery ground that greets rationalists who venture beyond positivism. In theater, that ground was claimed mainly by theatricalism and expressionism, and certain fundamental precepts of both those movements can be discerned in Hagenbeck's project.

Hagenbeck's Tierpark opened in Hamburg, Germany, in 1907. It was the first zoo to move its captives into the open air and place them in naturalistic landscapes that sought to mimic their natural environments. Hagenbeck's professed goal was twofold, mixing in equal parts concern for the animals' well-being, and concern with the enjoyment of their human spectators. The radical incommensurability of these two goals conveniently escaped Hagenbeck, as it has many of his successors in zoo culture.

Like all progressive zoo thinkers after him, Hagenbeck wanted animals to enjoy more freedom than was allowed by the sanitized interior enclosures of nineteenth-century zoos. These zoos, self-proclaimed models of scientific empiricism and taxonomic inquiry, took elaborate pains to present their captives as objects of study: singled out, set apart, abstracted from reality, labeled, explained. A host of design elements helped to concretize the scientific frame: animals were grouped according to scientific classification rather than geographical origin, cages were harshly lit and coldly tiled to resemble laboratories, extreme cleanliness and odorlessness were sought by extreme means (cages were designed so they could be flushed like toilets), and animals were scrupulously "protected" from what were considered unhealthy drafts of fresh air and disease-carrying exposure to natural soil.

The scientific zoo was a self conscious alternative to the genre of animal display that Hagenbeck himself had been most closely linked to by his personal history. Having started out with six performing seals at a local fairground, Hagenbeck had rapidly built one of the world's largest animal dealerships. His first Tierpark, which attracted huge paying crowds, was in fact a modern exemplar of that ancient ancestor of the zoo: the menagerie. Dating back thousands of years before the Christian era and spread around the world, the practice of collecting and displaying exotic animals either in cages or in enclosed parks was originally affordable only to a tiny elite. In the early modern period, however, colonial expansion and commercialization gradually increased both the supply of, and demand for, exotic animals. The private menageries that had been status symbols for European royalty since the sixteenth century were slowly transformed into more "democratic" institutions, relocated from palace gardens like Versailles and Windsor Castle to public parks like Paris's *Jardin des Plantes* and the Zoological Gardens of London.[14] Here, in keeping with the Baconian idea that not only words but also *things* were viable instruments of knowledge and instruction, and with the help of the growing terminology of scientific classification, the spectacle of the caged animal could delight the masses under cover of instructing them. Like its contemporaneous theatrical form, naturalist melodrama, the scientific zoo supplied sensation dressed as sober truth.

The kind of zoo that Hagenbeck envisioned in the early years of the twentieth century had a markedly different ideal. "I desired, above all things," Hagenbeck writes in his autobiography, "to give the animals the maximum of liberty." His very next lines show, however, that this desire was partly construed in theatrical rather than actual terms: "I wished to exhibit them not as captives, confined within narrow spaces, and looked at between iron bars, but as free to wander from place to place within as large a limit as possible, and with no bars to obstruct the view and serve as a reminder of captivity" (20). The supposed natural freedom of animals could not simply be asserted; it had to be *shown*, translated into visual terms for spectators. The animals had to be *seen* to be free, "as they really were," going about their natural lives in natural ways. This meant that spectators had to be helped to disregard the reality of the animals' captive state, to forget the vast distance they had been moved from their natural habitats to this site of display. In short, the bars of the cage had to be replaced by an invisible fourth wall. The familiar paradox of realist theater came into play: the more authenticity sought, the more illusion required. Hagenbeck embarked upon an elaborate design project, experimenting with terraces, platforms, panoramas, and vistas to create the illusion of natural habitats.

But the emphasis on freedom was not merely aesthetic. It was, in fact, a key element of a certain (prevalent though not dominant) view of animality, one that is also embedded in Marinetti's contrast between circuses and zoos. This view, of which the extreme and most elaborated philosophical statement came from Nietzsche, equates animality with vitality, health, freedom, even sanity. It stands in partial opposition both to the mechanistic view of animals inherited from Cartesian rationalism (and coded in the protocols of the scientific zoo) and to the religious view of animals coded in medieval and early modern schemas like the Great Chain of Being. While both those views inferiorized animals in relation to human beings—the Cartesian with regard to consciousness and feeling, the Christian with regard to morality—the romantic, Nietzschean view idealized them, especially in relation to modern Western humanity. This account of animality, then, proved particularly attractive to counter-traditional artists seeking metaphors for a critique of repressive modern civilization. The romantic, vitalist, view of animality persists throughout the century, appearing in dramatic works like Peter Shaffer's *Equus*, and, more recently (2002), Mabou Mines's *Ecco Porco*.

O'Neill's *The Hairy Ape* is a complicated and self-contradictory version of this view of animality, reflecting the clash of romantic and populist discourses within American ideology. The inspiration for the play was the story of a sailor whom O'Neill had briefly known in his seafaring days, and who committed suicide by throwing himself overboard in mid-ocean. O'Neill wondered, why this man, "*so proud* (as he put it) *of his animal superiority and in complete harmony* with his limited conception of the universe, should kill himself" (qt. in Falk 136).

The driving force of O'Neill's play is the question of what it means to be "in harmony" with the universe; or, in Yank's favorite phrase, "to belong." That the zoo should be Yank's last resort in his quest for identity and belonging is, of course, deeply and intentionally ironic, although the irony intended is tragic rather than, as I read it, discursive and ideological. In the remainder of this paper I want to read O'Neill's final scene through its setting, which encapsulates many of the material and ideological contradictions by which the modern zoo assists in the boundary-work necessary for framing modernist forms, including modernism's tragedies of self-consciousness.

The zoo that is explicitly called for in O'Neill's play, the New York Zoo, had a few years before been the venue of an extraordinary piece of boundary-work. In 1906, the New York Zoo had for a period of time displayed in its Monkey House an African man named Ota Benga. Ota Benga had been brought to the United States from the Belgian Congo in 1904 by the explorer Samuel Verner and displayed along with other Africans at the 1906 World's Fair in St. Louis. He was then transferred to the Bronx Zoo, where he was housed with many monkeys, several chimpanzees, a famous gorilla, and an orangutan. The accounts of Ota Benga's experience are chilling: "There were 40,000 visitors to the park on Sunday. Nearly every man, woman and child of this crowd made for the monkey house to see the star attraction in the park—the wild man from Africa. They chased him about the grounds all day, howling, jeering, and yelling. Some of them poked him in the ribs, others tripped him up, all laughed at him" (Bradford and Blume 269). Under threat of legal action from local Black clergy, the director of the zoo compromised to this extent: during the day, Ota Benga was allowed to leave his cage. He had to circulate around the zoo in a white suit, and he returned to the monkey house every night to sleep. After repeated protests by Black clergy, Ota Benga was eventually released from this captivity, soon after which he committed suicide.

The practice of exhibiting "exotic" humans alongside animals dates back to antiquity, and was a regular feature even of Carl Hagenbeck's first Tierpark, where a group of Lapps were displayed in full Arctic regalia, including skis and reindeer, and Eskimos paddled around in kayaks, supposedly hunting seals (Croke 145). This kind of boundary-blurring was, of course, also a kind of boundary-making, part of the metropolitan zoo's project of defining Western civilization and its inhabitants as superior not only to nature but to nature-identified, "primitive" populations who would not be entirely out of place in the inferiorizing space of the zoo.

The final scene of O'Neill's play, in which a man exchanges places with a zoo animal, encapsulates the role of the zoo in the kind of boundary-work that then serves human culture's ideological programs. It shows clearly how the zoo is a site of boundary-blurring and identity crises, which facilitate the demeaning classifications and oppressive identifications by means of which cultural power is wielded. In O'Neill's scene, the gorilla is set apart from other animals, but they are not far away. The presence of a horde of monkeys, unseen but chattering loudly, confirms his animality. At the same time, and crucially for Yank's tragic purposes, he is also humanized, explicitly and specifically, as follows: *"The gigantic animal himself is seen squatting on his haunches on a bench in much the same attitude as Rodin's 'Thinker'"* (O'Neill 195).

O'Neill's zoo exemplifies several other versions of the permanent identity crises that characterize zoo animals. The first of these is what might be called the "crisis of individuality." The stage direction reads: *"In the monkey house at the Zoo. One spot of clear gray light falls on the front of one cage so that the interior can be seen. The other cages are vague, shrouded in shadow from which chattering can be heard. On the one cage a sign from which the word 'gorilla' stands out"* (228). By convention and necessity, zoos usually have only one or two animals standing in for the entire species. Their representational status is often (as is the case in O'Neill's play) signaled by the signage on their enclosure: they are labeled generically: "Gorilla," "Chimpanzee," etc., rather than "A gorilla." This abstraction is dictated by the putatively educational mission of the zoo. But the embodiedness of animals, their seductive "flesh and blood" reality, militates against the official generalizing impulse. Visitors mostly prefer to relate to the animal as a unique individual rather than a representative type, a preference which has led to the interesting and now highly controversial phenomenon of "zoo pets," animals who are singled out for special attention and various anthropomorphizing treatments, including naming, costuming, even performances, by both zoo keepers and zoo visitors. (The orangutan with whom Ota Benga was exhibited in the Bronx Zoo was named Dohung and was trained to ride a bicycle. The sign on Ota Benga's cage combined both conventions: it gave his name, but it also identified him as "The African Pygmy.") The zoo pet inconveniently disrupts the scientific boundary-work of zoos, but it usefully mediates between the divergent agendas of exhibitors and spectators, a mediation that pays off economically.

Another identity dilemma for the zoo comes from the fact that not all animals are equally fascinating or adorable to human beings. Visitors' preference for the more striking-looking animals— "charismatic mega-fauna," as they are sometimes called, or, as one writer dubs them, "National Geographic animals"—conflicts with the modern zoo's commitment to context, accuracy, and completeness in its account of animal life. O'Neill's gorilla—as well as his real-life counterpart in the Bronx Zoo at that time—falls into this category. The gorilla's "high-exhibition value," as it is called, was reflected in a pamphlet published by the New York Zoo around the same time as O'Neill's play. It contains the following chilling information and advice:

> [The Gorilla] is very rarely seen in captivity. The only specimen which up to 1911 had ever reached America alive lived but five days after its arrival. Despite the fact that these creatures seldom live in captivity longer than a few months, they are always being sought by zoological gardens. The agents of the New York Zoological Society are constantly on the watch for an opportunity to procure and send hither a good specimen of that wonderful creature; and whenever one arrives, all persons interested are advised to see it *immediately*—before it dies of sullenness, lack of exercise, and indigestion.
>
> (Hornaday 1921)

Amazingly enough, the author of this pamphlet is William T. Hornaday, the first director of the Bronx Zoo, and the man who had overseen and defended the exhibition of Ota Benga in the Monkey House. A visionary animal advocate and a leader of the movement to enlist zoos in the cause of wildlife preservation, Hornaday's attitudes furnish some of the most vivid examples of the ideological complexity and internal contradictions of human discourse on animals. His love and admiration of animals was balanced by contempt for certain human beings, some of them visitors to his zoo, whom he described as "low-lived beasts who appreciate nothing and love filth and disorder" (1915: 63).

The rhetorical use of animals in the articulation of racial and class prejudice has been amply documented by cultural historians.[15] Hornaday's example alerts us to the sobering and politically confusing fact that the source of discourses of bestialization can sometimes be animal lovers and advocates. A well-known and sensational example is the following story about Adolf Hitler watching an animal film: "During the scenes showing men savagely torn to pieces by animals, he remained calm and alert. When the film showed animals being hunted, he would cover his eyes with his hands and asked to be told when it was over. Whenever he saw a wounded animal, he wept" (Payne 461). A more complicated and perhaps more disturbing example is that of primatologist Dian Fossey, whose defense of endangered gorillas often involved serious disregard and disrespect for the rights and needs of native Rwandans (Armbruster 218). Her racial prejudice is apparent in the binary formulation she offered for the species' endangered status: it was, she said, because of "the encroachment of native man upon its habitat—and neglect by civilized man" (Fossey).

The native–civilized dichotomy is of course pervasive in O'Neill as in other early modernists. But in *The Hairy Ape* the mediating role played by animals in that dichotomy emerges most clearly. Yank's moment of tragic self-consciousness crucially involves a construction of the animal as fundamentally and blessedly territorial, unalienable, beyond the reach of the debilitating geopathologies of modern human beings. Yank concludes that the gorilla "belongs" while he himself doesn't:

> Youse can sit and dope dream in de past, green woods, de jungle and de rest of it. Den yuh belong and dey don't. Den yuh kin laugh at 'em, see? Yuh're de champ of de woild. But me—I ain't got no past to tink in, nor nothin' dat's coming', on'y what's now—and dat don't belong. Sure, you're de best off! ... You belong! Sure! Yuh're de on'y one in de woild dat does, yuh lucky stiff!
>
> (230)

Yank's construction of animality as essentially territorial is implicitly contested by its setting. The zoo is the place where the modern world stages its account of the "place" of animals. The semiotics of the zoo, however, make that account profoundly paradoxical and self-contradictory: the zoo is the place of animals who have been displaced from their "real" places, animals whose real places are too distant from urban centers to allow easy access. Indeed, it is the most distant, most "exotic" animals who were and remain the zoo's *raison d'être*, and zoo visitors' desire for proximity to these animals has challenged zoo designers from Carl Hagenbeck and his famous bar-less enclosures to the designers of Disney's Animal Kingdom and their notion of "environmental immersion" for both animals and spectators. To overcome the physical and conceptual distance that separates modern city-dwellers from wild animals requires presentational techniques consonant not only with changing views of particular animals and of animals in general, but also with the ever-changing conventions of dominant visual media. These conventions are often in stark conflict with the zoo's more ecological agendas. For example, when plate glass windows replaced iron bars as the means of containment, the intended gain in freedom was entirely the spectator's, who could now escape from the unpleasant and symbolically powerful materiality of cages and iron bars. For the animal, however, it was just one more sensory deprivation, one more concretization of the geopathology that began with its capture in the wild.

The zoo animal leads a remarkable bifurcated ideological existence, inscribed on the one hand within the modern zoo's increasingly high-minded claims of education, ecological consciousness-raising, preservation of endangered species, and, on the other, the persisting low-brow voyeurism of zoo-goers, which even the most serious zoos still cater to, with practices like public feeding-times and even public mating.[16] The zoo inherits and extends the culture's double-coding of animals as objects of knowledge and objects of fantasy. The very first elephant ever to be seen in America was first exhibited on Broadway (well, the corner of Broadway and Beaver Street!) and then at the first commencement of Harvard University! (Hancocks 87) Conversely, the great touring menageries of the Ringling Brothers and Barnum and Bailey advertised themselves as "Traveling Universities of Natural History," and boasted thousands of animals "advantageously displayed in electric-lighted dens, where they may be studied at close range" (qt. in Hancocks 87).

The coexistence of knowledge and fantasy in human beings' dealings with animals unsettles and disproves Marinetti's contrast between zoo and circus with which I began. *The Hairy Ape*, however, suggests why this contrast, tenuous as it is, is ideologically useful. In the film version of the play, made in 1944, the scene with the gorilla was moved from its climactic position, and placed several scenes before the end. Rather than concluding a tragedy of self-consciousness, the meeting with the caged animal initiated a comedy of social conformism. Instead of killing himself, Yank saves various people, including his former upper-class tormentors, and ends up cheerfully well-adjusted to his station in life! Interestingly enough, the encounter with the gorilla does not take place in the New York Zoo. It takes place in the tent of a traveling circus. Yank goes to the circus after seeing a poster featuring its chief attraction, a gorilla named Goliath. The poster shows Goliath holding a swooning young white-clad woman in his arms. The story's displacement from tragedy to comedy, zoo to circus, mirrors its ideological transformation from O'Neill's romantic socialism to Hollywood's pacifying fatalism. Whereas O'Neill's animal had emulated Rodin's heroic human thinker, Hollywood's working-class man is made iconographically to mirror that exemplary spectacular beast of the popular modern imagination, King Kong.[17]

In modernism, Baudrillard has said, "Animals must be made to say that they are not animals" (129). The modern zoo is a principal site of this paradoxical program of loud silencing. But the zoo stories of the modern theater are actively involved in it as well. A final and current example: Steven Berkoff, writing about his recent monologue "Dog," remarks: "Naturally the desire to be beast is overwhelming." Then he adds: "and what better beast than a fascistic, football-loving lager lout who owns a pit bull."[18] Playing both roles—man and dog—Berkoff reminds us that the modern theater, no less than the modern zoo, is an important site for the ceaseless boundary-work that is the chief burden of the beasts.

Notes

1 Anderson 1998: 276.
2 Qt. in Chris Dercon 1990: 19.
3 See Ham 1997.
4 Reinhardt's famous *Grosses Schauspielhaus* in Berlin was the refurbished Shuhmann Circus.
5 DeGrazia 1996.

6 Some important recent works are: Arnold Arluke and Clinton R. Sanders, *Regarding Animals* (1996); Alan Bleakley, *The Animalizing Imagination* (2000); Susan Davis, *Spectacular Nature: Corporate Culture and Sea World* (1997); Aubrey Manning and James Serpel, *Animals and Human Society: Changing Perspectives* (1994); Bob Mullan and Garry Marvin, *Zoo Culture* (1987; 1999); Chris Philo and Chris Wilbert, *Animal Spaces, Beastly Places: New Geographies of Human–Animal Relations* (2000); Paul Shepard, *How Animals Made Us Human* (1996); Roy Willis, ed., *Signifying Animals* (1990).

7 *Performance Research* 5 no. 2 (Summer 2000).

8 See, for example, Jean Baudrillard, *Simulacra and Simulation* (1994); Gilles Deleuze and Félix Guattari, *A Thousand Plateaus: Capitalism and Schizophrenia* (1988); and Jacques Derrida, "The Animal That Therefore I Am (More to Follow)" (2002).

9 See Bliss 1994.

10 The film *Scotland, PA* offers a hilarious and provocative rumination on the relationship between power and animality in *Macbeth*. The transformation of the Macbeths into pioneers of the fast food hamburger chain reads like a gloss on the title of Carol Adams's famous book, *The Sexual Politics of Meat: A Feminist-Vegetarian Critical Theory* (revised edn. 2000).

11 See Wolfe and Elmer 1995.

12 In *Zoo Story*, Jerry ironically asks: "Say, what's the dividing line between upper middle-middle-class and lower-upper-middle-class?" (20).

13 Didion 1991.

14 The former in 1804, the latter 1847.

15 See, especially, Steve Baker 1993.

16 In the 1990s, the San Diego Zoo offered a tour called "Night Moves" billed as "a unique dating experience" "focusing on the wild courtship and mating rituals of the facility's exotic—and erotic—residents." Quoted in Malamud 1998: 236.

17 "The original monstrosity of the beast, object of terror and fascination, but never negative, always ambivalent, object of exchange also and of metaphor, in sacrifice, in mythology, in the heraldic bestiary, and even in our dreams and our phantasms—this monstrosity ... has been exchanged for a spectacular monstrosity: that of King Kong wrenched from his jungle and transformed into a music-hall star." Jean Baudrillard, "The Animals: Territory and Metamorphosis," in *Simulacra and Simulation* (1994), 135.

18 Berkoff 2002.

Works cited

Adams, C. (2000) *The Sexual Politics of Meat: A Feminist-Vegetarian Critical Theory*, revised edn. New York: Continuum.

Albee, E. (1959) *The Zoo Story*, in *Two Plays by Edward Albee*. New York: Signet.

Anderson, K. (1998) "Animals, Science, and Spectacle in the City," in J. Wolch and J. Emel (eds.) *Animal Geographies: Place, Politics and Identity in the Nature–Culture Borderlands*. London: Verso, 27–50.

Arluke, A. and Sanders, C.R. (1996) *Regarding Animals*. Philadelphia: Temple UP.

Armbruster, K. (1997) "'Surely, God, These Are My Kin': The Dynamics of Identity and Advocacy in the Life and Works of Dian Fossey," in J. Ham and M. Senior (eds) *Animal Acts: Configuring the Human in Western History*. London: Routledge, 209-30.

Baker, S. (1993) *Picturing the Beast: Animals, Identity, and Representation*. Manchester: Manchester UP.

—— (2000) *The Postmodern Animal*. London: Reaktion Books.

Baudrillard, J. (1994) *Simulacra and Simulation*. Ann Arbor: U of Michigan P.

Berkoff, S. (2002) "Dog," Director/Writer's Program Note, program for *One Man*. The Culture Project @ 45 Bleecker Street, January 23–March 10.

Berry, E. (2001) *Shakespeare and the Hunt: A Cultural and Social Study*. Cambridge: Cambridge UP.

Bleakley, A. (2000) *The Animalizing Imagination*. London and New York: Macmillan and St. Martin's P.

Bliss, M. (1994) "Property or Performer?: Animals on the Elizabethan Stage." *Theatre Studies* 39: 45–59.

Bradford, P.V. and Blume, H. (1992) *Ota Benga: The Pygmy in the Zoo*. New York: St. Martin's P.

Croke, V. (1997) *The Modern Ark: The Story of Zoos, Past, Present and Future*. New York: Scribner.

Davis, S. (1997) *Spectacular Nature: Corporate Culture and Sea World*. Berkeley: U of California P.

DeGrazia, D. (1996) *Taking Animals Seriously: Mental Life and Moral Status*. Cambridge: Cambridge UP.

Deleuze, G. and Guattari, F. (1988) *A Thousand Plateaus: Capitalism and Schizophrenia*, trans. B. Massumi. Minneapolis: U of Minnesota P.

Dercon, C. (1990) "Many Dreams of Many Gardens," trans B. Groeneveid, in *Theater Garden Bestarium: The Garden as Theatre as Museum*. Cambridge, MA: MIT Press.

Derrida, J. (2002) "The Animal That Therefore I Am (More to Follow)." *Critical Inquiry* 28 no. 2: 369–418.

Didion, J. (1991) "New York: Sentimental Journeys." *The New York Times Review of Books*, January 17. Online.

Falk, D. (1982) *Eugene O'Neill and the Tragic Tension* [1958]. New York: Gordian P.

Fitzsimmons, M. and Goodman, D. (1998) "Incorporating Nature: Environmental Narratives and the Reproduction of Food," in B. Braun and N. Castree (eds) *Remaking Reality: Nature at the Millennium*. London: Routledge, 193–219.

Fossey, D. (1970) "Making Friends with the Mountain Gorillas." *National Geographic* 137: 574–85.

Hagenbeck, C. (1910) *Beasts and Men*, trans. H.S.R. Elliot and A.G. Thacker. London: Longmans, Green.

Ham, J. (1997) "Taming the Beast: Animality in Wedekind and Nietzche," in J. Ham and M. Senior (eds) *Animal Acts: Configuring the Human in Western History*. London: Routledge, 145–64.

Hancocks, D. (2001) *A Different Nature: The Paradoxical World of Zoos and their Uncertain Future*. Berkeley: U of California P.

Hornaday, W.T. (1915) "The Police and the Public," in *Nineteenth Annual Report of the American Zoological Society (1914)*. New York: Clark & Fritta.

—— (1921) *Popular Official Guide of the New York Zoological Park*.

Malamud, R. (1998) *Reading Zoos: Representations of Animals in Captivity*. New York: New York UP.

Manning, A. and Serpel, J. (1994) *Animals and Human Society: Changing Perspectives*. London: Routledge.

Marinetti, F.T. (1972) *Marinetti: Selected Writings*, trans. R.W. Flint. New York: Farrar, Strauss and Giroux.

Mullan, B. and Marvin, G. (1999) *Zoo Culture* [1987]. Urbana: U of Illinois P.

O'Neill, E. (1995) *Anna Christie, The Emperor Jones, The Hairy Ape*. New York: Vintage Books.

Payne, R. (1960) *The Life and Death of Adolf Hitler*. New York: Prager.

Performance Research (2000) vol. 5 no. 2.

Philo, C. and Wilbert, C. (2000) *Animal Spaces, Beastly Places: New Geographies of Human–Animal Relations*. London: Routledge.

Scotland, PA (2001) Film, dir. W. Morrissette. Lot 47 Films.

Shepard, P. (1996) *How Animals Made Us Human*. Washington, DC: Island P.

Willis, R. (ed.) (1990) *Signifying Animals*. London: Unwin Hyman.

Wolch, J. and Emel, J. (eds) (1998) *Animal Geographies: Place, Politics and Identity in the Nature–Culture Borderlands*. London: Verso.

Wolfe, C. and Elmer, J. (1995) "Subject to Sacrifice: Ideology, Psychoanalysis, and the Discourse of Species in Jonathan Demme's *Silence of the Lambs*." *Boundary 2: An International Journal of Literature and Culture* 2 no. 3: 141–70.

Animalizing Interlude

Zoöpolis

By Una Chaudhuri and Marina Zurkow

All images courtesy of Marina Zurkow.
Google Street View images © 2010 Google.

Zoöpolis *is a collaborative project located at the intersections of urban theory, site-specific eco-art, and animal studies. Our point of departure is the recognition that, while the modern city is an animal habitat as much as a human one, urban animality is both physically and conceptually constricted: each category of animals is confined within an identity which is also a location: pets in the home, meat in the freezer, pests out of sight. Challenging this restrictive spatialization of species,* Zoöpolis *seeks to imagine the city as a space of shared animality, an eco-system capable of supporting the lives, pleasures, and freedoms not only of its human citizens but also of an expanded population of members of other species. The project draws its inspiration—and its title—from urban theorist Jennifer Wolch's similarly-titled article,[1] which envisions a new "ethic, practice, and politics of caring for animals and nature" in the postmodern city.*

The images, by Marina Zurkow, develop in dialogue with the texts, by Una Chaudhuri. The images—collages built on top of Google Street View shots of New York City—play with the aura of authority and veracity that now attaches to Google's mapping "services," and with the fact that Google Street View acts as an immersive digital double of the cities it represents. As such, it is a form of public space that has elicited a range of activities and responses, from accusations of privacy violation, to staged parades and absurd performances directed at Google's camera rig. Zoöpolis *treats the panoramic images offered by Street View as sites of artistic and ideological intervention, using these surfaces to imagine new conjunctions between the lives dictated by urban spaces of many kinds—encompassing various social classes, activities, and histories—and the natural behaviors of the other animals.*

"The Shock is Metaphysical"

In a *New York Times* opinion piece entitled "Wildlife," Brent Staples writes about the increasing numbers of wild animals—especially raccoons—that have been invading Brooklyn backyards lately. After describing a recent close encounter of his own, one that was harrowing enough for him to call 911, he protests: "Suburbanites and rural folks are no doubt laughing at us. But city slickers are entitled to be unnerved. Meeting 20 pounds of fangs and claws in a fenced-in urban yard and glimpsing the masked animal in a grassy country meadow make for two very different experiences. The shock is metaphysical" (3). *Zoöpolis* amplifies the shock that Staples calls "metaphysical" but that is perhaps more ontological, and certainly ideological. The presence of any animals, not just wild ones, in the city is governed by—and responded to in terms of—assumptions and norms developed over centuries of concerted territorialization, a long history of literally mapping human dominion onto multi-species landscapes. The question of who belongs where has always been both sentimental and brutal—sometimes aglow with the welcoming hearth but just as often coldly shutting out the unwanted outsider. For animals, both those affective poles of the concept of belonging are vastly magnified. Animals judged to belong with humans are invited into the most intimate of places, given catchy names and special diets, their presence normalized within civic and domestic space: these are our beloved pets, coddled and pampered at home, shown off and admired in the street. By contrast, those animals who are judged not to belong with humans are made to disappear: exterminated, eradicated, excluded, forgotten.

The prevailing "pet or pest" binary organizes the vast multiplicity of animal species from the perspective of human convenience, ignoring all other kinds of needs—on the part of both humans and non-humans—for more varied and complex interactions among species. *Zoöpolis* wants to remember and imagine those other kinds of needs. *Zoöpolis* wants to speak back to what Robert Michael Pyle has called the "extinction of experience" in modern life, the sad diminishing of opportunities to be in the presence of, to feel, touch, observe, smell and think about, forms of life that lie beyond the compass of human utility and instrumentalization (4). This thinning of experience is dangerous not only to the diversity-reliant environment, but also to humanity, feeding a deadly cycle of increasing homogeneity and anthropocentric cocooning.

Invited back in, the animals alter the metaphysic. Already, the raccoons are changing the rules. The laws of mega-buck advertising make one gigantic billboard enough for any single product, company, or service. But the raccoons ignore economics and are swarming onto adjacent boards. The fundamental Deleuzian law of animality—the law of the pack, the herd, the flock, the law of collective identity—is tearing the medium and the message away from their investments in singularity. Henceforth anything that multiplies will be called a raccoon. Proliferation will be called raccoonation. Later, all those who believe in concerted collective action will be called the Raccoon Nation.

The raccoons are also revealing the rules. They show that business and pleasure, work and play, selling and sliding are not the separate worlds they are purported to be. They are two sides of the same coin, two slips down the same slide. Another fundamental law of Deleuzian animality—freedom from faciality—is boldly and brazenly proclaimed from the very citadel of individualism: the celebrity face, the monumental portrait.

The secret is out: the clamorous claims to uniqueness and originality are tedious and outworn. Sliding between identities might be lots more fun. In Zoöpolis, there are slides at many intersections, and free raccoon masks.

Zooground Zero

The Animals in War Memorial was unveiled in Park Lane, London, in November 2004. Its ruptured wall—symbolizing the ramparts of war as well as the boundary between life and death—is adorned with bas-relief representatives of many species, including elephants and camels. Four realistically sculpted bronze animals—two mules, one horse, and one dog—take their places on either side of the wall: the burdened mules struggle wearily toward it, heads bowed, while the horse and dog walk free beyond it, in apparent pursuit of their lost companions. The memorial commemorates the many millions of animals that the British and Allied forces "enlisted," according to the memorial's website, "to serve and often die alongside their armies." The website goes on: "These animals were chosen for a variety of their natural instincts, and vast numbers were killed, often suffering agonising deaths from wounds, starvation, thirst, exhaustion, disease and exposure." ("Information about Animals in War")

The number of animals honored by the London memorial pales in comparison to the numbers of those who will be remembered by the only memorials that will be erected in *Zoöpolis*: memorials to those countless billions who have been thoughtlessly slaughtered and sacrificed in the course of that most ancient of all conflicts: the human war on animals. Before those monuments can be built, however, the first order of business will be to convert all previously planned monuments and memorials, as well as those currently under construction, into refuges for rescued animals. Whenever possible, the refuges will include play areas for the young of various species, including humans. Raccoon slides will be prominently featured, as will monkey bars and parrot perches.

The Raccoonae

Procyon lotor (that is, surprisingly, the scientific name for the raccoon) was back in the news today, this time on the front page of the Arts section. Theater critic Ben Brantley's experience of *The Bacchae* in Central Park, was, he forthrightly admits, shaped by an unintentional (as far as we know) opening ritual:

> I saw a wonderful raccoon at the Delacorte Theater the other night. It appeared, as serene and silent as a rising moon, at the far edge of the open-air stage in Central Park where the Public Theater presents its summer productions. Its face a shining-eyed mask, this creature froze for just a second to scrutinize the audience from the spotlight before being followed in unhurried procession into the darkness by two other raccoons.

Animals, especially animals in masks, struck Brantley as uncannily apt portals into this particular play, their performance "an appetite-whetting prologue to a play about the animal in humanity." The raccoons were, for Brantley—as they had been for Brent Staples in the story that brought the raccoons into *Zoöpolis*—"reminders of the mysterious and often forgotten coexistence of the natural and urban worlds in New York City." Sadly for Brantley (and for audiences of this *Bacchae*) the production failed utterly to tap into this potentially enriching coexistence, this framing Big Picture of human and non-human animality which was the wellspring of Greek tragedy, making its characters' actions deeply—that is, ontologically and ethically—consequential. Performed literally against the backdrop of nature, the Central Park production shared with Greek theater something that has been lost to Western theatricality since—"outsideness," open air, a location in something one could call "actual nature" (however culturally constructed most of it might be).

Yet the presence of a surrounding world of trees and breezes and birdsong did little to rescue this production from the claustrophobic, anthropocentric, socio-psychologism that has made theater the least environmentally aware, most eco-alienated, and nature-aversive of all the arts of the Western world. Far from amplifying or extrapolating from the charged moment of human–animal encounter at the heart of Euripides' play, this production did what so much theater since the Greeks has done: it exchanged the "more-than-human" Big Picture for the petty rivalries between rulers and intruders, wise old sages and cocky young princes. No wonder that Brantley "kept thinking about those raccoons all through the 90 minutes" of the play: "those animals had everything that this show lacks: mystery, grace, charisma and (though they didn't bare them) teeth."

Of course they didn't bare their teeth: the raccoons are not interested in tragedy, or even melodrama. They have been busy pursuing the classic marriage plot of comedy, showing little interest in the pity and fear, the catharsis and *peripeteia* of tragedy. They availed themselves of *Zoöpolis*'s diurnal rhythms—chiefly, the fact that no one is out and about at 5 a.m.—to give their friends a wedding to remember. (One of them did have to stop a cab and get the driver to take a stoned kid home, but that did nothing to impair the jubilation of the masked wedding party.)

The Columbus Circle Wedding Party: is this the twenty-first-century incarnation of Cocteau's *Eiffel Tower Wedding Party*? That surreal Parisian group's story ended when they all walked into an old-fashioned hooded camera; our group emerges from the ubiquitous cameras of Google Street View. Have they been waiting for almost a century to return? What were they waiting for? The raccoon masks, of course. They were waiting for *Zoöpolis* to furnish the means for what Joseph Meeker (in one of the first works ecocriticism) called *The Comedy of Survival*. They are proposing that the genre that *Zoöpolis* must cultivate is the one that celebrates beginnings rather than commemorating endings.

Ark Dreams

Like the raccoons who are swarming over Brooklyn backyards (and, in *Zoöpolis*, all over downtown billboards), water—in sudden, large quantities—transforms and overwhelms the cityscape. Like the raccoons—refugees of natural habitat destruction—the catastrophic hurricanes that have been turning street grids into a network of canals are symptoms of climate change. Unlike the raccoons, however, the floods of global warming do not offer new modes of habitation. They portend the opposite: the undoing of domicile, the un-grounding of our lives. The annual images of distant Bangladeshi peasants waist-deep in ruined paddy fields are now matched by looped videos of Katrina's roof-marooned. Lately newspapers and websites seem to overflow with images of canoes in watery streets, children on shoulders, and stranded figures in watery landscapes. The cover of Dave Eggers' book, *Zeitoun*, shows a man in a boat in a flooded city street—New Orleans. The *New York Times*'s Arts section had a picture from Josh Neufeld's graphic novel, *A.D.: New Orleans After the Deluge*, a two-toned, two-page aerial view of a drowned city, where two men on a sloping roof are turning in for the night, black waters eddying around a few feet below them.

These rising tides of a heating world, recalling the twin myths of the Flood and the Ark, have a particular resonance for *Zoöpolis*: they remind us that we share certain vulnerabilities with the other animals—we are creatures of the land, like so many of them—but also that we are capable of sharing more: we can share our shelter, our ingenuity, our care. They offer an opportunity to re-imagine the Noah myth (itself a version of Mesopotamian nature myths, commemorating rare downpours in a desert region).[2] Unlike Noah, who was ordered by his god to include other animals in his survival plan, many inhabitants of New Orleans, we learned, saved their companion animals—and those of their fellow citizens—voluntarily, often heroically, risking their own safety to save terrified dogs and cats stranded in drowning houses.

The new Ark that these rescuers bring into view might also be one that—unlike Noah's—wants to achieve more than simple survival. In its conscious embrace of other species, the Ark of *Zoöpolis* aims not merely at continued existence but at renewal, a conviction that the flood this time must teach a different lesson: not the old one of a sinful humanity punished by an angry god, nor that of a single righteous man's family spared and charged with

replenishing an emptied world, but rather a story of the realization that a lonely world is not worth saving, that the fate of humanity at every level—physical, psychological, spiritual—depends on the well-being of the other animals with whom we share this sadly damaged planet.

The Ark of *Zoöpolis* will undoubtedly require levels of ingenuity as high as those imagined by generations of biblical commentators when they were confronted by the mathematically precise specifications found in Genesis: arguments raged about the shape, size, structure, and functionality of the vessel that Noah had built. One fifteenth-century explicator described "the vent in the habitation of the […] animals through which dung was conveyed to the sentina. Noah and his sons collected the dung and cast it by means of an orifice into the sentina so that animals would not rot in their own offal" (Alfonso Tostado, qt. in Allen 76). In the mid sixteenth century the geometrician Johannes Buteo worked out that, "after subtracting the space occupied by stairways, partitions, beams and joists, there was usable space in the ark of 350,000 cubic cubits," including an aquarium (which, however, Buteo was not sure was needed) (Cohn 40).

More than the considerable technological challenges that face *Zoöpolis* in the age of melting icecaps, unprecedented levels of imaginative and ideological ingenuity will be called for. This Ark, intended not only to see us through the heavy weather ahead but also to see us to a new—post-anthropocentric—way of living must surely turn, for specifications and instructions, not to god but to the other animals. What can *Zoöpolis* learn from animal habitations— from the nests, lairs, dens, hives, webs, burrows, and warrens of our fellow earth-dwellers? How can we honor and commemorate their animal life(styles)? And what new spaces can we create that will serve not only that "poor, bare, fork'd animal" that Lear speaks of in his extremity, but other creatures like him, "unaccommodated" by catastrophe?

"I have a dream … "

The hopeful, idealistic, ameliorative phase of the environmental movement is decidedly a thing of the past. That was the phase shaped by the Sixties counter-culture, Deep Ecology, ecofeminism, the Gaia hypothesis. Its central image was the "blue planet" photograph of earth from space, and its central trope was Back to the Garden. In those early stages, going "back to nature" usually meant getting as far away as possible from the city, preferably with drumming added. In time, that impulse found a home in the city, in the Green Spaces Movement: vertical gardens, rooftop farms, planted street medians, more city parks.

Zoöpolis wants to take this impulse one step further, and open ourselves up to the potent doses of irony and danger that lie beneath another, closely related dream, that of the Peaceable Kingdom, where the lions shall lie down with the lambs. The irony of this fantasy is packed into its oxymoronic title, which covers over the sovereign power principle with a promise of unexplained harmony. The danger behind it brings us face to face with species difference, with the laws of predation and self-preservation, and with the violence and competition they entail. In *Zoöpolis*, then, the dream of the garden accommodates a measure of risk and uncertainty, the awareness of a few snakes in the grass.

No lions or lambs presented themselves right away, so Zoöpolians must lie down with coyotes and deer instead. Also, they can run with the wolves and swim with the trout (no dolphins around either). And what better place to stage this revised spectacle of interspecies harmony than Times Square, home of both spectacular theater and sober factuality: all that jazz, and all the news that's fit to print. The dream of *Zoöpolis* grows out of—and into—the most cherished institutions of the metropolis. It takes root in the arts, in leisure, in the media; it branches into work rules, lunch hours, office

attire. The frenetic electronic billboards are turned off. The gigantic paper ones begin to fray and mold. Zoöpolians cultivate an "alternative hedonism".[3]

"I have a nightmare ..."

Today's ecological imagination is dominated by apocalyptic thought and imagery, accompanied by feelings of shame, guilt, and despair. These strip-mined hills, deforested mountains, chemically contaminated lands, oil-soaked wetlands, melting glaciers, broken ice shelves, bleached coral reefs, and—above all—these thousands of extinction-threatened species, might not they be better off without humans? A seductive new trope emerges: "Earth Without Us." The Church of Euthanasia's slogan instructs: "Save the Planet, Kill Yourself." As BP digs "relief wells," many sense there will be no relief from the speeded-up "natural disasters" and failed climate summits. *Zoöpolis* is in search of affective and political responses to ecological devastation that can help to lift the ecocidal malaise that is descending on us like some final stifling smog.

One impulse: learn to play in the world we have made. The transformed landscape prompts the invention of new games, the changing of old rules. So, in the new obstacle race, you have to go backwards, edging carefully down stairs you can't see, down piles of debris that shifts as you put one foot behind another. The idea came from the animals, who adopted the technique so as to conserve energy (it's much slower going and uses fewer calories). Thoroughbreds and circus horses, cantering backwards, teach the new ways. The ruined monumental sites of obsolete practices (like mail) make excellent racetracks and obstacle courses.

This new rule also favors the new slowed-down tempo of *Zoöpolis*, a leisurely pace that befits a city with blocked streets and buried cars. (Google's naturalizing of an automotive world—a world seen exclusively from drivable surfaces—is often undone in *Zoöpolis*.) Walking backwards, negotiating a shifting topography, going slow: from these imperatives a new cityscape emerges. One looks more closely, notices many more details, cherishes old things anew. The animals of *Zoöpolis*—both the human and non-human ones—dig beneath the broken asphalt surface and paddle in the muddy ponds for food and fun.

Notes

1 "To allow for the emergence of an ethic, practice, and politics of caring for animals and nature, we need to renaturalize cities and invite the animals back in, and in the process re-enchant the city. I call this renaturalized, re-enchanted city *Zoöpolis*. The reintegration of people with animals and nature in zoöpolis can provide urban dwellers with the local, situated, everyday knowledge of animal life required to grasp animal standpoints or ways of being in the world, to interact with them accordingly in particular contexts, and to motivate political action necessary to protect their autonomy as subjects and their life spaces. Such knowledge would stimulate a thorough rethinking of a wide range of urban daily life practices." Jennifer Wolch 1998.

2 Cohn 1996.

3 Kate Soper writes: "I have been urging the potential significance of what I have termed an 'alternative hedonist' disenchantment with consumerism. This rests on two main claims. The first is that the affluent, 'consumerist,' Euro-American mode of consumption that has become the model of the 'good life' for so many other societies today, is unlikely to be checked in the absence of a seductive alternative, an altered conception of what it is to flourish and to enjoy a 'high' standard of living. In this sense, the chances of developing or reverting to a more ecologically sustainable use of resources, and hence of removing some of the key sources of social and environmental exploitation, are dependent on the emergence and embrace of new modes of thinking about human pleasure and self-realization, especially, in the first instance, on the part of the affluent global elites. An anti-consumerist ethic and politics should therefore appeal not only to altruistic compassion and environmental concern but also to the more self-regarding gratifications of consuming differently: to a new erotics of consumption or hedonist 'imaginary.'" Soper 2008.

Works cited

Allen, D.C. (1949) *The Legend of Noah*. Urbana: U of Illinois P.

Brantley, B. (2009) "God vs. Man in an Open-Air Fight." *New York Times*, August 24, http://theater2.nytimes.com/2009/08/25/theater/reviews/25 bacchae.html?ref=arts

Cohn, N. (1996) "Mesopotamian Origins," in *Noah's Flood: The Genesis Story in Western Thought*. New Haven: Yale UP, 1–9.

"Information about Animals in War" (2016) *The Animals in War Memorial*, www.animalsinwar.org.uk/index.cfm?asset_id=1375

Pyle, R.M. (1998) *The Thunder Tree: Lessons from an Urban Wildland*. Lyons Press.

Soper, K. (2008) "Alternative Hedonism: Cultural Theory and the Role of Aesthetic Revisioning." *Cultural Studies* 22 no. 5: 567–87.

Staples, B. (2009) "The City Life: Wildlife." *New York Times*, July 14, www.nytimes.com/2009/07/14/opinion/14tue4.html

Wolch, J. (1998) "Zoöpolis," in Jennifer Wolch and Jody Emel (eds.) *Animal Geographies: Place, Politics and Identity in the Nature–Culture Borderlands.* London: Verso.

Chapter 6

Becoming Rhinoceros
Therio-Theatricality as Problem and Promise in Western Drama

> *The dust raised by the animal spreads across the stage.*
> (Eugène Ionesco, stage direction in *Rhinoceros*)[1]

The eponymous animal of Tennessee Williams's play *The Night of the Iguana* is typical in one way: animals tend to be heard rather than seen on the stages of Western theater. By its being trapped in the wings, the captivity and suffering of Williams's reptile are not only marginalized but rendered *obscene*—quite literally so, if we accept the contested etymology of the word, from the Greek *ob-skene*: off-stage (McKay). This obscuring and "obscening" of the animal is the hallmark of the dominant tradition of Western theater, a tradition that is obsessively anthropocentric, dedicated to repeatedly constructing and enshrining the human as "the paragon of animals" (*Hamlet* 2.2.297) by derogating or excluding all others.

However, the Western theater's repression of animality—like the many other such repressions through which humanist cultures are produced—comes at the cost of a profound ambivalence, an anxiety that the repressed will return when least expected and will dissolve the vaulting edifice of self-importance into a quintessence of dust. To manage this anxiety, the theater fills its spaces with animal effigies, symbols, masks, and meanings: signs of a disavowed animality which, taken together, amount to a shadow-tradition, a "therio-theatricality" through which drama peers into what John Berger calls "the narrow abyss of noncomprehension" that separates humans from the other animals (5). Rooted in antiquity and flourishing through early and later modernity, this shadow-tradition reaches the limits of its ideological usefulness and psychological value at the dawn of the postcolonial era, when accounts of otherness proliferate to the point of shaking the rigidly binary foundation of humanist ideologies. In the "experimental" European drama of this period (starting in the middle decades of the last century), animal visitation is often the means by which humanist certitudes are dismantled rather than confirmed.

Eugène Ionesco's mid-century play *Rhinoceros* is a paradigm of therio-theatricality, not only because of its boldly proclaimed animal subject but equally because that very subject has for so long been systematically ignored and skirted by the play's critics. The fact that the animal can *fail* to register in the critical reception and scholarly discussion even of a play *named* for an animal is in itself an interesting phenomenon, further evidence of the programmatic disavowal just mentioned. The reasons why this can happen—and the logic by which it is made to happen—have to do with the Western theater's traditional characterology, according to which viable dramatic identity is forged in a long, lonely, and above all *verbal* journey. In this paradigm, therio-theatricality lurks in the wings, erupting periodically to activate the rich materiality that is the hallmark of theater: its seductive traffic in bodies, objects, spaces, and sounds.

When *Rhinoceros* received a high-profile revival at the Royal Court Theatre in 2007, the critical reception closely resembled that of the equally high-profile revival of another well-known animal play the same year, Peter Shaffer's *Equus*. The reviews were uniform in their admiration for various aspects of the *production*, especially the performances of the lead actors. On the play itself, however, there was nothing like such unanimity. Indeed, many critics explicitly framed their praise of both productions as a matter of transcending the limitations of weak and dated dramatic sources. In the case of *Equus*, this response closely resembled the one to its premiere, back in 1973, where the critical consensus could be summed up as: "great theater, bad play" (see Chaudhuri 1984).

In 2007, both animal plays were characterized by several critics as intellectually shallow and hopelessly dated. Michael Billington of the *Guardian* said Ionesco's central metaphor was "so vague as to be meaningless: you could apply it with equal validity to Nazism, communism or capitalist consumerism." The play was not only "intellectually woolly and predictable," he said, it came dangerously close to implying that "every minority is right." Paul Taylor, writing in the *Independent*, agreed that this "Absurdist fable about the pressure to conform (Fascist, Communist, you name it) has not survived its own occasion." It was, he said, "dated and dead." Similar dismissals greeted "the hokum" of *Equus*, with its R.D. Laingian "creed"—now long out of vogue—"of communing with one's inner madman" (Brantley).

Yet for all their intellectual inadequacy the plays were, the critics agreed, vastly entertaining and engaging as theater events. There was no dearth of explanations: sometimes, the credit went to "the wit of Martin Crimp's translation," at others to the production-values, which were widely praised as exemplary, "from the trumpeting noises of Ian Dickinson's sound design to the rhino-heads by Jonathan Beakes" (Billington). Or it could have been that this "stunning production" was directed by "possibly the most gifted director in the country," who knew how to "whip up the tension brilliantly," making for a staging that "was lucid, expertly orchestrated" (Taylor). In the case of *Equus*, the theatrical triumph was also explained, according to the critics, by another non-dramatic feature: the pitch-perfect casting of child- and teen-idol Daniel Radcliffe as Alan Strang, a character who is, as Ben Brantley cleverly observed, "a tidy inversion of Harry Potter. Both come of age in a menacing, magical world where the prospect of being devoured by darkness is always imminent."

The critical values underlying this reception tacitly privilege text and ideas over performance and production elements. In so doing, they are building on a key feature of therio-theatricality: the equation of animality with physicality and materiality—with bodies and things—and the correlated association of the human with mind, soul, thought, ideas, and meaning.

It is not surprising, therefore, that the one feature of these plays that never came up in the discussions of their theatrical strengths and dramatic weaknesses was the fact that each has, at its thematic center as well as a key element of its scenic discourse, the figure of an animal. Ionesco's play is, of course, about an "Invasion-of-the-Body-Snatchers"-style epidemic that overtakes and transforms all but one inhabitant of a French town. *Equus* is famously based on the horrifying true story of a young man who inexplicably blinded a stableful of horses (Shaffer 9). Both play-texts incorporate extensive directions for, and descriptions of, zooësis, both mimetic (shown) and diegetic (narrated). Ionesco's pachyderms are first heard, then seen, and the climactic scene of the play features a protracted becoming-rhinoceros,[2] one of the most famous transformation scenes in world drama. Shaffer's horses are also first heard ("the Equus Noise" is described in a prefatory note as "a choric effect ... composed of humming, thumping, and stamping" [16]), and then seen. Here too, the climactic scene is one in which a becoming-animal occurs, though here the terms of transformation are ritualistic and psycho-sexual rather than—as they are in *Rhinoceros*—political and emotional. Yet in spite of this extensive and explicit animal presence in these plays, the subject of animals and animality, and of the human–animal relation has never been afforded a central critical focus. Never has a critic asked the question Shaffer's tortured protagonist, Dr. Dysart, famously identifies: "Why me? Account for me" (108).

This is, of course, "the question of the animal,"[3] a question that has haunted philosophy at least since Aristotle, the question that was bluntly shut down for several centuries by Descartes, and that was taken up with increasing vigor and urgency in the course of the past century. It is a question that *Rhinoceros* engages with far more extensively than the critical tradition on the play suggests. To approach the play from the perspective of the animal and its "question"—which is, essentially, the question of animal alterity, of the similarities and differences between animals, including human animals—is to discover in it an encapsulated history of the modern animal as well as a lively demonstration of its role in the production—and later dismantling—of Enlightenment subjectivity. The history spans the period from the Cartesian *cogito* to the post-Darwinian naked ape, though that history's formulations are presented not discursively or chronologically but rather as a stampede of more or less contradictory ideas, rushing at and around each other. This intellectual disorder is a crucial element of the play's zooësis, which amplifies these historical fragments with a powerfully chaotic scenic and performative discourse. The animal presence that builds steadily and confidently in the course of the play culminates in an aesthetic transformation that contributes as much to the play's discourse of species as do the tortured existential heroics of its protagonist. In the last scene of the play, a stage direction tells us that:

> *Powerful noises of moving rhinoceroses are heard, but somehow it is a musical sound. On the up-stage wall stylized heads appear and disappear; they become more and more numerous from now on until the end of the play. Towards the end they stay fixed for longer and longer, until eventually they fill the entire back wall,*

remaining static. The heads, in spite of their monstrous
appearance, seem to become more and more beautiful.

(94)

The "stylized heads" that gradually fill the walls of the stage recall
an influential artistic movement of early twentieth-century
modernism: primitivism. Cultivating an aesthetic based on the
monstrous and the savage, primitivism was, as Philip Armstrong
has argued, a version of the modernist turn to *wildness* as a valued
ideal, which included a radical revaluation of animality:

> Rejecting the complacencies of Victorian modernity, the
> modernists aimed also to dispense with—or in some ways,
> reform—the legacy of the last great literary revolution,
> Romanticism, which they felt had been tamed by intervening
> generations. The wildness of Romanticism has been
> domesticated; its sublime potency reduced to mawkishness; it
> was time for art to break loose, go feral, and return to a
> revitalizing savagery. As this rhetoric suggests, the modernist
> break with the past entailed, and in many ways depended upon,
> a revaluation of human–animal relations.
>
> (134)

The result of this development is what Armstrong calls a new "therio-
primitivism," a distinctively modernist mode of relating animality to
an archaic, essential, humanity (142). More or less explicit versions
of therio-primitivism inform such foundational discourses of
modernism as the Nietzschean, Darwinian, Marxian, and Freudian,
each bequeathing a different equation between their respective
normative human subjects and animality, and thus prescribing a
different trajectory—toward or away from—that animality.

In both its affirmative and its skeptical versions, this therio-
primitivism is one of the underlying discourses of *Rhinoceros*'s
ambivalent account of animality, efficiently correlating with each of
its two opposite allegories. *Rhinoceros* is the theatrical equivalent
of the famous duck/rabbit optical illusion: looked at one way, it is
an indictment of the human capacity to adapt to horror. This is
certainly how the play's leading critics read its narrative of a mass
transformation of humans into animals, in which the lure of
conformity and the willingness to compromise with coercive mass
movements sweeps over all but one of the inhabitants of a town,

leaving him defiantly proclaiming his humanity on an empty stage. Looked at another way, it is a drama of liberation from the bonds of bourgeois conformity, a joyful return to nature and a cathartic embrace of animality. While the dominant reading is supported by and relies on the play's intellectual discourse—in particular the ideological awakening of its protagonist Berenger—the latter perspective emerges when attention is paid to the play's scenic discourse, with its proliferating parades of animal heads and its oddly exhilarating animal chorus, as well as to its most famous scene (and most challenging performance): the physical transformation of Berenger's pompous friend Jean into a rhinoceros.

The negative version of therio-primitivism, which "conceives of animality as a state out of which the human must be forged, or from which it must travel," underlies the allegory that has dominated the critical tradition of the play, according to which the embrace of animality is politically and culturally regressive, a betrayal of all the hard-won achievements of modern civilization (Armstrong 142). A different, "redemptive," therio-primitivism subtly informs the characterization of the protagonist, Berenger, complicating the meaning of his later conversion to the position of defender of civilization. A second complicating factor in reading Berenger's story is the species of animal selected to represent the ideology that proves so seductive to every single one of his human companions. Had Ionesco chosen to mine traditional bestiaries and anthropomorphic fables for his satire on cowardice and conformity, the play might have been entitled "Sheep," or "Lemming," or even "Chicken." These options might have produced a more straightforward allegory, but they would also have forsaken much that is enigmatic and original—not to mention dark and disturbing—in the play. The choice of an animal with few (if any) specifically cultural associations spins Ionesco's allegory in an unexpected way, making it, in a performatively important way, uncontrollable. Much of the ambivalence that the play registers—and elicits from its audience—is a function of its animal choice. The rhinoceros is the wild animal par excellence, rarely seen, rarely evoked in myth or fable, the subject almost exclusively of arcane natural history taxonomies, like the one Ionesco makes brilliant theatrical hay with in Act 1: "The Asiatic rhinoceros has one horn and the African rhinoceros has two. And vice versa" (32). This importation of wildness into the space of civilization pushes the play's zooësis beyond political allegory, affording instead (or in addition) a kind of encounter with *animal ambivalence* that theater, as an art form, is particularly well suited to provide.

Ionesco's animals gain much of their meanings and effects because they—like all stage animals—are fundamentally *out of place*[4] on stage, in the theater, and in what has been, since the sixteenth century, the classic scene of comedy, the town square.[5] This archetypal setting is vividly realized in the play's first scene, its grocery and café sharply etched against a "Blue sky; harsh light; very white walls" (4). This quintessentially urban scene is the ideal setting for a drama of animal ambivalence, the city being, by many accounts, the epitome of de-animalized space. The ancient history told by Protagoras, for instance, posits a strictly causal relationship between wild animals and cities:

> ... man lived at the beginning in scattered units, and there were no cities. So they began to be destroyed by wild beasts, since they were altogether weaker. Their practical art was sufficient to provide food, but insufficient for fighting against the beasts— for they did not yet possess the art of running a city, of which the art of warfare is part—and so they thought to come together and save themselves by founding cities.
>
> (qt. in Ridout 115)

The intrusion of animals into this exclusively human space puts them in a very special category of animals: those who encroach upon areas designated off-limits to them, spaces from which they have been deliberately and vigorously excluded. This is the category of the pest. Animal artists Snæbjörnsdóttir and Wilson, writing about their project on pests, entitled "Uncertainty in the City," note:

> Long ago, settlements and therefore latterly cities were predicated on the concept of refuge, and a physical division of culture and nature. Clearly such division has proved increasingly porous as more and more animals and birds consider concentrations of human population an attraction rather than a deterrent because of the opportunities such cultures provide in terms of habitat and feeding.
>
> (5)

Reactions to the many animals who return to areas marked human are many and varied, ranging from fear and disgust to fascination and delight. In general, however, the pest elicits negative reactions, and the list of these provided by Snæbjörnsdóttir and Wilson is an admirable summary of many of the feelings expressed in Ionesco's play:

Fear of disregard of individual territory
Fear of a disregard of manner and protocols
Fear of an implicit erosion of boundaries
Fear of disruption of our own patterns of behavior
Fear of those setting up residence without permission
Fear of aural disturbance
Fear of damage to property.

(5)

The choice of species to play the role of pest—the rhinoceros—is as different as possible—in size, in familiarity, in provenance—from the species who usually play that role: rodents and insects. This "re-casting" of the pest is key to the play's therio-theatricality, its use of the animal as a lens to see human sociality in new—non-anthropocentric, non-zoophobic—ways.

The play begins, then, in a phobically clean and bright space. As the first act proceeds, the pristine space of civilization is engulfed with the dust of stampeding herds. (Other versions of this space of civilization in later scenes of the play—first an office, then a home—will suffer even worse damage, splintering and collapsing in a way that seems to characterize animal visitation in drama.)[6] At present, however, the only animals here, besides the human ones who will soon reveal their animality in all sorts of ways, are the unseen ones in the grocery freezer and the one that accompanies the first person to enter the stage, a housewife clutching an exemplar of that obligatory humanized animal of modern life, the pet.

The housewife's pet cat makes an ideal point of departure for the play's soundings of modern animality because it exemplifies the cultural animal practice, pet-keeping, through which modernity has increasingly compensated for the growing "ontological and material separation of human and animal" (Armstrong 13). Keith Thomas notes that "[by] 1700 all the symptoms of obsessive pet-keeping were in evidence. Pets were often fed better than servants … and they became an increasingly regular feature of painted family groups" (qt. in Armstrong 13). The housewife's treatment of her cat is nothing if not obsessive, and includes an absurdist version of the pet-keeper's delusional anthropomorphizing: "He was so gentle, just like one of us. [...] He was devoted to us. [...] He could almost talk—in fact he did" (31–32). Fittingly, the housewife's cat—this token of modern humanity's presumed control over the natural world—will be the first victim of the wild animality that is soon to engulf the world of the play.

The archetypal set of comedy and the humanized animal of modernity frame the ironized Nietzschean dyad of the play's two main characters. The unkempt, hung-over Berenger is a debased instance of the Dionysian ideal, with the appearance and comportment of an exhausted satyr. He lives, according to his censorious friend, "in a thick haze of alcohol" which is "clouding [his] brain." A rampant physicality –"I'm conscious of my body all the time," he says (18)—and uncontrollable appetites link him to animality and alienate him from the de-animalized world that (in the person of his punctilious friend Jean) criticizes and scolds him:

> You're in a bad way, my friend. [...] You're dropping with fatigue. You've gone without your sleep again, you yawn all the time, you're dead-tired ... You reek of alcohol [...] Your clothes are all crumpled, they're a disgrace! Your shirt is downright filthy, and your shoes ... What a mess you're in!
>
> (5–6)

Jean's contrasting rendition of the Apollonian ideal is even more pitiful and attenuated, its intellectual clarity and moral order now reduced to a smug and self-satisfied conformism: "The superior man is the man who fulfills his duty. [...] His duty as an employee, for example" (7). When Berenger confesses that he sometimes wonders "if I exist myself," Jean confidently proffers a Cartesian solution: "You don't exist, my dear Berenger, because you don't think. Start thinking, then you will" (19). Jean's faith in the *Cogito* links him to the most notorious source of the binaries—reason/ passion, thought/emotion, mind/body, human/animal—that came to structure Enlightenment thought. René Descartes's denial of animal sentience produced the "beast-machine" against which a new ideal of humanity would be counter-posed: man as rational animal, ruling his passions and in control of his body.

Besides his Dionysian aspects, Berenger is also the play's link to another modernist discourse with a complex and ambivalent relation to animality: Freudian dream theory. Although Berenger explicitly rejects the word "instinct" in favor of "intuition" to describe the source of his convictions ("No, that's not what I mean, it's the rhinoceros which has instinct—I feel it intuitively, yes, that's the word, intuitively" [85]), his association with sleeping, dreaming, and day-dreaming throughout the play suggests that he, more than any other character in the play, is struggling not only with demanding social beasts but also with the monstrous animals of the unconscious. The final act begins with Berenger asleep in his room:

[He seems to be having a bad dream, and writhes in his sleep.]
Berenger: No. [Pause] Watch out for the horns! [...] No!
[He falls to the floor still fighting with what he has seen in his dream, and wakes up. He puts his hand to his head with an apprehensive air, then moves to the mirror. [...] He heaves a sigh of relief when he sees he has no bump] (71).

Berenger's self-scrutiny in the mirror reaches an obsessional pitch in the last section of the play, after his last human companion, his girlfriend Daisy, has abandoned him, preferring "the ardor and the tremendous energy emanating from all these creatures around us" to "what you call love—this morbid feeling, this male weakness. And female, too" (xx). Indeed it is precisely while Berenger "continues to examine himself in the mirror" that Daisy leaves (105). From that moment onwards, until the end of the play, Berenger will return to the mirror repeatedly, checking his face against the proliferating animal heads all around him: "A man's not ugly to look at, not ugly at all! *He examines himself, passing his hand over his face.* What a funny-looking thing! What do I look like? What?" (106). This classic image of self-absorption— the individual scrutinizing his reflection—takes on a different connotation in the animalized context of the last scene, where the human face is somehow being expected to "face down" its animal counterpart. Berenger even attempts to address the quantitative superiority of his antagonists by putting up pictures he claims to be of himself. Chillingly, the stage direction reports: "*When he hangs the pictures one sees that they are of an old man, a huge woman and another man. The ugliness of these pictures is in contrast to the rhinoceros heads which have become very beautiful*" (106). Once again, an aesthetic intervention complicates the existential allegory emphasized by most critics of the play.

Berenger's trajectory, it suggests, is not so much a triumph of individualism as a fraught and unfinished passage through modernism's ambivalent animalities.

The mirror of the last scene returns us to the mirror of Scene 1, held up to Berenger not by himself but by the censorious Jean, who carries it in his pocket, along with a tie and a comb. One of the most striking things about the play is the way its two protagonists appear to change places as the play goes on. Jean's transformation is, of course, the most extreme and astonishing, taking him from cartoon Cartesianism ("I'm master of my own thoughts, my mind doesn't wander. I think straight, I always think straight" [61]) to Darwinian caricature:

Jean:	Moral standards! I'm sick of moral standards! We need to go beyond moral standards!
Berenger:	What would you put in their place?
Jean:	Nature! [...] Nature has its own laws! Morality's against nature.
Berenger:	Are you suggesting we replace our moral laws by the laws of the jungle?
Jean:	It would suit me, suit me fine ... We've got to build our lives on new foundations. We must get back to primeval integrity. [...]
Berenger:	Just think a moment. You must admit that we have a philosophy that animals don't share, and an irreplaceable set of values, which it's taken centuries of human civilization to build up ...
Jean:	When we've demolished all that, we'll be better off! (67)

Jean's transformation from Man of Reason to Naked Ape is not merely a change of mind; Ionesco's confident theatricality renders it as a change of just about everything, including, of course, of body. En route to that final animalization, Jean—whose first moments on stage had marked him as a fastidious dresser and stickler for social codes, tears off his clothes, shouting: "Hot, far too hot! Demolish the lot. Clothes itch, they itch. [...] The swamps! The swamps!" (68)

Of course, Jean is hardly the only rationalist to succumb to the beasts. The play provides a range of positions that correlate with various versions of modernist species discourse, beginning with a Swiftian satire on the fetishization of certain modes of thought:

Logician:	Here is an example of a syllogism. The cat has four paws. Isidor and Fricot both have four paws. Therefore Isidor and Fricot are cats.
Old gentleman:	My dog has four paws.
Logician:	Then it's a cat. [...] Another syllogism: All cats die. Socrates is dead. Therefore Socrates is a cat.
Old gentleman:	And he's got four paws. That's true. I've got a cat named Socrates. (18–19)

A more familiar ideal of rationality is articulated by Dudard, who clothes his passivity and cowardice in the guise of moderation and tolerance:

> My dear Berenger, one must always make an effort to understand. And in order to understand a phenomenon and its effects you need to work back to the initial causes, by honest intellectual effort. We must try to do this because, after all, we are thinking beings. I haven't yet succeeded, as I told you, and I don't know if I shall succeed. But in any case one has to start out favorably disposed—or at least, impartial; one has to keep an open mind—that's essential to a scientific mentality. Everything is logical. To understand is not to justify. [...] I'm trying to look the facts unemotionally in the face. I'm trying to be realistic. I also contend that there is no real evil in what occurs naturally. I don't believe in seeing evil in everything. I leave that to the inquisitors.
>
> (83)

Berenger's own transformation, from chronic outsider ("I feel out of place in life, with people ..." [17]) to reluctant defender of human civilization follows an opposite trajectory of therio-primitivism, from sensual oblivion to a kind of instinctual self-preservation. Berenger begins his journey in a state of extreme alienation, so bored as to seem in need of something like a herd of rhinoceroses to revitalize him. As the thunderous offstage noise announcing their arrival grows in volume, and as all the characters on stage, one after the other, abandon their activities and conversations to look at the amazing sight unfolding just out of the audience's view, Berenger alone remains unaware and unmoved. The only animalistic human in the group seems oblivious to the animals invading his environment. Later, in sharp contrast to the repeated exclamations and ejaculations that follow the animal visitation, Berenger alone offers a few plausible explanations: perhaps the rhinoceroses have escaped from the zoo, or from a traveling circus, or perhaps they've simply been hiding "in the surrounding swamps?" (14) Jean's increasingly impatient and bizarre retorts ("there's been no zoo in our town since all the animals were destroyed in the plague" [15]), along with his ridiculous repeated pronouncement that "it shouldn't be allowed!", quickly moves the animal figure in the direction of allegory that has been highlighted in criticism of the play, making it a stand-in for all that disturbs the surface calm of a mediocre and self-satisfied society, a kind of corporate antagonist for anyone loyal to the civilization of the bright town square where the play begins (13). And indeed this strain of meaning runs throughout the play, signposted periodically by such observations as the following: "You get used to it, you know. Nobody seems surprised anymore to see herds of rhinoceroses galloping through the streets. They just stand aside, and then carry on as if nothing had happened" (91).

But the Nietzschean theme introduced through the main characters cuts across the allegory that has dominated the critical tradition on the play. Berenger's animality, while being a far cry from ecstatic Dionysian embodiment, is nevertheless on a continuum with the rapturous wildness that increasingly defines the world of the play, captivating one character after another. His resistance to it requires him to draw upon reserves of restraint and self-regard that have previously been the hallmarks of the insufferable Jean. He even begins to sound like Jean, huffing that "your duty is to oppose them, with a firm clear mind" (93). Is Berenger's final "triumph," then, actually a regressive return to the humanism of the Enlightenment subject, compulsively "cleansed" of animality, disembodied and denatured? And what is it that has routed Berenger's Dionysian instincts and embodied sensualities? The answer may lie in the characterological opposition itself, the sharp contrast between the two protagonists established at the outset. Their professions of friendship, especially Berenger's, suggest a commonality and kinship that is belied by the schematic difference called for in their performances, which demand strongly contrasting appearances and behavior. When Jean holds a mirror up to Berenger in the first scene, it is pointedly to show him how different he, Berenger, is from Jean himself. Yet the evolving dynamic of this central relationship seems to contradict the very recognition—of personal identity, of essential individuality—that

lies at what has been assumed to be the philosophical—humanist—
heart of the play.

The epic scene of Jean's becoming-animal begins with a moment
of mutual non-recognition, forecasting the massive case of mistaken
identity to come:

Jean: I didn't recognize your voice.
Berenger: I didn't recognize yours either. (59)

As the extraordinary scene proceeds, with the Jean actor
performing human animalization through every semiotic register
available in theater—voice, costume, gesture, movement,
physicality, vocalization—Berenger's responses mark the
transformation not as un*natural* but as un*characteristic*: "I'm
amazed to hear you say that, Jean, really! [...] It's not like you to
say a thing like that. [...] You're not yourself!" Berenger, who had
earlier confessed to being unsure of his own existence, becomes
increasingly focused on the question of identity: "I'm frightened
of becoming someone else," he now confesses (73). Indeed, his
desperate colloquy with the mirror in the play's final moments
suggest that his is not so much a drama of individual self-discovery
as it is one of tenuous *human construction*, made arduous not
only by the presence of animality but of a particularly challenging
and seductive kind of animality: the kind produced by modernism's
therio-primitivism. This is, after all, a *wild* animality, bringing
with it the sultry breezes of "The swamps! The swamps!" and
inspiring a dreadful and a joyful awe: says Daisy: "They're
beautiful. [...] They're like gods!" (68, 104)

Above all, they are *many*, and it is this feature of the animals that
Ionesco's dramaturgy realizes most vividly. Long before Berenger
tries to match their numbers by putting up pictures of human faces
on his wall, their *quantity* has been terrifying him. As he tries to
escape from Jean's apartment after Jean has become a rhinoceros,
he finds all his exits blocked: the porter has turned into a rhinoceros,
and so have Jean's neighbors. He tries to escape through the window
between the stage and the auditorium *"but gets back again quickly,
for at the same time, crossing the orchestra pit, move a large number
of rhinoceros heads in line.* There's a whole herd of them in the
street now! An army of rhinoceroses, surging up the avenue ...!"
(70) As theatrically realized in this play, from the momentous first
sighting in Act 1 to the "trumpetings, hectic racing, clouds of dust"

that accompany the proliferating animal heads of Act 3, it is as a *multiplicity* that the animal most seriously challenges human identity. As Jacques Derrida argued in his late animal texts, the animal has the paradoxical effect, in the realm of autobiography, of correlating the individual to multiplicity:

> ... my animal figures multiply, gain in insistence and visibility, become active, swarm, mobilize and get motivated, move and become moved all the more as my texts become more explicitly autobiographical, are more uttered in the first person.
>
> (35)

The singularity that might be assumed to be the quarry and ideal of the autobiographical project—the discovery of the uniqueness that distinguishes the self from all others—is contradicted by animal presence. When animals enter into autobiography, it would seem, they do so in numbers and with urgency, "lunging more and more wildly in my face" (35). Their appearance seems to invite the autobiographical self *to rethink itself beyond singularity*, to seek more pluralistic modes of self-knowledge. It is an invitation that lies on the far side of the excruciating choice that appears to torture Berenger in the last moments of *Rhinoceros*. His "either/or" concept of human animality has him lurching painfully between a feral primitivism and a "purified" humanism, both equally impossible to inhabit permanently.

One conceptual foundation for an alternative account of the self, a "zoo-autobiography" as Derrida calls it, is found in Alphonso Lingis's challenge to the habitual association between singular form (such as a body) and individuality:

> How myopic is the notion that a form is the principle of individuation, or a substance occupying a place to the exclusion of other substances, or that the inner organization or the self-positing identity of a subject is an entity's principle of individuation! A season, a summer, a wind, a fog, a swarm, an intensity of white at high noon have perfect individuality, though they are neither substances nor subjects.
>
> (39)

Lingis extends his pluralized vision to human identity, recasting individuality and agency as vast collaborative processes:

Human animals live in symbiosis with thousands of species of anaerobic bacteria, 600 species in our mouths which neutralize the toxins all plants produce to ward off their enemies, 400 species in our intestines, without which we could not digest and absorb the food we ingest. [...] The number of microbes that colonize our bodies exceeds the number of cells in our bodies by up to a hundred fold. Macrophages in our bloodstreams hunt and devour trillions of bacteria and viruses entering our porous bodies continually. They replicate with their own DNA and RNA and not ours; they are the agents that maintain our borders. They, and not some Aristotelian form, are true agencies of our individuation as organisms.

(38–39)

Another generative concept in animal philosophy, Deleuze and Guattari's becoming-animal, offers another perspective on identity beyond singularity. Allan Smith explicates the concept as involving "conditions of acute intensity, of demonized volatility; of contagious transport of impersonal affects and teeming multiplicities" (160). In Smith's reading as in others, becoming-animal is closely related not only to excess and intensity but also to *multiplicity*, and to Deleuze and Guattari's interest in the aggregative or collective nature of animals, to the fact that, as Philip Armstrong puts it, "animals are never one but always 'as one'" (7).

The human response to this perceived pluralization of animal identity is deeply ambivalent. On the one hand, there is a long tradition of recognizing, even celebrating it in language, as captured in James Lipton's much-loved volume *An Exaltation of Larks*, a delightfully illustrated collection of animal group names—or "terms of venery," so-called because of their origin in hunting culture. The impulse to capture something essential about a species in the group name assigned to it leads from the familiar "a pride of lions" to the chilling "a murder of crows," to a host (so to speak!) of witty coinages that leave the animal world far behind ("a flush of plumbers," "an annoyance of cellular phones").

More recently, a new representational technology has brought the exhilaration of animal multiplicity to film animation. Boids, invented by Craig Reynolds, are distributed behavior models that simulate the behavior of the individual birds in a flock. They are hi-tech, vastly amplified versions of the kinds of synchronized performances, both human and animal, that have always and everywhere delighted audiences, from the ritual dances of early cultures to the Rockettes of Radio City Music Hall. Indeed, the practice of training humans and animals to perform in unison could itself be a consequence of ambivalent feelings toward animals: on the one hand, a desire to imitate the dance-like beauty of the natural movements of their herds and flocks; on the other, an effort to master and control the energy generated by their multiplicity and bend it to our will and pleasure. Spectacles of animal multiplicity then, be they boid animations or Lipizzaner stallions, exist on a continuum with phenomena like animal collections (actual or virtual) and even odd events like the "cow parades" that have sprung up around the world in recent decades.[7] Part civic-celebration, part commercial racket, these so-called "public art" events can be read as safe and domesticated versions of the kind of animal visitation Ionesco envisions in *Rhinoceros*.

Alphonso Lingis argues that animal multiplicities "exert a primal fascination on us," because they echo and mirror "the multiplicities in us. What is mesmerized in us are the inhuman movements and intensities in us, [...] the micro-organic movements and intensities in the currents of our inner rivulets and cascades" (166-7). Animal multiplicities charm and fascinate. As frequently, however, they provoke unease and anxiety, even terror. Though avian flocks may exalt the spirit, they also threaten, as Hitchcock demonstrated, to swoop and smother. As for hordes, packs, and swarms: they are often, in fiction as well as in political theory, figures for dangerous crowds: "fringe groups, nomad armies, raiding parties, gangs, cabals, crime societies" (Smith 160). This is undoubtedly the association that is uppermost for Ionesco's Berenger, as for most critics of his play. But when *Rhinoceros* is unfolding on a stage, with all channels of theatrical semiosis fully engaged, this disturbing connotation of multiplicity is only one among several folded into the play, and not necessarily a strong one.

Ionesco repeatedly reminds us that the herds that so frighten Berenger are not the only ones in his town. The behavior of his fellow citizens at many junctures in the play can most accurately be described as herd behavior, beginning with the identical and reflexive reactions they all have to the first sighting: phrases like "Well, of all things!" and "Oh, the poor thing!" (10) (this in reference to the housewife's crushed cat), are repeated endlessly, with every character taking his or her turn, and often by groups of characters in unison. That human beings are pack animals is established long before they start jumping species. Ironically, it is this very feature of the human animal that also underlies the bio-dynamics of Ionesco's plot: as character after character joins the herd, the biological foundations of social behavior come into view. The social behavior we humans prize and regard as a sign of our superiority is a product of natural selection, "found in members of species with better survival chances in a group than in solitude. The advantages of group life can be manifold, the most important being increased chances to find food, defense against predators, and strength in numbers against competitors" (de Waal 9).

Multiplicity—both human (as sociality) and animal—is the challenging context of the drama of human recognition that lies at the heart of *Rhinoceros*. And it is closely related to the play's greatest challenge to humanism, its demonstration of the instability of identity. When Berenger comes to Jean's house at the beginning of the transformation scene he knocks on the door and calls Jean's name. A man answers, but it is not Jean. In a pitch-perfect use of illogic that was to become one of the hallmarks of Absurdism, Ionesco has the man, who is Jean's neighbor, inform Berenger that "I thought it was me you wanted. My name's Jean too" (58). The conflict between Berenger and Jean turns out to be something other than the two versions of the human—(cartoon) Dionysian and (cartoon) Apollonian—with which they began. Rather, their battle unfolds in the ideological and aesthetic arena of which a key feature was the unraveling—and eventual death (Fuchs)—of the traditional notion of dramatic character. The reading of *Rhinoceros* that I have offered here shows the extent to which that unraveling was bound up with a resurgent therio-theatricality. Long exiled to the wings of Western theater, the animal returns to join late modernism's posthumanist project. As for the human animals who must now—at long last—share the stage of Western representation with other species, I hope I have shown here that they will find few better resources than those of theatricality—of live, embodied performance—for joining in the great drama of animal alterity.

Notes

1 Ionesco 1960: 9.
2 Gilles Deleuze and Félix Guattari's notion of "becoming-animal" is one of animal philosophy's most aesthetically productive concepts, as well as one of its most enigmatic. In an article reporting on a sustained theatrical exploration of the concept, my co-author and I wrote: "[...] the most

challenging of Deleuzian definitions [...] was the idea that becoming is antithetical to imitation: 'We fall into a false alternative if we say that you either imitate or you are. What is real is the becoming itself, the block of becoming, not the supposedly fixed terms through which it passes' (Deleuze and Guattari 238). Becoming resists metaphor and mimesis. It courts fleeting synecdoches, momentary metonymies, shifting interstices. For actors, it offers an opportunity to indulge and unleash creative impulses without pointing them towards externally (conventionally) settled images" (Chaudhuri and Enelow 2006: xx).

3 This phrase, "the question of the animal," appears as the subtitle of at least two influential works of animal philosophy (Wolfe 2003; Calarco 2008).

4 As Nicholas Ridout puts it, "The impropriety of the animal on the theatre stage is experienced very precisely as a sense of the animal being in the wrong place. In the circus there are still a few tawdry reminders of nature. [...] The theatre, by contrast, rigorously excludes nature" (2006: 98).

5 In 1545, the influential Renaissance architect and theorist Sebastiano Serlio proposed three stock settings for drama, one each for tragedies (palaces), comedies (a town square), and pastorals (country scene). See Nagler 1959.

6 Elizabeth Egloff's wonderful animal play *The Swan* concludes with the following stage direction: "There is a huge noise: glass breaking, the world breaking, a tree cracking" (54). In Edward Albee's extraordinary exploration of the animal roots of tragedy, *The Goat*, the dialogue is punctuated by one character smashing one decorative object after another on the floor.

7 "CowParade is the largest and most successful public art event in the world. CowParade events have been staged in over 75 cities worldwide since Chicago in 1999." www.cowparade.com/

Works cited

Armstrong, P. (2008) *What Animals Mean in the Fictions of Modernity*. London: Routledge.

Berger, J. (1980) "Why Look at Animals?" *About Looking*. New York: Pantheon.

Billington, M. (2007) Review of *Rhinoceros*. *The Guardian*, September 27.

Brantley, B. (2008) "In the Darkness of the Stable." *New York Times*, September 26.

Calarco, M. (2008) *Zoographies: The Question of the Animal from Heidegger to Derrida*. New York: Columbia UP.

Chaudhuri, U. (1984) "Drama in the Spectator/The Spectator in Drama." *Modern Drama* 27 no. 3: 281–98.

—— (2007) "Defacing Animals: Zoösis and Performance." *TDR/The Drama Review* 51 no. 1: 8–20.

—— and Enelow, S. (2006) "Animalizing Performance, Becoming-Theatre: Inside Zoösis with the Animal Project at NYU," in *Theatre Topics* 16 no. 1: 1–17.

Deleuze, G. and Guattari, F. (1987) "Becoming Intense, Becoming Animal," *A Thousand Plateaus: Capitalism and Shizophrenia*. Minneapolis: U of Minnesota P.

Derrida, J. (2008) *The Animal That Therefore I Am*, ed. Marie-Louise Mallet, trans. David Wills. New York: Fordham UP.

de Waal, F. (1996) *Good Natured: The Origins of Right and Wrong in Humans and Other Animals*. Cambridge, MA: Harvard UP.

Egloff, E. (1994) *The Swan*. New York: Dramatists Play Service.

Fuchs, E. (1996) *The Death Of Character: Perspectives On Theater After Modernism*. Bloomington: Indiana UP.

Ionesco, E. (1960) *Rhinoceros and Other Plays*, trans. D. Prouse. New York: Grove P.

Lingis, A. (1999) "Bestiality," in H.P. Steeves (ed.) *Animal Others: On Ethics, Ontology, and Animal Life*. New York: SUNY UP.

Lipton, J. (1968) *An Exaltation of Larks; Or, The Venerable Game*. New York: Grossman.

McKay, C. (2010) "Murder Ob/Scene: The Seen, Unseen and Ob/scene in Murder Trials." *Law Text Culture* 14 no. 1: 79–93.

Nagler, A.M. (1959) "Serlio's Three Scenes," *A Source Book in Theatrical History*. New York: Dover Publications, 52.

Reynolds, C.W. (1987) "Flocks, herds, and schools: A distributed behavioral model." *Proceedings of the 14th Annual Conference on Computer Graphics and Interactive Techniques* (SIGGRAPH'87), ACM.

Ridout, N. (2006) *Stage Fright, Animals, and Other Theatrical Problems*. Cambridge: Cambridge UP.

Shaffer, P. (1973) *Equus*. New York: Penguin.

Shakespeare, W. (2008) *Hamlet*, ed. G.R. Hibbard, *The Oxford Shakespeare* series. New York: Oxford UP.

Smith, A. (2007) "Bill Hammond's Parliament of Foules" in *Knowing Animals*, eds. L. Simmons and P. Armstrong. Brill, 160.

Snæbjörnsdóttir, B. and Wilson, M. (2010) *Uncertainty in the City*. Berlin: Green Box.

Taylor, Paul (2007) "First Night: *Rhinoceros*, Royal Court, London: A fine performance but the wrong choice of opener." *Independent*, September 27. Online.

Williams, T. (2009) *The Night of the Iguana* [1961]. New York: New Directions.

Wolfe, C. (ed.) (2003) *Zoontologies: The Question of the Animal*. Minneapolis: U of Minnesota P.

Chapter 7

Bug Bytes

Insects, Information, and Interspecies Theatricality

> Are insects, then, animals that are always on stage?
> (Eric C. Brown, "Performing Insects in Shakespeare's *Coriolanus*")[1]

Tracy Letts's 1996 play *Bug* joins the ranks of many works—dramatic and otherwise—that are unexpectedly activated (I am tempted to say "reanimated") when seen through the lens of the emerging field of animal studies. That lens is characterized by a kind of stereoscopy: it reveals the double nature of animal representation, the fact that the animal, which was for so long and so unquestioningly treated as a symbol or metaphor, a stand-in for human ideas and feelings, is now seen to be, and to always have been, also a representative of the real species to which it belongs. Whatever animals may "stand for" in works of art, literature, and film—and in the art of a self-obsessed species like ours, they will inevitably stand for myriad human concerns—the animal studies framework insists that they *also* be read as standing for, and signifying about, *themselves*. Seen thus, the animal figure in art becomes a productive site for the ecological revisionism called for by the accelerating crises of climate change.

In the case of Letts's *Bug*, the animal studies lens not only reminds us that the bugs of the imagination have painfully real counterparts, it also reveals how volatile the current stage of human–insect relations is—more volatile and complex perhaps than ever before in its long history. The complexity includes a dawning recognition, alongside a reluctant admission, that insect species may not be as alien as we have styled them. In *Bug*, as in a variety of other recent insect representations, a revisioning of the insect imaginary seems to be linked to a digitally inflected posthumanism whose murky logic is partially captured in the exchange below, from an interview with insect artist Catherine Chalmers:

> *Chalmers:*   I've often wondered if our hatred of insects ... doesn't have something to do with this ancient memory that we must have in an evolutionary sense as mammals, of a time when we lived with the dinosaurs, and we had to be in tiny little holes because these giant reptiles ruled the earth, and so there was a time when mammals had to be very skittish because we were living around these enormous things, and of course it was only with their demise that we were able to rise as a group and take over the planet. And I wonder if somewhere in the back of our deep-seated memory there isn't this insecurity about another animal coming and taking over from us as we lose control.
>
> *Interviewer:* I guess that would be computers?

(Chalmers 2004)

Computers are only one of several new threads recently added to the tangled skein of human beings' thoughts and feelings about insects. The threatened extinction of whole species and bioregions from climate change and other global ecological crises adds a new dimension to the profound ambivalence that characterizes humans' relations to insects. Traditionally, this ambivalence was rooted in the fact that insects, whom we so often experience as enemies (because they feed on us) or rivals (because they feed on our food), are also, as pollinators, absolutely vital to our survival. Our ambivalence turns to anxiety and then, often, to murderous rage when we find ourselves cast in the helpless role of mere onlookers in the dance of fertility that insects perform with the organisms, especially flowers, whose beauty moves us as much as it draws them. In the lush drama of vegetal fertility—a multi-sensory scene saturated with seductive colors, intoxicating smells, astonishing shapes, and surprising sounds—the human becomes a mere voyeur, envious and excluded or, at best, curious and excited.

In Western culture, that curiosity and excitement have often found expression in the arts of collecting and display, and of their more scientific counterparts, taxonomy and anatomy. Insects have, of course, played central roles in all these endeavors, filling countless wonder cabinets and testing the limits of scientific counting. (It is estimated that the number of unknown insect species—that is, species as yet uncataloged by science—far exceeds that of known ones.) Today, the race to name and describe all insect species appears more desperate than ever, being run, as it seems, under the sign of extinction, and especially of the kind of guilt-filled loss associated with our time—the Anthropocene, the age of human ecological dominance.[2] This new major theme in insect discourse turns up the volume on the habitual ambivalence just mentioned because, once again, the insects are both our rivals and our vital allies. Thus the cockroach today not only evokes, as it did before, fear and disgust, but also resentment because of the oft-repeated claim that it could survive many of the catastrophic events, including nuclear holocausts, that could wipe out most other species, including, of course, our own.

This is the context invoked by Chalmers in her remark that our hatred of insects may be tied to a fear of being toppled from our perch as top species, a fear she traces to an evolutionary past before our current dominance, a fear that is escalating now as ecological crises make us more conscious of our vulnerability. Chalmers' musings ring true in our growing recognition of the role our species may be playing in aggravating the "sixth extinction"—a mass die-off that threatens to halve the number of species on earth within the next hundred years.[3] The wide reporting of the unexplained deaths of large numbers of bees, bats, and frogs in recent years has raised the issue of animal extinction to public consciousness, with greatest alarms sounding around the bees and the disturbing (and disturbingly named) phenomenon of "colony collapse disorder." A recent award-winning documentary film on the subject, *Queen of the Sun*, has a subtitle that captures something essential about today's insect imaginary: *What Are the Bees Telling Us?*

The idea that the behavior and fate of these insects is a message to our species is the current—we could call it the "Anthropocenic"— incarnation of an old association between insects and secret knowledge, a kind of *entomancy* rooted in the unnatural and difficult modes of apprehension that are thrust upon our species by the strangeness of insect forms and insect natures. In particular, the smallness of insects, combined with their styles of mobility, makes them particularly challenging objects of our attention and knowledge and arouses fantasies of forbidden facts and secret truths.

Entomology itself—the scientific study of insects—participates in this entomancy, the microscope being its crystal ball (as Emily Dickinson astutely noted),[4] invented in response to one of the most psychologically affecting of insect characteristics: size. It is not simply that, as Chalmers notes, "if insects were the size of dinosaurs our relationship to them would be vastly different. Creatures smaller than our feet tend to be stepped on"; things are actually more complicated than that. While it is true that the individual diminutive insect is at the mercy of big-footed humans, size matters in a very different way for insect collectives. The human obsession with knowing insects, which is also, for our scopophilic species, an obsession with seeing, arises from a combination of their small size with their vast numbers. Multitudes are frightening enough in any context, but multitudes of invisible or near-invisible creatures are truly terrifying.

The terror is doubled, and redoubled, by two other characteristics of insects: their disregard of territorial boundaries, and the nature of what they bring with them. Insects flout the borders we guard most obsessively: the walls of our homes—*home* is, of course, the most emotionally turbulent of geopathological sites—and the skin that encases our bodies. Sneaking into private domains and personal interiors, insects turn their relative-size disadvantage to a distinct advantage; they are stealthy, uninvited visitors, squatters, and traffickers in our most intimate spaces. Furthermore, the matter they are able to convoy in the course of their unauthorized travels into our private interiors makes their diminutive size, vast numbers, and creeping mobility ultimately threatening: insects are vectors of disease, spreading deadly contagions capable of wiping out vast human populations. This infectious potential makes them (as we will see played out in the work I discuss below) ideal figures for imagining, registering, and resisting what Michel Foucault theorized as *bio-power*: the increasing state control over citizens' biological lives, the politicization of biology.[5]

The project of seeing insects, then, of flushing their tiny forms out of hiding and exposing them to view—with the hope of then destroying, or at least controlling, them—is bound up with our sense of species survival, but it is always historically inflected and the will-to-see is tinged with widely varying affects and associations at different times. For example, as Richard Leskosky demonstrates in his survey of "big bug" films (a genre whose insectivorous voyeurism rivals that of scientific entomo-microscopy), the scary overgrown bugs of 1950s horror films were figures of the nuclear imagination and the Cold War, giving monstrous form to the then pervasive fears of invasion, contamination, and wholesale destruction by toxic radiation. By the twenty-first century, however, "radiation seems to have gone well past its half-life in the popular imagination," and the big bug films of the new millennium clearly "suggest that DNA research and genetic engineering are of greater popular concern than nuclear war or radiation contamination" (Leskosky 331). This new entomological imagination aligns closely with growing recognition of the vast and ubiquitous bio-political threats to human life and freedom, the ability and tendency of governments of all kinds, from democratic to totalitarian, to monitor and interfere with the biological lives of citizens, their modes of nourishment, reproduction, health, enjoyment, and death.

Coincidentally (perhaps), a bug is the most famous illustration of a theory that has been energizing animal studies of late, and that has particular resonance for performance theory. The lowly tick,[6] and its astonishingly attenuated sensorium, is currently the best-known example of Estonian biosemiotician Jacob von Uexküll's increasingly influential *Umwelt* theory,[7] invoked repeatedly in the animal philosophy of Gilles Deleuze and Félix Guattari, as well as in the opening chapters of *The Open: Man and Animal*, Giorgio Agamben's signal contribution to animal philosophy. The word *Umwelt*, which translates as "environment" or "milieu," is usually left untranslated in discussions of Uexküll's theory in order to convey its special valences and connotations, its notion of *environment as something that differs from species to species, even from individual to individual*, surrounding each organism like a bubble that moves with it and provides it with its distinctive experience of existence. As further explicated recently by Elizabeth Grosz, who credits Uexküll with making "the earliest attempt to develop a phenomenology or biosemiology of animal life," *Umwelt* theory offers an understanding both of species and their evolution that is characterized by radical interdependence (40). It asserts that species cannot be properly understood other than in relation to the environments they inhabit, and specifically to those aspects of their environments that are relevant to their existence and with which they are involved "in a kind of coevolution" or, in Uexküll's own favorite metaphor, in a kind of "contrapuntal musical performance" (Grosz 40).

The tick makes such a good example of Uexküll's theory because of how starkly limited its points of interaction with its environment are. Blind, deaf, and mute, the tick relies upon photosensitivity, smell, and taste to fulfill its life cycle. The former sense, drawing it toward the light, makes it move up a twig, where it assumes a waiting position at a relative height to the animal it needs in order to continue its life cycle. Its second sense is developed to detect a single smell, that of butyric acid, which is present in the sweat of all warm-blooded mammals—the kind of creatures the tick feeds on. When such an animal passes below the branch upon which the tick is waiting—sometimes for as long at eighteen years!—its acid odor prompts the tick to let go, fall onto the creature below, and embed itself in its flesh. The warmth of the animal triggers the tick's sucking reflex and it begins to fill with blood. When fully engorged it drops off its host, deposits its eggs, and dies.

In Uexküll's terms, the tick's *Umwelt* consists entirely of three elements: the warmth of the sun and of the mammal's skin, the smell of butyric acid, and the taste of blood. Everything else in the environment, including every other feature of the mammal that is to be the tick's host, is irrelevant to the tick. Describing the matter in terms of Uexküll's preferred trope, Grosz writes: "The tick lives in a simplified world, a harmonic world of its own rhythms and melody, a melody composed by its Umwelt, the conjunction mammal-twig-sun, in which it is a connective, an instrument" (42).

The organism as an instrument, conjured up by nature to play the melody of a particular *Umwelt*; or rather, to *attempt* to play that melody, since success, or even smooth functioning, is far from guaranteed. This notion aligns with the new relational ecology that has been gaining ground in recent years based on growing recognition of the anti-essentialist and nondeterministic implications of Darwinian evolutionary thought.[8] It also invites an engagement between ecological thought and performance, understood as including, though not limited to, Uexküll's favored art form, music. This is the invitation I propose to take up here by discussing *Bug*, a play that explores both contemporary cultural experience, as well as theatricality, using, as a point of departure, the idea of overlapping and contesting *Umwelts*.

Interestingly, the play's use of insects to explore both these levels of experience, and especially the theatrical, played a major role in the failure of its film version. The tension between our desire to see insects (discussed above) and the fact of their natural invisibility played out strangely and unexpectedly in the transfer from stage to screen. Although blest with an excellent director, cast, and script, the film completely flopped because it was marketed as a horror film and hence deeply disappointed the audiences it drew, which expected all insects in horror films to be of the magnified, spectacularly monstrous variety.[9] This film, however, like the play on which it was based, was most deeply engaged with the very opposite of insect spectacle, being interested in the ways that we can be driven crazy by what we *don't* see. Indeed, Letts's play offers a unique contemporary artistic engagement with insects by means of a brilliant challenge to the visual limits of theater, limits that the theater resists and resents in its dedication to *showing* rather than *telling*—a dedication that is coded even in its etymology: the Greek *theatron* means "the seeing place."

Like all plays, *Bug* creates a fictional world whose elements selectively resemble or diverge from its spectators' lifeworlds, the worlds they feel themselves to inhabit; however, the special strategy of *Bug*, as of other works of what I call a "theater of species" [see Chapter 8] is to manipulate both the resemblance and divergence enough to create a new awareness and experience of human life *as species life*, a mode of being as fully defined by the material and biological factors of existence as by sociopolitical or psychological ones. The conduit to this experience in *Bug* is, appropriately, a reliance upon the non-visual elements of theater, especially upon those we associate with insects: vibration and sound.

Bug launches its experiment in entomological staging with a clever twist on an old theater joke: during rehearsals for a show, especially during tech-rehearsals, whenever there is a sound that should not be there or whose source cannot be traced, it elicits the comment: "It's crickets." (This is perhaps the theater's version of the showbiz trope of "crickets chirping," which refers to the awkward silence following a bad joke.) In *Bug*, the "chirp" of the cricket turns out to be the sound of the smoke alarm signaling its need for new batteries. This is also one of the play's savvy moments of folding the spectators' lifeworlds into the play: providing an early moment of "verification"—of audience assent—in a play that is increasingly about discerning truth from delusions or lies. Here, the assent is achieved simply by invoking a phenomenon that is familiar, although uncanny, to most of us (the chirp the smoke alarm gives off when it is out of batteries).

This association of insect and everyday technology initiates what is to become the play's main preoccupation: namely, the alliance through invisibility and hyper-miniaturization between technology and insects, and the impact of this on the species life of us human animals. Besides the cricket, two other sounds serve to keep our sonic experience of contemporary life keyed to insects: there is an air conditioner that shuts off and turns on throughout the play, and a helicopter is heard whirring in the sky "outside" periodically. The uncannily whimsical behavior of the air conditioner, which seems to operate (as so many machines in the modern world seem to do) independently of human control, contributes to the sense, which will grow as the play proceeds, that the space of human habitation here—these humans' *Umwelt*—is largely shaped by unseen, hostile, and mechanized forces. As for the helicopter, it provides an aural proof of the protagonist's claim of government-sponsored infestation (and the fusing of warfare and entomology); in the final moments of the play, its sound transforms fully into the sound it has reminded us of all along—that of "a swarm of bugs" (92). The transformation serves as aural confirmation that one lifeworld, that of the protagonist, Peter, has prevailed over others that have contested it—including, initially, the audience's.

Bug tells the story of Peter, a Gulf War veteran, who meets and moves in with a waitress, Agnes, who lives in a motel room. Agnes's backstory emerges quickly: a failed marriage, a lost child—literally lost, as in *missing*—that have left her desperate, depressed, and drug-dependent. Peter's story is far less clear, emerging in a context that is tainted with unreliability. Peter appears initially as a familiar American type, the paranoid loner with a shady past and an overwrought cultural analysis: "You're never really safe. One time, maybe, a long time ago, people were safe, but that's all over. Not anymore, not on this planet. We'll never really be safe again. We can't be, not with all the technology, and the chemicals, *and the information*" (30, emphasis added). The last element in Peter's list of dangers, information, links the play's exploration of insects and human life to the idea expressed in the spontaneous response of Chalmers' interlocutor quoted earlier. Misunderstanding her, the interviewer assumes that the new species whose ascension human beings today fear must be computers.

This slippage of perceived threat, from the realm of biology to that of technology, is neither idiosyncratic nor illogical; indeed, it forms the basis of an entirely new field of research and technological innovation. The foundation of the field is the recognition that Chalmers discusses playfully in one of her blog posts, that of the resemblance between insects and networked media: "Ants invented a sophisticated, networked communication system that rivals the

Internet. Without central command—individual antennae touches are like Google hits—complex decisions are made. At some point a message goes viral. If only I could write an algorithm to better decipher the data" (Chalmers 2013).

Just such algorithms as Chalmers imagines, although intended to mimic the data rather than decipher it, are the quarry of a field whose relevance to art and performance is explored in Jussi Parikka's wonderfully original study, *Insect Media*. Parikka's point of departure is the burgeoning field of digital technology modeled on the behavior and characteristics of so-called social insects: insects that exist in, and appear to only thrive in, collectives, such as swarms and hives. What makes insects so promising to digital programmers is their apparent ability to share agency and decision-making, which is also the ability to function in non-hierarchical and non-centristic ways. As Eric Bonabeau and Guy Théraulaz report:

A growing community of researchers has been devising new ways of applying swarm intelligence to diverse tasks. The foraging of ants has led to a novel method for rerouting network traffic in busy telecommunications systems. The cooperative interaction of ants working to build their nests leads to more effective control algorithms for groups of robots. The way in which insects cluster their colony's dead and sort their larvae can aid in analyzing banking data. And the division of labor among honeybees could help streamline assembly lines in factories.

(42)

Studies and applications of "swarm intelligence" have progressed to the point that, as Parikka points out, the insect collective has decisively displaced the cyborg—that once so promising and exciting figure of posthumanism—as "a model for designing artificial agents that expressed complex behavior, not through pre-programming and centralization but through autonomy, emergence, and distributed functioning" (xi).

While the shared agency and decentered collaboration of insect collectives might resonate with progressive, populist, or anarchistic political positions (a resonance I will return to at the end of this essay), these same features can be experienced as a kind of scary and threatening "headless animality," a mindless, unmotivated malignity poised to infect and destroy without reason or provocation (Thacker 138). This is the perception that lies behind the interviewer's reflexive response to Chalmers in which the slippage from bugs to computers occurs. The same perception undoubtedly underlies the use of words like "bug" and "virus" to designate intentional disruptions of computer programming, especially those maliciously intended to spread undetected beyond the initial site of infection.

The first documented case of a computer virus "in the wild"— that is, affecting personal computers rather than industrial mainframes—occurred in 1981 and was named "Elk Cloner." When it infected a computer, the monitor displayed the following message: "It will get on all your disks / It will infiltrate your chips / Yes it's Cloner! / It will stick to you like glue / It will modify ram too / Send in the Cloner!" (qt. in Bardini 147). Elk Cloner's threat of unwelcome proliferation and contamination reveals and contests the fantasy of a technology capable of sanitizing and purifying human life, producing zones where abstract thought can flourish undisturbed by organic matter. Elk Cloner and its vast progeny bespeak a different desire in which dysfunction and disorder play a role, as do those invisible challengers of human supremacy, the bugs of the world. And, in what seems like an act of highly deliberate mischief on the part of nature, the use of "bug" to refer to computer-code infections has an actual insect lurking in the history (or at least the folklore) of computer science. Admiral Grace Murray Hopper, a pioneer of U.S. computing, writes of an incident that occurred in 1945, when she and a group of Harvard programmers were building Mark II, an early electromechanical computer:

> We were working in a World War I temporary building. It was a hot summer and there was no air-conditioning, so all the windows were open. Mark II stopped, and we were trying to get her going. We finally found the relay that had failed. Inside the relay—and these were large relays—was a moth that had been beaten to death by the relay. We got a pair of tweezers. Very carefully we took the moth out of the relay, put it in the logbook and put Scotch tape over it (qt. in Harpold and Philip 1–2).

If the body of a real bug preceded its virtual avatars in the computer world, real bugs remain closely connected with those avatars in *Bug*. The bugs that Peter claims to be dealing with are simultaneously real and informatic, organic and technological; they are tiny cyborgs implanted beneath the skin of unsuspecting "subjects" to spy on and then control them. Their prototype is "the Intelligence Manned

Interface biochip, a subcutaneous transponder, a computer chip imprinted with living brain cells" (Letts 2006: 83). In linking biological bugs with viral information, Letts's play might be thought of as playing the metaphorical association (the one underlying the term "computer virus" or "computer bug") backwards, rewinding our digital anxieties—the ones spontaneously expressed by Chalmers' interviewer—back to their entomological origins. In doing so, it identifies the theater as a productive space for thinking about the kinds of swarm-like experiences and opportunities that digital "insect media" are making available to us, along with the ideological and ecological promises, and pitfalls, they present.

Bug dramatically activates the anxiety of infiltration by redefining the theater as an inherently *infested* space. It reminds us that (to paraphrase Brown's idea that serves as the epigraph to this essay) no stage is ever free of insects—invisible or nearly invisible, they are always there. That uncomfortable reality is cleverly, one might even say diabolically, exploited in the first "insect scene" of the play. The scene begins, significantly, in darkness, the first of the play's systematic challenges to theater's reliance upon visuality. It unfolds slowly—I am tempted to say creepily. I quote this section at unusual length here to do justice to the painstakingly constructed process by which one character's (Agnes's) experience becomes the bridge for the spectator to cross over into the lifeworld being asserted by Peter:

Peter: Motherfucker.
[Long pause.]
            Motherfucker.
[Long pause.]
            You little—
[Long pause.]
            Come here, you ...
[Beat.]
            Fucking ... motherfucker.
[Beat.]
            Fuck. Fuck FUCK! FUCK IT, MAN!
[Agnes wakes, turns on a bedside lamp. Peter is scratching his wrist.]
Agnes: What's the matter? Is it—? ...
Peter: Fucking bug, a fucking bug bite, fuck this— ...
[Peter snaps on his bedside lamp.]
            Where are you, you little motherfucker... .
Agnes: I don't see it—

Peter:	There.
Agnes:	What.
Peter:	Right there.
Agnes:	Where.
Peter:	There.
Agnes:	Where?
Peter:	There, you see it?
Agnes:	What.
Peter:	The bug.
Agnes:	Where.
Peter:	Right there.
Agnes:	I don't ...
Peter:	Right. There.
Agnes:	This?
Peter:	No. This. That. There.... Well, do you see it?
Agnes:	I'm not sure.
Peter:	Right there. It's really small (33–36).

The insistence on the insect's diminutive size and near invisibility serves to remind us of bugs' resistance to theater's scopocentric regime, a resistance that afforded one of the pleasures of that most unlikely of performance forms, the flea circus.[10] As often happens, this feature of the insects is soon linked to the second characteristic that is both disturbing and crucial to the association being installed here, between insects and information—namely, their vast numbers:

Peter:	There might be more.
Agnes:	There's not any more. We would've seen 'em.
Peter:	You almost didn't see that one.
Agnes:	Well, it's small.
Peter:	That's my point, Agnes, they're small. We might not have seen them (37–38).

By the end of the act, Agnes has begun seeing things (literally) Peter's way: "*She spies something in his hair, picks it out, studies it*" (46).

The second act has Agnes's friend R.C. mounting a counter-attack against Peter's account of reality. That account is, to be sure, complete with a paranoid conspiracy theory: "I don't know that I'm not carrying some disease with me, some contagion. Jesus, you know that's how they start, typhoid, Legionnaires' disease, some government screwup, AIDS with those fucking monkeys in Africa. They're after me. These people don't fuck around, Agnes" (46). In Peter's account of the world (and of his body), there is an intimate connection not only between insects and (illicit) information, but also between those two and warfare. Again, there is much that is familiar about this conjunction, based on both fact and fiction: not only have countless Hollywood films traded on the idea of nefarious chemical warfare, but, as environmental historian Edmund Russell shows in his book *War and Nature: Fighting Humans and Insects with Chemicals from World War I to Silent Spring*, the actual interdependence of pesticide production and chemical warfare has been responsible for such increasing scales of human and natural destruction as to make fear like Peter's inevitable, even rational. Recently, DARPA (the Defense Advanced Research Projects Agency) proposed a plan to weaponize insects by inserting electronic devices into insect pupae, devices that would become part of the insect after its metamorphosis, allowing the "cyborg insect ... [to] then be controlled and used as a spy tool for army covert operations. Who would suspect a lone moth or a bumblebee?" (Parikka x).

The close relationship between entomology and warfare is vividly staged at the start of Act 2, when Peter is revealed sitting "*in front of a child's footlocker where he has set up his 'lab': a kiddie chemistry set, with microscope, magnifying glass, petri dishes, glass slides, and vials*" (47). These traditional tools of the human obsession with seeing and knowing insects, the microscope in particular, are accompanied here by the "*weapons of a bug war ...: cans of bug spray, from the cheap, over-the-counter items to the industrial tub with a metal spray hose; fly strips, hung from the ceiling, the lamps, the painting; roach motels, in the corner, on the table, by the fridge, under the bed; a flyswatter*" (47). This transformation of the fictional space of the play signals the imminent defeat of R.C.'s efforts to resist the reality that Peter is asserting, efforts that she is making not only on behalf of Agnes, but also on behalf of us, the audience. We learn that she has taken Agnes to a doctor to look at her alleged bug bites:

Peter: What kind of doctor?
R.C.:   A dermatologist.
Peter: And what did he find?
R.C.:   No bugs.... . He said they didn't even look like bug bites.... . He said her sores were "self-inflicted" (59–62).

R.C.'s challenge to Peter's lifeworld is unequivocal and blunt: "There ain't no bugs in the microscope, on your skin, *in* your skin. In the room. *There ain't no fuckin' bugs*" (62, original emphasis). This is a decisive line in the sand, and it marks the boundary that Agnes and the audience are going to be asked to negotiate for the remainder of the play. It is worth emphasizing that the boundary in question depends on trusting, or otherwise, the evidence of one's eyes. It is therefore equally a boundary about the limits of theatricality, and the remedies for those limits. One of those remedies—the move from mimesis to diegesis, from showing to telling—is immediately invoked following R.C.'s combative declaration. In what appears to be a direct response to her refusal of Peter's claims, he moves from merely claiming (telling) to performing (showing) the infestation: "*Peter suddenly slaps his neck, brushes at his hair. He staggers backward, slapping at his arms, his face, his hair, his neck, the air in front of him.... His slapping and brushing becomes frantic, panicked. He grabs a coat hanger, beats himself with it, spinning in a circle, screaming.... Peter goes into a frenzy, scratching, slapping, shrieking*" (64). Agnes covers him with a blanket, pulls him to the floor, and holds him down until he calms down. Then she harshly sends R.C. packing, throwing her lot in with Peter, essentially crossing over into his lifeworld. "*From this point on,*" a stage direction tells us, "*Agnes and Peter often kill bugs, swat them away from their faces, et cetera.*"

The insects that come to inhabit the stage of *Bug* are, we might say, *gestural insects.* They are known by the actors' physical, behavioral response to them, a response that courts the audience's assent in the very same way that all stage behavior by actors does: by its verisimilitude, its apparent authenticity. In the case of bugs, however, the audience's assent is complicated by the fact that, as Brown's remark reminds us, there always *are* insects onstage and an actor might, at any moment, be bitten or stung. A gestural insect onstage, therefore, is always equivocal: a piece of convincing acting *or* an instinctive reaction to a real stimulus.[11] *Bug* cleverly exploits this inherent equivocation by dividing its reading among different characters: Peter is essentially accused by various characters of faking the insects (either intentionally or delusionally), while he himself violently asserts their reality.

All this would be familiar dramatic fare were it not for the fact that the gestures in question, the gestures of itching, scratching, swatting, and so on, produce, over time, a somatic sympathetic response in many members of the audience. These gestures are, like yawns, affective and contagious—they are *catching*. Watching other people scratching themselves can cause people to start feeling an itch themselves. At the performance of *Bug* I attended, many audience members kept exchanging sheepish grins as they began to experience this response to Peter's and Agnes's gestural insects. This somatic response, along with the play's association of it with paranoia and madness, plunged the spectators into an epistemological quandary very similar to the one that was, according to Peter, the prevailing cultural norm: profound and potentially lethal uncertainty rooted in the vulnerability of the human body, the permeability of its surfaces, the extreme miniaturization of technology, and the pervasive reach of the state. Enlisting the spectators' bodies as much as the powers (and limits) of theatricality, *Bug* stages the contemporary *Umwelt* of extreme biopolitical vulnerability.

Bug ends in cataclysm. The stage direction reads: "*He strikes a match. Blackout. Fire, buzzing*" (55). In the original New York production, this was interpreted as an explosion so loud and so blindingly bright as to obliterate the stage world and threaten the real one. This conclusion locates the play firmly at a particular stage in the development of the entomological imagination, the stage in which infestation was equated with abjection and eventual destruction at the hands of those wielding informatic biopower. But the entomological imagination has recently taken a turn that suggests other outcomes and affects for the kind of biologically activated space that the play has actualized. Although it links insects and information, *Bug* does not register—or, more accurately, fails to anticipate—the social and imaginal transformation of recent decades, when the digital phenomenon that Parikka calls insect media has begun to alter and denaturalize the negative affects long evoked by "creepy crawlies." As digital technologies become more and more ubiquitous, increasingly making everyday life a digitally mediated experience, "an emergent reality principle in its own right," the entomological imaginary undergoes a transformation, allowing feelings of admiration, friendliness, and even kinship to displace, at least partially, the old feelings of revulsion and suspicion (Kroker and Kroker 7). Thoroughly and, for the most part, pleasingly networked as we humans now are, we are finally able to find reflections of our species' sociality in that of many insect species. This newfound friendliness may account, for instance, for the invention of something like the "solar powered garden insect theatre," a contraption whose description on an eco-friendly website suggests that our species may be ready for some new genres of insect performance, beyond those of horror movies and embalmed collections:

> If you need some front porch evening entertainment but aren't into the cruelty of the traditional bug zapper, you can try the solar powered Garden Insect Theatre. Like the bug zapper, it draws insects in at night with its bright light. But unlike the bug zapper, it won't electrify them. Instead, when the insects fly in to get closer to the light, you can watch them flutter around for a while until they find their way out though the holes in the side. Odd? Uh huh.[12]

I read the garden insect theater as a simplistic and commercialized instance of a new, post-digital "insect gaze," a vastly expanded affective field that has opened between humans and insects and that is being explored in searching and complex ways by artists like Chalmers, Tessa Farmer, Poul Beckman, Amy Youngs, Jennifer Angus, Jan Fabre, and Damien Hirst.[13] A number of these artists regard their practice as an "interspecies collaboration," an approach that Chalmers articulates eloquently in one of her blog posts: "On grant applications I check the box next to—Artist. It never occurred to me to select—Art Collective. But, perhaps I should. I never work alone. My collaborators just don't happen to be human. Early on I raised my colleagues—fed them, housed them, cleaned up after them. The dialogue was between me and the cockroach, me and the praying mantis, me and the frog" (Chalmers 2011). Her artistic "colleagues" join hosts of other animal species in a rapidly expanding field of contemporary zooësis with great aesthetic and ideological potential. Viewed in this way, the infested, somatized stage of *Bug* points toward a theater of species that could contribute to the search now underway for an *affirmative* biopolitics, one that reconceptualizes biopower away from the brutal associations of its Foucauldian source.

Philosophers like Antonio Negri and Michael Hardt, seeking a way of thinking about vulnerable bodies not only as targets and victims of state power, but also as sites of resistance to it, mobilize the increasingly activated association between swarms and networks (discussed above) for political theory in the figure of the multitude.[14] In search of a politics capable of responding to the rapidly multiplying modes and venues of biological manipulation in contemporary life—from mass migrations of human and non-human species, to biotechnologies (with both therapeutic and threatening applications), to pharmacological controls on behavior and rights, to radical reconfigurations of notions of public and private—an affirmative biopolitics posits a new kind of group and political agency, one that is different from the kind associated with groups like "the masses," "the public," or "the people": "The multitude is not just a large number that has been unified, homogenized, rendered a body-above-the body (a body politic); it is also defined by its constitution, which is labile, permeable, and morphological. What keeps the multitude from being 'one' is that it is defined by a set of diverse interests, affects, and relations" (Thacker 2004).

Conceptualized in relation to the distributed intelligence and collaborative yet diversified agency found in the swarm, the concept of the multitude allows political thought to shift its fundamental question from "How can this group be governed?" to "How will this group govern itself?" (Thacker 2004).[15] To be sure, the shift from governance to self-governance is at present only a utopian pathway toward a "coming community,"[16] but it is one that the theater, with its own potent utopianisms,[17] will surely follow productively. As the infested stage of *Bug* demonstrates, the bodies of human and non-human animals, and of their different though overlapping *Umwelts*, co-perform the emerging realities of the changing world they share.

Notes

1 Brown 2006: 37.
2 The word *Anthropocene* was originally coined by ecologist Eugene Stoermer by analogy with *Holocene*; it was later popularized by atmospheric chemist Paul Crutzen. It is now widely used to name the era we are living in, and to mark it as a time of vast anthropogenic—man-made—changes in the geophysical environment, most notably in the phenomena of climate change.
3 "There have been five great die-offs in history. This time, the cataclysm is us." Elizabeth Kolbert, "The Sixth Extinction?" (2009).
4 "'Faith' is a fine invention / When Gentlemen can *see*— / But *Microscopes* are prudent / In an Emergency." Emily Dickinson, *Final Harvest* (1961: 20).
5 Foucault 1976; 1998.
6 Ticks are not, technically, insects, but arachnids.
7 Uexküll 2010.
8 For a brief, provocative, and highly influential introduction to this discourse and its relevance to literary studies, see Timothy Morton's "Queer Ecology." Morton says that "[e]volution means that life-forms are made of other life-forms. Entities are mutually determining: they

exist in relation to each other and derive from each other. Nothing exists independently, and nothing comes from nothing" (2010: 275).

9 In an interview published on the Hermitosis blog, Letts called this "the worst [ad] campaign in the history of motion pictures. It was just an absolutely *abysmally* conceived and executed plan. When they first talked about opening the thing on 2000 screens, Bill and I both said, 'You're crazy! Why would you do that? This is not that kind of movie, this is a small picture, you need to open this in New York and LA, and put it on the festival circuit to let it find its audience. But they had this plan in mind to open on all these screens and con kids into thinking it was *Saw* or *Hostel* to bring them into the theater. As a result, people who would have enjoyed the film didn't go see it, because they were put off by the marketing campaign, and kids who were enthusiastic to see the movie advertised were *furious*. Why are these people talking?'" (Letts 2008, emphasis in original)

10 While many flea circuses, past and present, use real, "trained" fleas, some merely produced the illusion of live insect involvement by other means, like gesture, behavior, and movement.

11 And to complicate matters further, an actual reaction can easily be misread by onlookers. A recent ITV television drama titled *Collision* spun several hours of mystery and detection out of the fact that the gesture of swatting away a wasp can also look like an expression of anger.

12 See Helmbuch 2009.

13 These and other artists are presented in an early double issue on insects of *Antennae: The Journal of Nature in Visual Culture* 3 nos. 1–2 (Autumn 2007).

14 See Negri and Hardt 2005.

15 "In current political theory, the key issue is a shift in the way the question of the multitude is posed. The question is no longer that of choosing between the priority of the individual and the priority of the group... the multitude is neither the individual nor the group. It is positioned somewhere in between, or somewhere else entirely" (Thacker 2004).

16 Giorgio Agamben in *The Coming Community*, 1993. Agamben imagines a new kind of community arising from the recognition, formulation, and valuing of a new notion of identity, which he calls "whatever singularity"—an identity asserted and granted without any requirement of explicit group affiliation. This kind of identity is, for Agamben, utopian though not impossible because its implacable enemy, the state, can be defeated.

17 See, among many other sources, Jill Dolan's capacious essay, "Performance, Utopia, and the 'Utopian Performative'" (2001).

Works cited

Agamben, G. (1993) *The Coming Community*. Minneapolis: U of Minnesota P.
—— (2004) *The Open: Man and Animal*, trans. K. Attell. Stanford: Stanford UP.
Antennae: The Journal of Nature in Visual Culture (2007) 3 nos. 1–2 (Autumn).

Bardini, T. (2008) "Hypervirus: A Clinical Report," in A. Kroker and M. Kroker (eds) *Critical Digital Studies: A Reader*. Toronto: U of Toronto P, 143–57.

Bonabeau, E. and Théraulaz, G. (2008) "Swarm Smarts." *Scientific American* 18 no. 1: 40–47.

Brown, E.C. (2006) "Performing Insects in Shakespeare's *Coriolanus*," in E.C. Brown (ed.) *Insect Poetics*. Minneapolis: U of Minnesota P, 29–57.

Chalmers, C. (2004) "Chalmers, Crickets, Kafka." Interview on *Studio 360*, episode 514, April 3. NPR.

—— (2011) "The Original Social Network" (blog), March 14, www. catherinechalmers.com/blog/

—— (2013) Blog, January 10, www.catherinechalmers.com/blog/

Chaudhuri, U. (2012) "The Silence of the Polar Bears: Performing (Climate) Change in the Theater of Species," in W. Arons and T. J. May (eds) *Readings in Performance and Ecology*. New York: Palgrave Macmillan, 45–58.

Collision (2009) Television drama, writers A. Horowitz and M.A. Walker, dir. M. Evans. ITV.

Dickinson, E. (1961) *Final Harvest*. Boston: Little, Brown.

Dolan, J. (2001) "Performance, Utopia, and the 'Utopian Performative.'" *Theatre Journal* 53 no. 3: 455–79.

Foucault, M. (1998) *The History of Sexuality*, vol. 1: *The Will to Knowledge* [1976]. London: Penguin.

Grosz, E.A. (2008) *Chaos, Territory, Art: Deleuze and the Framing of the Earth*. New York: Columbia UP.

Harpold, T. and Philip, K. (2000) "Of Bugs and Rats: Cyber-Cleanliness, Cyber-Squalor, and the Fantasy-Spaces of Informational Globalization." *Postmodern Culture: An Electronic Journal of Interdisciplinary Criticism* 11 no. 1.

Helmbuch, J. (2009) "Weird Solar Device of the Day: Solar Powered Garden Insect Theatre." *Treehugger*, December 18. Online.

Kolbert, E. (2009) "The Sixth Extinction?" *The New Yorker*, May 25. Online.

Kroker, A. and Kroker, M. (eds.) (2008) "Introduction," in *Critical Digital Studies: A Reader*. Toronto: U of Toronto P, 1–21.

Leskosky, R.J. (2006) "Size Matters: Big Bugs on the Big Screen," in E.C. Brown (ed.) *Insect Poetics*. Minneapolis: U of Minnesota P, 319–41.

Letts, T. (2006) *Bug: A Play*. Evanston, IL: Northwestern UP.

—— (2008) "Pulitzer-Winner Tracy Letts Explains Why *Bug* Deserves Another Look." Interview for *Hermitosis: Interviews and Obsessions From the Horrified Mind*, May 12, http://hermitosis.blogspot. co.uk/2008/05/pulitzer-winner-tracy-letts-on-his.html

Morton, T. (2010) "Queer Ecology." *PMLA* 125 no. 2: 273–82.

Negri, A. and Hardt, M. (2005) *Multitude: War and Democracy in the Age of Empire*. New York: Penguin Books.

Parikka, J. (2010) *Insect Media: An Archaeology of Animals and Technology*. Minneapolis: U of Minnesota P.

Queen of the Sun: What Are the Bees Telling Us? (2010). Documentary film, dir. T. Siegel. Portland, OR: Collective Eye Films.

Russell, E. (2001) *War and Nature: Fighting Humans and Insects with Chemicals from World War I to Silent Spring*. Cambridge: Cambridge UP.

Thacker, E. (2004) "Networks, Swarms, Multitudes: Part 2." *ctheory.net*, May 18, www.ctheory.net/articles.aspx?id=423

—— (2008) "Biophilosophy for the 21st Century," in A. Kroker and M. Kroker (eds) *Critical Digital Studies: A Reader*. Toronto: U of Toronto P, 132–42.

Uexküll, J. von (2010) *A Foray into the Worlds of Animals and Humans, with a Theory of Meaning*, trans. J.D. O'Neil. Minneapolis: U of Minnesota P.

Chapter 8

The Silence of the Polar Bears

Performing (Climate) Change in the Theater of Species

In 2006, a single picture launched a thousand articles about global warming. It ran in the *Sunday Telegraph*, the *New York Times*, the *Boston Globe*, the *International Herald Tribune*, *The Times* (London), and many other papers. It was said to have been taken by Canadian environmentalists and to show a pair of polar bears stranded on Arctic ice that was shrinking due to global warming. It made polar bears the poster animals of global warming, a status they retained even after the photograph's evidentiary status was discredited: it turned out that the photograph wasn't taken by environmentalists, but by a student of marine biology, who did not release the image herself and who never intended to convey that she was recording evidence of global warming. Moreover, the photo was taken in August, at the height of the Alaskan summer, when melting ice is normal. The ice floes pictured were not very far from land, and polar bears are good swimmers (Sheppard). Predictably, right-wing anti-environmentalists and global-warming deniers such as Rush Limbaugh were quick to use the episode to their own advantage, saying that this "fraud" was "a great little microcosm for the entire global warming escapade" (qt. by Zurkow).

But the iconicity that the image conferred on the animals did not dissipate. Rather, it intensified. Al Gore incorporated the image into his global warming slide presentation, adding a comment that goes to the heart of the images' power and appeal; these "beautiful animals," said Gore, are "literally being forced off the planet. They're in trouble, got *nowhere else to go*" (qt. in "Gore Pays for Photo," *National Post*, emphasis added).

Nowhere else to go. That forlorn phrase evokes a century or more of anguished negotiations with the concept of place, a history of what I have elsewhere called "geopathology" (Chaudhuri 1996: 55). The term refers, in the first instance and most generally, to the many problems related to *place*—as nation, homeland, neighborhood, environment, border—that largely defined the past century of dislocation. The term also seeks to name, and to recognize, a related phenomenon: the characterization of place itself *as a problem*, as a site of often-painful psychological impasse and as an ideological blind spot, with devastating consequences. The harsh political realities and untrammeled economic ambitions of the twentieth century produced movements of populations on an unprecedented scale. While millions moved voluntarily, to better themselves, millions more were forced to move, and millions more were simply stranded in refugee camps around the globe, with nowhere else to go. Today, the alarming phenomena of climate change have focused attention on the degree to which these vast human dislocations were also, inevitably, ecological devastations, and that other species have also paid an extraordinary price. The case of the polar bears is only one among many others that instruct us that geopathology is also, now, a zoöpathology: a disease of the ties that bind humans to other animals.

That this disease has a history in which the arts and representation are deeply implicated is achingly conveyed in an extraordinary work that combines a multiyear research project and art installation by Bryndís Snæbjörnsdóttir and Mark Wilson entitled *nanoq: flat out and bluesome*. Centered on the history of taxidermy and natural history collections, *nanoq* uses the figure of the polar bear to investigate and illuminate the relations among animal bodies, display, and place. The animal bodies in question are those of all the taxidermied polar bears the artists were able to find in the U.K. over a three-year period of research—thirty-four "specimens" of various sizes and in various states of repair, located in private homes, museums, shops, and (in one case) a pub. Once they had identified these emblems of a bygone era of conquest and adventure, the artists began a process that relocated the bears in complex ways: first by metaphorically returning them to their home places, by tracing the provenance of each taxidermied bear, learning as much as possible about the people and circumstances under which these magnificent living beings became, first, targets, and then trophies. This first metaphorical homecoming was followed by another kind of reinhabitation, as the artists sought and received permission to photograph the polar bears in situ, recording the bizarre transformation of these creatures from a freezing world into the differently frozen lives they lead in their new "homes" (fig. 8.1).

Figure 8.1 Somerset, from the project *nanoq: flat out and bluesome*, Snæbjörnsdóttir/Wilson.

Courtesy of the artists.

These photographs, displayed at various museums and printed in a beautiful book about the project, are exemplary documents of what might be called a "zoögeopathology": the infliction by humans, on the other animals, of the vicissitudes of displacement. Leafing through these brilliant photographs is like journeying through the very definition of the uncanny, in its etymological sense of "the unhomelike": the oddly estranged, the strangely out-of place (fig. 8.2).

The taxidermied bears, whose petrifaction is poignantly belied by their ferocious stances (many have been taxidermied in upright positions, as if ready to pounce), begin to speak a different language through the medium of photography. While taxidermy is a "fiction of liveness" paradoxically premised on death, photography is a fiction of presence paradoxically premised on the expectation of absence (and death, as theorized by Roland Barthes) (Desmond 159). The photographs of the polar bears seem to rescue them from their

Figure 8.2 Bristol (Misha), from *nanoq*, Snæbjörnsdóttir/Wilson.
Courtesy of the artists.

fake lives, *returning their deaths to them* in an act of delayed mourning. The *presence* in these photographs is not that of the bears but of the *places* they are in and the objects that surround them. Without exception, these places are "elsewheres" for these animals (notwithstanding the frequent attempts at recreating the bears' original habitats), making this a photographic record of the very principle that made polar bears the poster animals of climate change: the principle of the last resort, the endgame, the final corner, of nowhere left to go (fig. 8.3).

Yet the third stage of *nanoq* offers a startling coda to this apparent ultimatum. In a heroic effort of organization and logistics—reminiscent of the efforts that originally brought these polar bears to Britain (just as the first stage of the project is reminiscent of the hunts that originally sought them out in their distant habitats)—the artists borrowed a large number of the taxidermied bears and transported them to the contemporary art

Figure 8.3 Worcester, from *nanoq*, Snæbjörnsdóttir/Wilson.

Courtesy of the artists.

space Spike Island, in Bristol, where they were displayed in simple glass cases (fig. 8.4).

Steve Baker reports that "a crucial aspect of the project was the shift from the bears' singular use as educational museum exhibits or country house trophies" to an art context "with no indication of how they're to be read" (149). Baker quotes the artists as feeling that "it's in that sense of relocation, and the amassing, that everything becomes possible" (49).

Snæbjörnsdóttir and Wilson's "everything becomes possible" strikes me as a powerful countertext to the geopathological "nowhere else to go." Baker glosses the phrase as "new experiences of the bears, new interpretations of their histories, new emotional responses to them, and new understandings of the spaces that the bears might come to occupy" (154). The artists themselves characterize their project as "a notional community," made up of "animals that had shared a similar fate" (qt. in Baker 154). In the

Figure 8.4 Snæbjörnsdóttir/Wilson, *nanoq: flat out and bluesome*, installation of ten taxidermic polar bears, Spike Island, Bristol, 2004.

Courtesy of the artists.

age of climate change, that shared fate includes that of the human animals wandering the gallery space, turning that space, suddenly, into a space of ecological consciousness and—possibly—a platform for action.

The incarnation of *nanoq* as gallery installation opens a space of performance that I call "the theater of species," naming an emergent performance practice of our times. Climate change, which turns familiar sites into landscapes of risk or disaster, also reminds us that we humans are one species among many, among multitudes, all equally contingent and threatened. The theater of species restages all life as *species life*, highlighting and foregrounding the ecological dimensions of human life, which include not only biological, climatogical, and material factors but also the vast panoply of what Donna Haraway calls "naturecultures" in *A Companion Species Manifesto*: the ideas and practices through which human beings relate to the "more-than-human" world (1). The theater of species brings the resources of performance to bear on what is arguably the most urgent task facing our species: to understand, so as to transform, our modes of habitation in a world we share intimately with millions of other species. The theater of species addresses what we could call a "zoögeopathology"—the planetary health emergency that is challenging the anthropocentric geographies we have lived by for so long.

I turn now to two other works that offer divergent perspectives on the issues engaged by *nanoq*. Both works also use the figure of the polar bear, and both pair it with another figure—that of the child. This pairing imports a host of new frames, including those of genealogy and generation, psyche and psychoanalysis, kinship and biography, into their respective explorations of ecological crisis. The response to climate change that these works construct can be unpacked with reference to a provocative formulation offered by Jean Baudrillard. In a chapter entitled "The Animals: Territory and Metamorphosis," Baudrillard writes: "Animals have no unconscious, because they have a territory. Men have only had an unconscious since they lost a territory" (139). Curtly dismissing the Deleuzian association of animality with deterritorialization and nomadism, Baudrillard says that the idea that animals wander is "a myth," that animals have "never been deterritorialized" and that "their law is that of the territory" (140, 130).

Baudrillard's binary, *unconscious* versus *territory*, the postmodern version of the philosophically loaded modernist binary of map versus territory,[1] risks falling into the trap of human exceptionalism, which is pernicious even when it takes the form of critique (i.e., even when the characteristics identified as setting humans apart from animals are undesirable, as they are here, where the category associated with the human—the unconscious—is defined as repetitive mourning for the loss of a category associated with the animal—the territory). But that risk is worth taking in a context when it is precisely the breaking down of that binary that is the point. For is it not the case that the human exceptionalism (and humanism) that engendered the postmodern "hyperreal"—by replacing the "poetry of the map" with a "precession of simulacra"—also produced the zoögeopathology now afflicting us? (Baudrillard 2, 2, 1) This case of disastrously mistaken identity, by which we replace the challenging realities of the natural world with spectacular, digitally enhanced, and color-saturated worlds of our own making, is what the theater of species—among many other efforts—seeks to correct, by creating spaces from within which to re-recognize and rebuild our species life. In these spaces—the gallery of the *nanoq* installation is one—the binary of territory and unconscious is breaking down, being replaced by an uncanny space of shared animality.

Marina Zurkow's animated video installation piece *The Poster Children* (2007) brings the polar bears of global warming together with another figure of the contemporary pop-cultural imagination: the endangered children of post-Columbine America. Simply rendered figures representing the two groups inhabit the landscape, which consists of a watery expanse broken only by fragmenting ice floes and small islands of electronic waste. Posed disconsolately on their precarious stages, the animals and the children perform a listless and paradoxical drama of destructive survival: the animals ravenously tearing into bloodied flesh, the children compulsively firing guns (fig. 8.5). A more vivid or more poignant picturing of Al Gore's phrase—"nowhere left to go"—could hardly be imagined, and the fact that the predicament now applies not only to animals but also to the most vulnerable members of our own species makes for an instant and uncanny recognition that this is a crisis like no other.

These poster-animals and poster-children of possibly lost causes are pictured off-duty in this "anti-Eden," as the artist calls it, "allowed a break from their ideological duties as mercenary images-for-hire" (Zurkow 2008). Temporarily rescued from their jobs as environmental and cultural warning signs in the teeming mediasphere, the children and the animals display the characteristics of victims of trauma, their blank expressions and endlessly repeated actions pointing back to some experience that has interrupted normal growth, affect, and activities. To return to (and revise) Baudrillard's formulation: the territory they inhabit is saturated with the destructive unconscious impulses of our culture.

The disturbing repetitive behavior of Zurkow's characters links them to the characters in the second work I want to discuss here, a performance entitled *Polar Bear God*, by Deke Weaver, which also

Figure 8.5 Marina Zurkow, 2007, still image from animation work *The Poster Children*.

Courtesy of the artist.

engages questions of animals, humans, and place. Weaver's account of zoögeopathology involves one member of each of the groups in Zurkow's piece: one specific child and one specific polar bear. This polar bear, too, like those imagined by Al Gore and those clinging to ice floes in Zurkow's piece, has "nowhere else to go." While Zurkow's piece literalizes the idea of extreme verges and enforced endgames through its attenuated ice-shelves and pointless repetition, Weaver's piece literalizes it by focusing on an actual animal. The bear in this piece is Gus, the most popular "attraction" in New York's Central Park Zoo. A large part of the piece consists of an imaginative reconstruction of what it might feel like to be trapped as Gus is, with literally nowhere else to go.

Polar Bear God suggests some ways that performance can contribute to the goal of reversing the currently impoverished and exploitive relationship between humans and other animals. The pared-down style of the piece highlights the potential for performance to offer a kind of somatic knowledge, a way of understanding the Other by going beyond rationalizations and abstractions to embodiment and physicalization. The shift from one kind of knowledge to another is precisely marked in Weaver's performance: it happens at a specific moment during the section on the Central Park polar bear. Weaver tells us of being "fascinated" by the issue of cage size. He decided, he says, to do "some math," and talks us through a set of numbers. Then, after all his calculations and comparisons, the performer pulls out a square of fabric. It is, he says, the size his cage would be if it observed the same ratio of individual to natural range as the one that obtains in Gus's tank in the zoo. He holds up the square for us to see, then lays it down on the ground. And then he steps onto it (fig. 8.6).

Speaking from the cage he has painstakingly measured out for himself, the performer enters the life-experience of his subject. His language begins to take on the harrowing, repetitive rhythms of the caged bear, moving blindly between the two walls of his tormented existence: "Rock wall. Glass wall. Rock wall. Glass wall. Rock wall. Glass wall. Rock wall. Glass wall." When he speaks of the bear knowing his tank "exhaustively," with a knowledge that's "embedded in his bones, rooted deep in his muscles," he is speaking of a kind of knowledge that performance allows one to share. It is an embodied knowledge, and it allows the final move into the bear's subjective experience: "I feel like I can hear him moaning to himself, mmmm, mmmmm, mmmm."

Figure 8.6 Still image from Deke Weaver's performance of *Polar Bear God*, videographer Daniel Goscha.

Gus's behavior has a scientific name: such involuntary repetitive movements or sounds are called "stereotypies." Stereotypies characterize what some animal experts call "zoo psychosis"; they are symptoms of the trauma of being kidnapped, displaced, incarcerated, alienated, bored to death. Stereotypies are also characteristic behavior of people suffering from autism, and the second character in Weaver's piece is a victim of the frightening epidemic of that condition that is sweeping America. Gus swims back and forth, from rock wall to glass wall, hour after hour, day after day. Ellen's baby boy rocks back and forth, moaning to himself, hour after hour, day after day.

To link the two pathologies of zoo psychosis and autism is not to slight or trivialize the heartbreaking human experience of the victims of the condition. Nor is it to anthropomorphize or sentimentalize the animals' essentially unknowable suffering. Rather, it is to own up to the truth of our shared animality and our shared contingency in the anti-Edens we have been bringing into being. In giving both Gus and Ellen's baby boy the same voice, the same script, in imagining the wronged animal expressing itself with the moans of the afflicted child, the performer gathers their respective suffering into the attenuated space of his own bodily existence, and tests its capacity for embodied empathy.

The performative significance of Weaver's moaning characters emerges in contrast to a key feature of Zurkow's piece. As disturbing as Zurkow's figures are in themselves, what makes them deeply disquieting is that they unfold in complete silence. The video installation has no soundtrack. We hear no shots as the children pull the triggers, no splash as the bullets hit the water, no grunting as the bears tear into the flesh, no buzzing as the flies swarm around the floating piles of electronic waste. The seamless sound-image system of traditional animation—in which the soundtrack turns visual information into meaning and affect—is so entrenched in our experience of this genre that when it is suspended, as it is in *The Poster Children*, the absence feels like an ominous breakdown, a preamble to a more pervasive and irreversible collapse.

The absence of a soundtrack is particularly unsettling in the context of a story of animals and children, two groups whose natural distance from norms of rationalism and discourse has made them favorite targets of an investigative and rationalist humanism seeking to justify and impose its account of reality above all others. Baudrillard's analysis of this ideology recognizes the central role it assigns to language. To install itself at the normative center of reality, says Baudrillard, modernity must render all its Others— including children and animals—discursive. It must make them give up the silence that so threatens us with its intimations of autonomy, of distance and mystery. Everyone and everything must be conscripted into what Baudrillard calls the "empire of meaning":

> The mad, once mute, today are heard by everyone; one has found the grid on which to collect their once absurd and indecipherable messages. Children speak, to the adult universe they are no longer those simultaneously strange and insignificant beings—children signify, they have become significant—not through some sort of "liberation" of their speech, but because adult reason has given itself the most subtle means to avert the threat of their silence. [...] One had buried them under silence, one buries them beneath speech.
>
> (135–6)

The silence of the animals, however, seems to be able to survive all the many ways humanity has tried to render them discursive. This, Baudrillard seems to say, is their continuing gift to us. His formulation of this idea is particularly challenging:

It is not the ecological problem of their survival that is important, but still and always that of their silence. In a world bent on doing nothing but making one speak, in a world assembled under the hegemony of signs and discourse, their silence weighs more and more heavily on our organization of meaning.

(137)

From this perspective, the silence of *The Poster Children* reads not as deficit but as resistance, even as programmatic withdrawal from an "empire of meaning" that has so betrayed both humans and animals. By contrast, Deke Weaver's moaning wants to give voice to zoögeopathology without incurring the liabilities of language: while Zurkow's anti-Eden asks us to contemplate the possibility that our current predicament is an endgame, a last gasp before all bullets are spent and all places gone, Weaver makes voice and body the building blocks for a new creation. The last moments of the piece present a surprising theogony: the speaker's imagination gives birth to a ragtag collection of superspecialized deities, sitting in a waiting room somewhere, awaiting we know not what:

There's the floor mat god. Who's sitting next to the peeling paint god and the sheets that haven't been changed for three months and aren't you just the filthiest person I've ever met god. And sitting over there's the worn out left heel of the old dirty boots god and the broken zipper of your almost tossed out jeans god and the left leaf on the nearly bare maple tree god and the second turd out of the asshole of a 13 year old half dachshund, half German shepherd with arthritic hips and bad eyes god and the hairball god of all cats on 11th street and the god of the dish rack at the Odeon, downstairs on the left edge of the bar and the god of 64th notes and the god of breathing for asthmatics and the god of soaring for hawks and the god of those little bells made of seeds for parakeets and ... right over there is the god of ugly lawn mowing accidents.
All of these gods are sitting there. And hundreds of thousands more. They are calm. They are patient. They are waiting.

Like Zurkow's poster animals and children, like Weaver's own Gus and autistic child, these hyperspecialized and delimited gods may be waiting at some last resort, with *nowhere else to go*. Nevertheless, the re-sacralitization they represent is also an act of reclamation, a few shaky steps into a new space of shared animality and shared contingency.

That space—the theater of species—reorders the anthropocentric hierarchies of the past and challenges us to consider a new cast of characters. The human children and non-human animals in Zurkow's and Weaver's works recall and revise the long history—equally sentimental and coercive—by which our species has trained its young to view the other animals as enemies. The widely exploited cuteness of the polar bear cub—most recently celebrated in the story of Knut, the orphan cub in the Berlin zoo—is the other side of the coin of the alleged fierceness of adult bears, the excuse for their indiscriminate slaughter in centuries past (Ellis 46). The history of how animals and children have been silently co-conscripted into "the empire of meaning" is reflected in one of *nanoq*'s most arresting images: that of a bear positioned behind a statue of the boy who was to grow up to be his killer, the First Lord Somerleyton (fig. 8.7).

Figure 8.7 Statue of the first Lord Somerleyton, Sir Savile Crossley, as a boy, in front of one of two polar bear specimens shot by him in 1897, from *nanoq*, Snæbjörnsdóttir/Wilson.

Courtesy of the artists.

The drama that unfolds between and around these silent figures, boy and bear, child and animal, has a very long history, in which art, literature, and representation are deeply implicated. The theater of species begins to restage that drama and give voice to the shared animality on whose recognition the future of so many species depends.

Note

1 "But it is no longer a question of either maps or territories. Something has disappeared: the sovereign difference, between one and the other, that constituted the charm of abstraction. Because it is difference that constitutes the poetry of the map and the charm of the territory, the magic of the concept and the charm of the real. This imaginary of representation […] disappears in the simulation whose operation is nuclear and genetic, no longer at all specular or discursive" (1994: 2).

Works cited

Baker, S. (2006) "What can dead bodies do?" in B. Snæbjörnsdóttir and M. Wilson (eds) *Nanoq: flat out and bluesome: A cultural life of polar bears*. Bristol: Black Dog Publishing, 148-55.

Baudrillard, J. (1994) *Simulacra and Simulation*, trans. S.F. Glaser. Ann Arbor: U of Michigan P.

Chaudhuri, U. (1996) *Staging Place: The Geography of Modern Drama*. Ann Arbor: U of Michigan P.

Desmond, J. (2002) "Displaying Death, Animating Life: Changing Fictions of 'Liveness' from Taxidermy to Animatronics," in N. Rothfels (ed.) *Representing Animals*. Bloomington: Indiana UP, 159–79.

Ellis, R. (2009) *On Thin Ice: The Changing World of the Polar Bear*. New York: Vintage.

"Gore Pays for Photo after Canada Didn't" (2004) *National Post*, May 27, www.nationalpost.com/story.html?id=5961259b-de08-4532-850b-09d4753bed39&k=88988

Haraway, D. (2003) *A Companion Species Manifesto: Dogs, People, and Significant Otherness*. Chicago: Prickly Paradigm Press.

Sheppard, N. (2007) "Australian TV Exposes 'Stranded Polar Bear' Global Warming Hoax." *Newsbusters.org*, April 6.

Snæbjörnsdóttir, B. and Wilson, M. (2006) *Nanoq: flat out and bluesome, a cultural life of polar bears*. Bristol: Black Dog Publishing, 148–55.

Weaver, D. (2008) "Polar Bear God." *Aspect: The Chronicle of Media Art* 12: Vital (in DVD format). Fall.

Zurkow, M. (2007) *The Poster Children*. www.o-matic.com/play/poster

—— (2008) "Artist Statement." Gender on Ice Gallery. *S & F Online*, November 16.

Chapter 9

Queering the Green Man, Reframing the Garden

Marina Zurkow's *Mesocosm* (*Northumberland, UK*) and the Theater of Species

Current attitudes towards climate change are ruefully captured and skewered in the title of an ongoing solo performance series by California-based performance artist Heather Woodbury. Riffing on the title of a long-running, though recently canceled, daytime soap opera, Woodbury's work is called "As the Globe Warms." The title captures the disturbing way that one of the greatest catastrophes our species has ever faced is transmuted into yet another contentious and indecisive aspect of "the new normal," a vaguely unsettling yet instantly normalized account of social and political reality, produced and sustained by the mass media. Acknowledging the looming crisis while also characterizing it as inevitable, this discourse turns climate change into yet another weapon in the arsenals of biopower, the exercise of the state's control over the biological lives of its increasingly disempowered citizens. Like the programmatically endless "war on terror," the idea of an unavoidable drift towards climatic extremes helps to normalize events like state-mandated evacuations, removal of populations, increased monitoring and surveillance of public spaces, and mass medical interventions—all unfolding in the name of "protection" and "caution."

Within the mechanisms of biopower, the contested and mystified idea of climate change plays out not only on human bodies, but also on the vital links between human bodies and their physical environments, and more specifically on their modes of experiencing, thinking, and feeling those environments. To use a term with new traction in recent animal studies, climate change is played out on the human *Umwelt*. A key term in the biosemiotics of Jakob von Uexküll, the *Umwelt* consists of those aspects of an organism's environment that the organism responds or reacts to.[1] It is the organism's *experienced* world, and is located neither within the organism nor outside it, but rather streams between the two in a process of perpetual co-creation and mutual generation. Therefore, as a concept, *Umwelt* resists the operations of biopower that divide organisms from their environments through binaries such as inside/outside, self/other, and subject/object.

The rejection of binaries also makes the *Umwelt* a useful site for the elaboration of a new orientation toward the environment that is unfolding under the banner of "queer ecology." This discourse links queer theory's cultural critique of heteronormativity to recent scientific studies that challenge the ideological fiction of a heteronormative natural order by documenting the vast array of reproductive mechanisms and sexual and gender behaviors found in the natural world.[2] Queer theory's historic interest in unsettling established categories finds a congenial ally in the taxonomic anti-realism of Michel Foucault's account of the production of scientific knowledge, which throws the very idea of stable systems and fixed categories into question. Transposed into the realms of biology and ecology, queer theory's emphasis on "fluidity, uber-inclusivity, indeterminacy, indefinability, unknowability, the preposterous, impossibility, unthinkability, unintelligibility, meaninglessness, and that which is unrepresentable" initiates an ecocritical project that stresses the non-deterministic and non-essentialist implications of Darwinian theory (Giffney and Hird 4). As critic Timothy Morton puts it: "Evolution means that life forms are made of other life forms. Entities are mutually determining: they exist in relation to each other and derive from each other. Nothing exists independently, and nothing comes from nothing" (275). Adapting queer theory's program of "undo[ing] normative entanglements and fashion[ing] alternative imaginaries," queer ecology proposes a post-Romantic view of nature that vigorously deconstructs the nature/culture binary of traditional environmental thought and assumes an interdependency among life-forms, rejecting the view of organisms as bounded, holistic entities (Giffney and Hird 4). Most importantly, it sets a new goal for the ecological imagination different from the synoptic and sentimental one symbolized by the "blue planet" icon of earlier ecological thought: "Instead of insisting on being part of something bigger," Morton writes, "we should be working with intimacy" (278).

Intimacy and *Umwelt* are two key components of an ecological art practice I call "theater of species," which aspires to unsettle some of the assumptions upon which biopower rests. The practice exists at the intersection of several fields: ecocriticism, which studies how environmental realities and discourses are reflected in literature, art, and the media; animal studies, which explores the vast array of cultural animal practices that human beings are involved in; and theater and performance studies. While the latter may seem to be the odd one out, the first two have also, until recently, been disconnected. What has finally put them into the conversation is the looming specter of climate change and the long-overdue recognition that humans are one species among many that are facing unprecedented threats to survival. Climate change transforms familiar sites into landscapes of catastrophe, or at least into landscapes of risk and uncertainty. Those are the landscapes that the theater of species wants to acknowledge, create, examine, and inhabit.

An extraordinary example of such a landscape, Marina Zurkow's animated "landscape portrait" *Mesocosm (Northumberland, UK)*, exemplifies several strategies of the theater of species, the two most important being the *relocation* and *mobilization* of artistic experience. In this work, the former occurs through one of the richest of archetypal sites, the garden. The latter occurs through an engagement with the *frame*, a feature of visual art that recently received a powerful new Deleuzian theorization by Elizabeth Grosz. Its emergence, she writes, "is the condition of all the arts" because "the frame is what establishes territory out of the chaos that is the earth" (11). *Mesocosm* activates its own frame and presents a riposte to a long tradition of alienated and anthropocentric art, thereby participating in the movement of artistic exploration that Grosz characterizes as follows:

> If framing creates the very conditions for the plane of composition and thus of any particular arts, art itself is a project that disjars, distends, and transforms frames. [...] In this sense the history of painting, and of art after painting, can be seen as *the action of leaving the frame*, of moving beyond, of pressing against the frame, the frame exploding through the movement it can no longer contain.
>
> (17)

Though the temporality of *Mesocosm* is relaxed and capacious, its rendition of the human *Umwelt* is founded on a conception of life as volatile, capricious, random, and unpredictable.

Figure 9.1 Marina Zurkow, 2011, still image from software animation work *Mesocosm (Northumberland, UK)*, autumn.

Courtesy of the artist.

Mesocosm is a video animation representing the passage of one year on the moors of Northumberland, UK. One hour of world time elapses in each minute of screen time, so that a complete cycle lasts 146 hours: "Seasons unfold, days pass, moons rise and set, animals come and go," around a centrally located and almost omnipresent human figure. The figures that appear suggest an open, even infinite, set of beings and phenomena, unconstrained by taxonomic limits: there are cows, owls, ravens, squirrels, foxes, men, women, children, humans in animal costumes, butterflies, refugees, caterpillars, swarms of insects, bats, rabbits, dumpsters, trucks, steamrollers, vans, calves, dogs, hares, fairies, dragonflies, inchworms, midges, spiders, hikers, bikes, horses, ponies, sheep, lambs, swallows, clouds, smokestacks, fog, pollen, shadows, garbage, leaves, petals, pollen, snow, rain, sleet, and wind. This is indeed, as the artist says in her notes on the work, "an expanded view of what constitutes 'nature.'" It is also a capacious rendition of *Umwelt*, staging the endless communicative events and interactions that shape the experience of human and other animals.

No cycle is identical to the last, as the appearance and behavior of human and non-human characters, as well as changes in the weather, are determined by a code using a simple probability equation. This built-in indeterminacy is one of several features that align the work with queer ecology, which emphasizes the emergent, non-deterministic nature of evolution. In tandem with the work's long duration (to see a whole year unfold takes almost a week), this indeterminacy implies and encourages a special kind of spectatorship: more casual and peripheral than concentrated, more peripatetic and mobile than fixed. It is a spectatorship that accommodates the rhythms of everyday life, and construes the work as a frame and context for those rhythms as much as a repository of images, events, narrative, and ideas. Experienced as a frame for the spectator's ongoing lifeworld rather than as an alternate reality that is set against, intervenes in, or interrupts that lifeworld, *Mesocosm* functions like the landscape it depicts: a garden, that ancient and universal cultural framing of "nature" as a space for pleasurable visitation and temporary habitation.

The special kind of enjoyment offered by gardens makes them particularly rich sites for ecologically oriented cultural theory, because the recreation they offer involves contemplating the re-creation of the natural world. The garden is the site of a complex—and potentially queer—circuitry that links human creativity to organic growth and, as such, a space and practice that challenges the ideologically influential nature/culture binary. One classic formulation of the debate around this binary (in its "nature vs. art" version) appears in *The Winter's Tale*, where Shakespeare's characters argue about whether horticultural practices like grafting are natural or otherwise. Perdita's characterization of the cross-bred "gillyvors" in her garden as "nature's bastards" is challenged by Polixenes, who argues that:

> nature is made better by no mean
> But nature makes that mean: so, over that art
> Which you say adds to nature, is an art
> That nature makes. You see, sweet maid, we marry
> A gentler scion to the wildest stock,
> And make conceive a bark of baser kind
> By bud of nobler race: this is an art
> Which does mend nature, change it rather, but
> The art itself is nature.
>
> (IV.IV 89–97)

The interplay between art and nature that Polixenes asserts is nowhere better seen than in the garden, which also makes it a site for trying out, testing, or simply indulging—briefly and safely—new, non-normative identities. The central figure in Zurkow's work is,

I suggest, engaged in this experiment, and invites spectators to try out—or try on—an unaccustomed ecological role. Presence is a part of that role, but it is a strangely self-displacing, non-assertive presence, open to having the traditional boundaries of the individualistic self challenged and breached. This is a mobilized, aleatory, and queer presence, performing a new mode of species habitation.

One way to apprehend the key elements—as well as the creative potential and affective challenge—of this new role is to read it as a postmodern or queer version of the Green Man, another archetypal figure for the interdependence of art and nature. A common decorative motif of medieval sculpture, the foliate faces of this human–vegetable hybrid adorn the walls, doors, pillars, and windows of hundreds of churches, cathedrals, and secular buildings dating from the Middle Ages. Branches, leaves, and vines surround the faces of these figures, and often sprout from their mouths, noses, and ears. Figures of

Figure 9.2 Medieval wood carving of the Green Man. Parish church in Ludlow, Shropshire, England.

Photo by Simon Garbutt. CC BY-SA 3.0.

fertility and unbounded—not to mention boundary-breaching—growth, these species-crossing vegetable men were inherited from pre-Christian and pagan traditions of nature-worship.

But they are equally at home in the contemporary, non-deterministic, and anti-essentialist biologies that inspire queer ecology, where boundaries are, as Morton writes, "blurr[ed] and confound[ed] at practically any level: between species, between the living and the nonliving, between organism and environment" (275–76). The human figure at the (de-centered) center of *Mesocosm* is a living, moving Green Man for our age, a queer response to the increasing threat of biopower in the Anthropocene. He is the protagonist of a new theater of species.

Seeing *Mesocosm* as a theater of species begins with noticing a seemingly simple structural feature of the work: the ever-changing scene depicted in the work is bordered on two sides by an expansive black area. This area functions as a frame, but one that can be entered, crossed, and occupied—though not, it seems, inhabited. When animals walk or run into the black space around the narrow band landscape in the middle of the screen—and also when the human figure himself lumbers or strolls into or out of it—that space transforms into something like the wings of a proscenium theater, and momentarily turns the landscape into, as Zurkow writes in her description of the work, "a stage."

Figure 9.3 Marina Zurkow, 2011, still image from *Mesocosm (Northumberland, UK)*, spring.

Courtesy of the artist.

Mesocosm's landscape is haunted by the mode of theatrical representation that has dominated Western theater since Sebastiano Serlio introduced the principles of single-point perspective drawing into scene design in the sixteenth century. The theatrical aesthetic that developed soon after—illusionism—was greeted with great enthusiasm and launched a centuries-long love affair with realism that flourishes to this day.[3] I have argued elsewhere about the realist theater's complicity with anthropocentric and anti-ecological world views,[4] and recently Adam Sweeting and Thomas C. Crochunis have argued that the conventions of naturalist staging—especially its "rigidly dualistic conceptualization of space"—have shaped our experience of wilderness, and drastically limited the range of our imagination about nature and consequently our relationship to it (327). This is exactly the limiting structure that *Mesocosm* addresses through a playful engagement with some of the most powerful and entrenched conventions of theater.

The "gift" of illusionism was actually a costly exchange. With the illusion of depth now available to it, set design could supply astonishing effects of reality, but only—and always—within the confines of the picture frame, the proscenium arch. Pushed outside this frame, banished from the life–art dialectic that is the soul of theatrical process, the theatergoer went from being a participant to being a viewer. This new spatial order recast the spectator as a potential sovereign by suggesting an ideal position from which the perspectival effects are seen to perfection, known as the Duke's seat. Not merely a spatial site, the Duke's seat also modeled a new ideal of individuality, centrality, and authority for the ordinary theatergoer. But the bargain was a Faustian one: the average spectator's chances of actually sitting in the "Duke's seat" were just as bleak as his or her chances of actually "mastering" the social world.

The psychology of perspectival spectatorship is as obfuscating as its ideology. In his 1996 book, *The Experience of Landscape*, Jay Appleton famously related various sub-genres of landscape painting to a set of biological needs and urges derived from animal habitat theory. These genres, Appleton argued, are organized around certain strategic locations—prospect, refuge, and hazard—that are available to the predator or prey animal whose survival depends on successfully negotiating the various features of the land and its other inhabitants. Appleton singles out the picturesque genre as being especially pleasing because it places the viewer in a protected position, viewing the scene from a partially hidden and pleasantly shaded spot, the "refuge." Any framing of a natural scene that confers such a position of safety on the onlooker is an instance of the picturesque, a guarantee that it is "only a picture," and that the viewer is safely removed: "outside the frame, behind the binoculars, the camera, or the eyeball, in the dark refuge of the skull" (Mitchell 16). Proscenium staging is a similar instance of constructing the "picturesque spectator," the threatened or threatening human animal temporarily enjoying a moment of safety.

But as Gordon Rogoff puts it, theater is not safe—or rather, its special power is squandered in producing illusions of distance, separation, and protected privilege.[5] That spatial configuration supports both a theater of isolated individualism as well as an anthropocentric theater, framing the exemplary or heroic human figure and transforming everything non-human into mere scenery. Zurkow's theater-haunted landscape suggests ways to unseat the secure spectator and plunge him into the unpredictable terrain of life understood ecologically. The keys to this revisioning, or queering, of stage space are the position and behavior—and the astonishing art-historical lineage (from performance art, to painting, to video animation)—of the large human figure that dominates the foreground.

The main figure in *Mesocosm* is based on the Australian performance artist, designer, and drag queen Leigh Bowery, who helped to catalyze an extraordinarily interdisciplinary experimental art scene in London and New York in the 1980s. In Charles Atlas's documentary film *The Legend of Leigh Bowery*, a colleague of Bowery's describes him as "the greatest of the great outrageous Australians of the modern world," a man utterly committed to challenging every assumption, breaching every boundary, and destroying every artistic or social convention he could lay his gigantic hands on.

In his lifetime, Bowery's "legend" was keyed to the extraordinary costumes he designed, built, and wore—vast, molded carapaces of bright fabrics smothered in sequins and feathers. But, in a reversal that he himself would have relished, Bowery's posthumous image is likely to be resolutely *unclothed*. This is thanks to the surprising role that Bowery played toward the end of his short life, as muse and model to one of the greatest of modern painters, Lucian Freud. Atlas's documentary provides a delicious account of the moment this transformation occurred, this metamorphosis of a monstrously over-coded cultural icon into a mountain of flesh: Bowery had been invited to sit for Freud because his over-dressed style posed such a challenge to the renowned painter of disturbing, challenging nudes. But, while they were getting ready to start working, and while Freud's back was turned, Bowery took off all his clothes having assumed Freud would be painting him naked.

The central figure of *Mesocosm*, then, is an incarnation of Bowery who has escaped the "too, too solid flesh" of Freud's canvas to inhabit an eternity of jittery animation in a rural landscape. From his earlier life he has brought along another feature even more subversive here than it was in Freud's painting: he turns his back on us. In a recent article entitled "The Seated Figure on Beckett's Stage,"

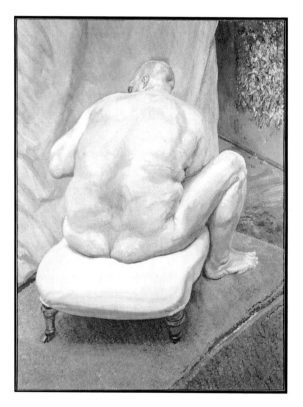

Figure 9.4 Lucian Freud, *Naked Man, Back View*, 1991–1992. Oil on canvas, 183.5 x 137.5 cm.

Image copyright © The Metropolitan Museum of Art. Image source: Art Resource, NY.

Enoch Brater shows how the absurdist master completes and deconstructs a historical process in which the seated figure on stage went from being an emblem of authority in the public sphere of Renaissance drama to a symbol of inwardness in the private worlds of nineteenth-century psychological realism.[6] The posterior view of the figure in *Mesocosm* initiates what I read as his challenging dialectic with anthropocentric stage presence, and thus as one strategy—though admittedly borrowed from painting—for the theater of species he anchors. The strategy involves a kind of insistent embodiment: foregrounding biological presence, "backgrounding" psychological being.

However, the two things that most surprise us about Zurkow's Bowery are also those that distinguish him from Freud's: First, as already mentioned, he gets up and walks out of the frame. Second, he allows various small creatures not only to climb on him and sit on him but also to feed on him, producing the only specks of color—blood red—in the work.

This scandalous symbiosis, based on a novel intimacy, suggests a queered updating of the ancient motif of the Green Man in the context of an anti-essentialist, relational ecology. The queer Green Man of *Mesocosm* contributes a personal and artistic history that is

Figure 9.5 Marina Zurkow, 2011, still image from *Mesocosm (Northumberland, UK)*, spring.

Courtesy of the artist.

Figure 9.6 Marina Zurkow, 2011, still image from *Mesocosm (Northumberland, UK)*, summer.

Courtesy of the artist.

deeply relevant to his role in this "expanded apprehension of what constitutes nature," a history that makes him the ideal protagonist for a post-anthropocentric, post-picturesque theater of species. His travels between genders and genres have prepared him for the more challenging transit ahead, the journey between species.

The confidence with which Zurkow's Bowery occupies this rural landscape represents the defeat of a long and contradictory cultural construction of the relationship between homosexuality and nature. As Andil Gosine writes in a recent article,

> Homosexual sex has also been represented in dominant renderings of ecology and environmentalism as incompatible with and threatening to nature. [The construction of this prejudice is related to the fact that] [i]n its early incarnations, streams of North American environmentalism were conceived as a response to industrial urbanization. As homosexuality was associated with the degeneracy of the city, "the creation of remote recreational wild space and the demarcation of 'healthy' green spaces inside cities was understood partly as a therapeutic antidote to the social ravages of effeminate homosexuality"[7].

(154–55)

Ironically, these very spaces began to be used by gay men looking for sex. When the gay practice of "cruising" forged an uncomfortable connection between homosexuality and public parks, it incited a new punitive discourse that sought to re-exclude homosexuals from nature, this time by equating their presence there with pollution, contamination, and danger to the community and its "family values."[8]

Seated center-stage yet unconcerned with the anthropocentric voyeurism, self-consciousness, and self-display of traditional stage presence, the Green Man of *Mesocosm* dwells in a theater of species—all species—and nonchalantly performs a scandalous form of species companionship and ecological intimacy. The transgressive ethos and outrageous aesthetics of Leigh Bowery's performance art and the extravagant physicality of Lucian Freud's figures come together to queer the fragile landscape of the Anthropocene.

Notes

1 See Uexküll 2001.
2 See Bagemihl 2000, and Roughgarden 2009.
3 Notwithstanding the fact that Brechtian and other avant-gardes spent the last century exposing its complicity with essentially conservative (though ostensibly progressive) humanist ideologies and individualist psychologies.
4 Chaudhuri 2002.
5 Rogoff 1987.
6 Brater 2011.
7 The source quoted by Gosine in this citation is Catriona Mortimer-Sandilands's article "Unnatural Passions? Notes Toward a Queer Ecology," in *Invisible Culture: An Electronic Journal for Visual Culture* 9, page 10.
8 Gosine cites the large number of reports of arrests of gay men in parks that explicitly mentioned the "trash" found at the sites of arrest—specifically condoms, condom wrappers, and tissues.

Works cited

Appleton, J. (1996) *The Experience of Landscape*. London and New York: Wiley Print.

Atlas, C. (dir.) (2002) *The Legend of Leigh Bowery*, documentary film.

Bagemihl, B. (2000) *Biological Exuberance: Animal Homosexuality and Natural Diversity*. New York: Stonewall Inn Editions.

Brater, E. (2011) *Ten Ways of Thinking About Samuel Beckett: The Falsetto of Reason*. London: Methuen Drama.

Chaudhuri, U. (2002) "Land/Scape/Theory," in *Land/Scape/Theater*, eds. E. Fuchs and U. Chaudhuri. Ann Arbor: U of Michigan P.

Foucault, M. (1994) *The Order of Things: An Archaeology of the Human Sciences*. New York: Vintage Books.

Giffney, N. and Hird, M. (eds) (2008) *Queering the Non/Human*. Aldershot: Ashgate.

Gosine, A. (2010) "Non-White Reproduction and Same-Sex Eroticism: Queer Acts Against Nature," in C. Mortimer-Sandilands and B. Erickson (eds) *Queer Ecologies: Sex, Nature, Politics, Desire*. Bloomington: Indiana UP, 149–72.

Grosz, E.A. (2008) *Chaos, Territory, Art: Deleuze and the Framing of the Earth*. New York: Columbia UP.

Mitchell, W.J.T. (2002) *Landscape and Power*. Chicago: U of Chicago P.

Morton, T. (2010) "Guest Column: Queer Ecology." *PMLA* 125 no. 2 (March): 273–82.

Rogoff, G. (1987) *Theatre is Not Safe: Theatre Criticism, 1962–1986*. Evanston, IL: Northwestern UP.

Roughgarden, J. (2009) *Evolution's Rainbow: Diversity, Gender, and Sexuality in Nature and People*, 2nd edn. Berkeley: U of California P.

Shakespeare, W. (1997) *The Winter's Tale*, in *The Norton Shakespeare*, ed. S. Greenblatt. New York and London: W.W. Norton.

Sweeting, A. and Crochunis, T.C. (2001) "Performing the Wild: Rethinking Wilderness and Theatre Spaces," in K. Armbruster and K.R. Wallace (eds.) *Beyond Nature Writing: Expanding the Boundaries of Ecocriticism*. Charlottesville: UP of Virginia, 325–40.

Uexküll, J. von (2001) "An Introduction to Umwelt." *Semiotica* 134: 107–10.

Zurkow, M. (2011) *Mesocosm (Northumberland, UK)*, www.o-matic.com/play/friend/mesocosmUK/indexPlay.html

Chapter 10

War Horses and Dead Tigers
Embattled Animals in a Theater of Species

The theater season in the fall of 2011 was an interesting time in New York for someone who (like me) works on both theater and animal studies. Just about everyone I knew or met asked me if I'd seen *War Horse*, and if I'd loved it as much as they had. In time I learned to couch my answer in terms that would make it less disappointing to my interlocutor, by saying that, actually, the animal play that I'd been really impressed by was *Bengal Tiger at the Baghdad Zoo*. This 2010 Pulitzer Prize Finalist by the American playwright Rajiv Joseph reached nowhere near the huge audience numbers as the London-bred *War Horse*, nor did it garner anything like the English play's accolades (*War Horse* won the Tony Award for Best New Play, among numerous other prizes). Nevertheless, most people I talked to had at least heard of it, if only because the Broadway production starred Robin Williams in the title role.

Sadly, this casting choice (no doubt partly box-office-driven) seriously derailed the disturbing logic of the play and undermined the very thing that makes the play so interesting from an animal studies point of view: namely, its use of an animal figure to explore something as troubling as George Bush's "pre-emptive," "regime-change war" in Iraq, and the strange, unwanted alliances that it forced into existence. As written and imagined, the Tiger in Joseph's play is a surprising, searching and healthily skeptical creature, a fitting lens through which to reevaluate the logics that transport individuals (of various species) into alien landscapes and cultures where they are doomed to be misunderstood, to suffer and to destroy. As played by Robin Williams, however, with his trademark teddy-bearish likability in full force, the Tiger turned into an avuncular fount of inexplicable insights, instead of—as he is written—a being fully immersed in, and expressing, the questions that arise from the radical displacements and dismemberments that characterize globalized warfare.

The Iraq war, it is now widely acknowledged, was the occasion—or, better, the induction—of a new logic of unending violence, loss, and pain that would inevitably ensue from the so-called "war on terror." The play's rendition—and analysis—of this new political condition arises from its deployment of a genuinely original "animal perspective": an orientation towards animals, including human animals, that manages to escape the sentimental and anthropocentric traditions that have stunted human–animal relations for so long, and to replace it with a genuine curiosity about how the other animals experience the world that we humans are increasingly shaping and defining for them. This animal perspective, increasingly common in visual arts and even literature, remains rare in the theater, where long traditions of animal symbolism—an especially complex and seductive form of disavowal—have tended to smother animal realities under thick layers of metaphor and sentiment.

As theater joins the other arts in "taking animals seriously," works like Joseph's play will surely reconfigure the ideological and affective force of the animal figure on stage (DeGrazia 1996). But the growing cultural awareness of and interest in animals will affect more traditional uses of the animal figure as well, and *War Horse* is a case in point. Although *War Horse* and *Bengal Tiger at the Baghdad Zoo* would seem to occupy opposite poles of a continuum that ranges from old-fashioned sentimentality to postmodern inscrutability, the works nevertheless share, each in its own way, in the cultural "animal uptake" that the field of animal studies participates in and comments on. The staging of the works—the live events they generate and the experiences they offer audiences—produces types of interspecies awareness that show how complex and layered—and therefore how promising—is the genre I want to imagine here, which I call the "Theater of Species."

Before describing this shared potential and defining this new genre, it is worth noting how much difference it is capable of bridging. At the level of plot, the two works could not be more different, the one a classic "boy meets horse, loses horse, finds horse" tale of interspecies loyalty in the context of vast inequalities and suffering, the other a credulity-straining tale of interspecies misunderstanding in the context of geopolitical insanity. *War Horse* is set during the First World War, and the play tells the story of the friendship between a horse, Joey, and a Devonshire farming lad,

Albert. When Albert's father, a cruel drunk, sells Joey to the cavalry, Albert lies about his age in order to enlist and follow his equine friend into war. The bulk of the play details the suffering of men and horses in newly technologized warfare (the valiant war horses are no match for the Kaiser's tanks, and their bodies suffer as much as human ones from that "ingenious and then new technology of pain, barbed wire"), reaching a climax when Joey escapes from his German captors and gets trapped in barbed wire between enemy lines, while Albert gets blinded by tear gas. Finally, after a few more twists of fate and near misses, the two friends find each other and get to return home to Devon, damaged but not broken by war. *War Horse* is, then, a bittersweet melodrama, a work that balances animal suffering with animal love, painting a familiar and unchallenging picture of humans, animals, and war.

Bengal Tiger at the Baghdad Zoo is a work of surrealistic history, its point of departure being a bizarre actual incident from that bizarre war: the fatal shooting of a tiger in the Baghdad zoo by American soldiers who were guarding the zoo. The tiger, it was reported, was shot when it bit off the hand of one of the soldiers, who was apparently teasing him. In the play, this tiger's death is anything but conclusive: he finds himself not only still in the world, but suddenly able to understand English and to think deep philosophical thoughts. Meanwhile, the soldier who shot him (Kev) and the soldier whose hand he bit off (Tom) find themselves negotiating strange aftermaths as well, while an Iraqi translator they work with (Musa) finds himself pulled, agonizingly, into the past against his will. The Tiger is not the only ghost in the play: Kev becomes a ghost after he tries to cut his own hand off, and two girls—one burned in a bomb strike, the other brutally assaulted by two men—also haunt the play. The assaulted one is Hadia, Musa's sister, and the two men who assaulted her are none other than Uday and Qusay Hussein—the sons of Saddam. In a feat of dramatic imagination that may be even more audacious than having the ghost of a Tiger as a protagonist, Joseph has these two characters appear as well, and play significant roles. They too haunt the play, Uday carrying around—and occasionally talking to—the severed head of Qusay. As if this were all not strange enough, the plot is thickened by successive thefts of certain outrageous items—a golden gun and a golden toilet seat—that had belonged to Uday and been stolen first by Tom, then Kev, then Musa. These objects, along with (as I will discuss below) one extremely peculiar landscape conjured by the play, are theatrically activated in relation to the Tiger, to the kinds of questions he asks, and to the kind of *space* his presence creates. It is the space of and for what I would want to call a Theater of Species, produced by engaging deeply with animal alterity.

Animal alterity, the radical *otherness* of the other animals, is a foundational insight of animal studies, and one that live theater is—I believe—especially well equipped to engage with. The constitutive alterities of theatrical representation—its ways of making meaning from the similarities and differences between actors and characters, stage and auditorium, spectacle and spectators—can be used to expose the kinds of distinctions that underlie various human understandings of the other animals. Those understandings range from the taxonomic ambitions of a Linnaeus to the scandalous homogenizations descried by posthumanism: "The animal," says Derrida, "What a word!," locating, in the unquestioned singularity of this word, the origins of logocentric humanism (23):

> animal is a word [...] that men have [...] given themselves the right [...] to give ... in order to corral a large number of living beings within a single concept ... at the same time according themselves, reserving for them, for humans, the right to the word, the name, the verb, the attribute, to a language of words, in short to the very things that the others in question would be deprived of, those that are corralled within the grand territory of the beasts: the Animal.
>
> (32)

A Theater of Species would seek to turn that corral of linguistically produced sameness into a space of embodied and productive difference, a means of encountering and considering *the particularities* of the bodies, territories, and limitations of specific animals, both human and non-human.

The questions that this theater of species might address are the following. To what extent have the conflicts that characterize human history been enabled by an anthropocentric value system, a way of seeing the world that obscures continuities between and within groups (and species) and instead emphasizes differences? If we are so easily able to bracket out the interests of the billions of other species with whom we share this planet, how could we not do the same to groups of our own species that we have similarly "othered" (often, indeed, by calling them "animals")? And, on the more positive, creative side of its inquiry, the theater of species might ask: what does the world look like, and how do people talk, feel, and think, when the many hierarchies that are founded on the primary human-over-animal one are no longer in effect, and when the interests of all species begin to matter to us? What is a geography of animal alterity? Of species difference?

The territories—places, nations, landscapes, habitats, enclosures—evoked in Joseph's play are all painfully subject to a key condition of the globalized present: *displacement*—the dislocation of entities from their places of origin and their sources of identity. The very title of the play indexes this feature of contemporary experience: the tiger's displacement from Bengal to Baghdad affects his identity—he jokes that he's now "Tiger of the Tigris"—and it also renders him, like many other characters in the play, radically, permanently, transient: "When you're this far from home," he says, "you know you're never getting back" (Joseph 150). The first place we encounter the Tiger is, of course, the zoo, an institution dedicated to displacement: the place for animals who have been removed from their own places.

Unsurprisingly, zoo histories and zoo cultures have received significant attention in animal studies, detailing the complex (and usually self-servingly anthropocentric) stories these institutions tell. The Baghdad Zoo itself became the subject of such a story, more narrowly nationalistic than anthropocentric. The zoo received huge media attention in the months following the American invasion of Iraq in 2003, even apart from the death of the tiger that gives Joseph his dramatic impetus. As Kathryn Denning shows in an article analyzing news coverage of the war, the Baghdad Zoo quickly became a favorite and complex metaphor for journalists and others, used to represent the invaded nation itself and to justify the invasion as a necessary "liberation." The poor conditions at the zoo were frequently treated as metonymic of Iraq's marginalized place in the international community, as evidence of backwardness and the necessity of external intervention, as well as a locus of liberation and symbol of recovery. For example, an article in the *Mirror* said of the zoo animals that, "unlike the people of Iraq, these prisoners of Saddam's cruel regime are still awaiting liberation" (qt. in Denning 64).

The fact that the zoo was in such terrible shape largely because it had been bombed by Coalition forces during the battle for Baghdad and then pillaged for food by hungry city dwellers was never mentioned in the media, buried under expressions of concern for the animals, reports of restoration, and implicit support for the idea that a zoo is a necessary feature of a great city. At the same time, the idea of the zoo was used in the opposite way, as the ultimate expression of contempt and conquest. An Iraqi was widely reported as saying of members of Hussein's regime: "Don't kill them. Put them in cages in a zoo. And then we can use the admissions fees to rebuild Iraq" (qt. in Denning 65). As often happens with animal metaphors, the zoo stood for diametrically opposed ideas: brutal degradation as well as compassionate civilization.

The media coverage of the zoo focused on what is called, in completely un-ironic zoo parlance, its "charismatic megafauna," such as the big cats. Besides the tiger, the other zoo animals who also gained fame and lost their lives in Iraq at that time were a group of lions who escaped from the zoo when it was bombed, roamed the city for several hours, and were finally gunned down by American soldiers. The lions later became the subject of a stunning graphic novel, *Pride of Baghdad* by Brian K. Vaughan and Niko Henrichon, which represents the war as an eco-apocalypse. Here, as Teresa Mangum and Corey Creekmur find in their analysis of the work, "the entire world is revealed to be a mere extension of a zoo or the military research facility" (Mangum and Creekmur 407). Like Joseph's play (and as I will elucidate further in my conclusion), this graphic novel travels deep into the space of animal alterity—a critical and productive space in which it is possible to celebrate the fact of kinship across species while also honoring the radical otherness of the other animals.

By contrast, the media coverage of the zoo was busy manufacturing cultural and national otherness. Contrasting the coverage of big cats in Iraq with that of big cats in the United States (there are more tigers in captivity in the U.S. than there are wild tigers in all of India, and thousands of cases of attacks, escapes, and abuse occur in the States each year), Denning finds that "the plight of tigers in America is portrayed as a consequence of the failure of the legal system, and of individual ethics, rather than a failure of the society itself, which was the clear insinuation regarding the big cats in Iraq" (68). Similarly, within the U.S., the luckier tigers are portrayed as being rescued from mismanagement, not liberated from oppression.

The big cats of Iraq were part of a perfect media storm that combined American exceptionalism and racism with the profound ambivalence human beings harbor toward wild animals. If the institution of the zoo is, as John Berger famously said, a monument to the disappearance of the animal from the modern world, the zoo in war-torn Baghdad became, perhaps, a way for the media to reframe its role in furthering one of the most deceitful and obfuscating rationales for invading a foreign country (26). Perhaps it also helped the American public feel a bit better about the whole adventure. The neat substitution of mistreated animals for missing WMDs is reflected in the title of one of several books about the zoo: *Babylon's Ark: The Incredible Wartime Rescue of the Baghdad Zoo* (Anthony and Spence).

The Baghdad Zoo in Joseph's play is emphatically not a setting for either sentimental musing or military swaggering. Instead of troping the animal the way the media did, the play deploys it surprisingly and anti-symbolically to open a new space for rethinking this and other wars in the context of ecology, environment, and species. Our first encounter with the Tiger highlights the principle of species *difference,* a skillful and (as imagined and written) extremely amusing preparation for the logic that will gradually turn the play in the direction of what I'm calling a Theater of Species. The Tiger's first speeches concern the lions who, he tells us, escaped from the same zoo two days ago, when a bomb blew their cage door open. The Tiger is full of disdain for these *"fucking Leos"* who, he reports, lasted only two hours on the outside (214):

> Leo, the head lion—I mean they were all named fucking Leo— Leo calls out to me just before he takes off: "Hey, Tiger! You gotta come with!" [...] *I gotta come with!* I'm still freaking locked up in here, Leo. What're you gonna do, steal the keys and *let me out*? These lions were dumb as rocks!
>
> (148–9)

This humorous rendition of species difference is interspersed, in the play's first scene, with an absurd—even grotesque—performance of cultural incoherence. While the Tiger muses on the stupidity of the lions, Tom and Kev discuss their own mystifying displacements and the fantasies that these engender, which range from "getting Iraqi pussy" to getting fabulously wealthy by selling the "*gold* toilet seat" they've stolen from Saddam Hussein's sons' mansion (153, 152 original emphasis). Just as the Tiger's journey from Bengal to Baghdad turns out to be only the first leg of a performance trajectory that goes on to transgress many boundaries—life and death, war and peace, human and animal, nature and culture, instinct and philosophy—so also the other characters in the play get caught up in events that intertwine the geopolitical with the biological. Tom's lost hand is replaced by a state-of-the-art prosthetic "Robocop" hand, which has one unfortunate effect (177):

> I've been whacking off since I was eleven. Always with the right hand. Probably twice a day since I was eleven, always with the right hand. That's a lot of whacking off. [...] It's not the same with the left hand. I broke in my right hand after all those years of yanking it every day. It had the right shape. It was familiar to me.
>
> (202)

Before the prostitute he's hired will do what he wants ("I want her to stand behind me and whack me off with her right hand") she asks to see his hand, smells it ("like milk," she says, which annoys Tom), and wants to know how he lost it (204, 208). The foregrounding of the physical lives of these characters, the recognition of the insistently, inescapably *embodied* nature of their experience frames a question that applies to all the characters, though it is the Tiger who confronts it most directly: what is the nature of my species, and how do the instincts and behaviors that arise from that nature relate to the world I find myself in? Recalling the moment when hunger led him to let down his guard and attack a pair of human children back in his home jungle, a moment of carelessness that led to his capture and transport to the Baghdad Zoo, the Tiger tries to suppress his carnivorous nature and become a vegetarian. The experiment lasts little more than a few hours before his species nature reasserts itself, leading him to wonder, "What if my every meal has been an act of cruelty? What if my very nature is in direct conflict with the moral code of the universe?" (187) In spite of his efforts to think otherwise—"It wasn't cruelty! It was lunch!"—the Tiger's philosophical awakening leads him, as it has so many, to reframe his question in religious terms, and to begin to wonder how his own species nature relates to the nature of whatever God may be in charge: "What kind of twisted bastard creates a predator and then punishes him for preying?" (187)

One striking response that the play offers to these questions takes the form of a strange landscape: a topiary garden (fig. 10.1), an extreme figure for breached boundaries and category confusion, and thus an apt setting for a Theater of Species. Musa, the Iraqi character who has been functioning as a military interpreter for much of the play, turns out to have been, in his pre-war life, the keeper of this garden. "I'm not a translator," he insists: "I am a gardener! [...] I am an artist!" (220) As a space where art is aligned with tending nature, a space for the dialogue of nature and culture, the topiary garden is the play's alternative site for interspecies accounting, a more honest memorial to our sadly compromised relationship to the non-human world than the zoo ever was. "First," says the Tiger, "they throw all the animals in a zoo, and then they carve up the bushes to make it look like we never left" (175). The condition of this garden—blackened and broken—bespeaks a state of crisis, or abject failure, of the nature–culture dialogue. The animals in the play's topiary are terribly damaged, their ruined forms mirroring the play's shockingly fragmented characters: Qusay Hussein is only a decapitated head, while others have lost their hands—to a tiger, or to a desperate suicide attempt, or to leprosy. These broken bodies, embodied as they must be on stage, perform and foreground the fragile species life that links humans with other animals. The topiary garden, we learn, was the site of the assault on Musa's little sister, and—as Uday recalls with brutal relish—that assault involved garden shears. The image he uses to describe what happened— "she burst like a ripe fruit"—horrifyingly furthers the category confusions that prevail in the world of the play, and whose sources and meanings the Tiger tries so hard to decipher.

Figure 10.1 Kevin Tighe in *Bengal Tiger at the Baghdad Zoo.* Center Theater Group, 2009.

Photo by Craig Schwartz.

As the play nears its conclusion, much of its hermeneutic and dramatic energy gets focused on the topiary garden. Various characters make different claims about it. The Tiger insists that it is "God's Garden" (reasoning that, "He likes gardens. He tests us in them, He tempts us in them. [...] It's like his fucking hobby") and that it holds a theological key to his salvation: "If this is God's garden, then maybe I need to become like these plants ... twisting and distorting my natural shape into something more pleasing to Him" (187, 214). His ghostly interlocutor, Kev (who has become "a straightup brainiac" in the afterlife, and an Arabic speaker to boot), uses his newfound rationality to speculate in another direction: "There's got to be some sort of relational algebraic equation that the three of us can factor into and solve our problem. Algebra was even invented here, you know? [...] the Arabic word *al jebr* means 'reunion of broken parts'" (214).

As the stage of Joseph's play fills with the broken parts of human beings and topiary animals, the Tiger's hope for a clarifying, unifying revelation from God becomes increasingly unlikely. When he tries to push Musa into the role of God, because Musa made the topiary animals, and pleads with him to speak, Musa replies: "God has spoken. This world. This is what He's said" (241). The Tiger's initial reaction is rage:

> *This?*
> This isn't enough! [...]
> You know what? You belong in a cage.
> We should hunt you down and lock you up like every other wild thing in the world.
> I can see it: God in a cage, right here. Finally get a look at You.
> All the great mysteries of creation could be revealed at the zoo!
> Come see the God exhibit! Come watch the beast play!
> And we, the lousy dead, innumerable and in constant parade, would finally have our Holy Land ... a cage in a garden in a burning city.
>
> (241–42)

Although the Tiger moves beyond this rage, and the play ends with him assuming a stance of quiet watchfulness, this striking image—a cage in a garden in a burning city—resonates as an indictment of the historical and continuing betrayals, by humans, of other species: the caged animals of zoo history, the destroyed landscapes of a war-torn world. The broken bodies and lives that have animated this theater of species find no algebraic—or reunifying—solution in the histories, traditions, religions, and spaces of the civilization they have inherited.

War Horse faithfully reproduces the past to the same degree that *Bengal Tiger at the Baghdad Zoo* rigorously rejects it. The landscapes and settings of *War Horse* are familiar to the point of being archetypal: the humble Devon cottage where the young hero's farming family lives, the fields in which he trains his beloved horse, Joey, and then the chaotic battlefields of the First World War, where the proud British cavalry is repeatedly devastated by the technologized weaponry—machine guns and barbed wire—of a new kind of warfare. The relationship between the boy and his horse (originally imagined in a 1982 novel for children by Michael Morpurgo, and adapted for the stage by Nick Stafford) is also familiar from movies like *National Velvet* and *Old Yeller*, and the play "speaks, cannily and brazenly," as the *New York Times* critic Ben Brantley puts it, "to that inner part of adults that cherishes childhood memories of a pet as one's first—and possibly greatest—love" (1). The widely shared view that the play is, to quote Brantley again, "steeped in boilerplate sentimentality [... and] keeps pushing buttons like a sales clerk in a notions shop," did not seem to bother its enthusiastic audiences at all (1). Indeed, as Lynda Birke disarmingly writes in a richly descriptive and affecting article on the play in *Humanimalia*, the horses are the heroes of the play, astonishingly realized and undeniably humanized:

> I am not an expert in theater studies, nor a historian of war, but I am passionate about horses, and have lived with them all my life. I too cried my eyes out throughout the production. If experts in stage production can criticize aspects of this dramatization, I simply focused on the characters of the horses. These are brilliantly done, making them believable—so believable that I had to look away and whimper when Albert ends the mare's suffering, and so believable that I too grieved for Topthorn.
>
> (126)

The credit for the extraordinary effect the horses have on audiences of the play goes to the designers Adrian Kohler and Basil Jones of the Cape Town-based Handspring Puppet Company, whose life-size puppets, each operated by several expert puppeteers, are the show's beloved scene-stealers. Gigantic forms made of clay, fabric and plywood, these figures single-handedly lift this production—in a way that the real horses of Spielberg's film, majestic and stirring as they are, could never do—out of a fundamentally anthropocentric sentimentality—the kind that makes us feel good about ourselves because we feel so sad for the animals that others among us exploit. The crocodile tears of that sentimentality are here alright, but here they are overshadowed by the heart-stopping effect of watching these hybrid creatures—stunning conglomerations of bodies and materials, of shapes and movement—bring *life itself* to life.

This is a Theater of Species of a different sort from the unsettling kind found in *Bengal Tiger at the Baghdad Zoo*: more visceral than cerebral, more addressed to the knowingness of the body than aimed at toppling the self-assured ascendancy of rational thought. The obvious care, skill, and patience conveyed by the *form* of the horse puppets as well as by the movements of their handlers tells its own interspecies story—and it is a different story from the familiar one about children and animals, and animals and exploitation. This is a story about how hard it is to know the other animals, and yet how vital, how rewarding, how *literally unspeakable* and therefore how *theatrically necessary* it is to try. The amazing animals of *War Horse* perform a mode of interspecies encounter and knowledge that could make the Theater of Species an essential site in the ongoing revaluation of animals in contemporary culture.

Coda: Species Lives and Globalized War

The Theater of Species that these two plays have helped me to imagine brings animality—ours, and that of the other animals—into view in new ways, staging a species life we have—to our great cost—been blithely ignoring. In closing, I want to discuss two other works—both emerging from the same horrifyingly botched and wasteful war as did Joseph's play—that use other media to pursue a similar goal, and as such will, I hope, situate the Theater of Species in the larger field of contemporary animal art and discourse. The first is the graphic novel I mentioned earlier, based on that other famous Iraqi animal tragedy: the lions who escaped from the zoo during the bombing of Baghdad, roamed the city for several hours, and were finally shot dead by American troops. *Pride of Baghdad*, by Brian K. Vaughan and Niko Henrichon, represents the war as an ecological apocalypse, an anti-Noah's Ark story of an epic betrayal of the human responsibility to the other animals. Using the conventions of the talking animal fable—even directly quoting from a famous example of that genre on the very first page ("The sky is falling! The sky is falling!")—the novel firmly refuses the traditional anthropocentric purposes of that genre and keeps its focus on the realities of animal lives, especially as these are distorted and circumscribed by human institutions (1). The novel's many scenes juxtaposing animal bodies with the machinery of war, or locating animals in blighted cityscapes, cumulatively produces a newly animalized vision of the global city, and begins recasting political agendas in terms of species life.

Human figures appear, for the first time in the novel, on its final pages. They are the American soldiers, seen only from the waist down—from the animals' point of view—as they stand over the dead bodies of the animals they have shot. "Where did they come from?" one terrified soldier asks. "They're not wild here, are they?" To which the other responds: "They're free." The exchange deconstructs a durable cliché, showing that the relationship between being wild and being free—a difference every zoo must obfuscate—is in urgent need of political attention. The American soldiers' presence in Baghdad—as displaced here as the Bengal Tiger was, they don't know what's native fauna here and what's not—indexes an ideology—American exceptionalism—that was as politically disastrous as another longstanding ideology—anthropocentrism—has been for all species, including our own.

Globalization's roots in imperialism link it, in an unbroken chain of connections, to a violent animal history, when the conquest of human populations was signified by the capture and display of exotic animals. The lions in Vaughan and Henrichon's graphic novel stage one end of that history. They do not indicate what forms might come to fill the space when—or if—the rubble of that history can ever be cleared. How a new kind of dialogue might develop as humans' and animals' lives continue to intertwine, locally and globally, is anybody's guess. The apocalyptic imagery and violence of the works I've discussed might even make the idea of future and continued dialogues seem unlikely and futile. But I want to conclude here with one tiny and quite surprising token of a more hopeful view.

One of my favorite animal artifacts of recent times—to call it an artwork would be too grandiose and would bely its modesty of scale and ambition—is a little book called *Birding Babylon*, subtitled "A Soldier's Journal from Iraq," written by Sergeant

Jonathan Trouem-Trend and published in 2006 by Sierra Club
Books. The writer, who was stationed in Iraq in 2004, is a lifelong
birdwatcher, and *Birding Babylon* is based on a blog he wrote, in
which he documented his bird sightings during his tour of duty. In
the Preface to the book, Trouem-Trend says the following:

> When I think of my time in Iraq, my thoughts turn first to the
> good things: to my friends, both Iraqi and American, and my
> time observing wildlife. Though my medical unit saw the terrible
> face of war, I also discovered a country rich in history and
> natural beauty, where I could pursue my lifelong love of nature.
> Iraq is full of people who love the natural world, with whom
> I felt a natural kinship, who would bring me insects or talk to
> me about birds and their names and where they could be found.

The experience conjured up here, along with the careful notations
and illustrations of the wildlife observed, is so radically different
from the norm to which we've been familiarized as to seem almost
bizarre, incoherent, unfathomable. Nor is it a sentimental and racist
exoticization of another culture. The global lives interacting here,
those of an American soldier and Iraqi birds (or rather, birds in
Iraq, since birds don't have nationalities!) are based on simple
appreciation and a respectful kind of curiosity that is, and has long
been, a powerful alternative to anthropocentric and exploitive
cultural animal practices. In its small and quiet way, it locates
animal lives in a shared space of political and ecological precarity.

I realize, of course, how painfully incommensurate this little
artifact seems with the ideological goals—the destabilization, if
not the overthrow of anthropocentrism—that I have claimed for a
Theater of Species. Yet perhaps it is precisely the diminutiveness of
this artifact that makes it resonate in a fresh and surprising way, by
contrast with the apocalyptic fantasies that are ignited by the
conjunction of war and globalization. As Timothy Morton remarks
in his proposal for a new, less grandiose, less synoptic, ecology:
"Instead of insisting on being a part of something bigger, we should
be working with intimacy" (278). The works I have discussed here
variously imagine new interspecies intimacies; they do not,
however, visualize the worlds in which such intimacies might
flourish. As the postscript to *Birding Baghdad* suggests, that is a
task for the future, requiring not only imagination but also hope
and a kind of species faith:

I hope to return to Iraq one day armed only with binoculars and a camera. Perhaps an Iraqi friend and I will drive around searching the deserts, the river valleys, and mountains for the birds I missed. We will talk about how wonderful it is to be free of the fences and to be able to go where the birds are instead of hoping they'll fly into our compound. No matter how long it takes to get to that future, I know the birds will be waiting.

Works cited

Anthony, I. and Spence, G. (2007) *Babylon's Ark: The Incredible Wartime Rescue of the Baghdad Zoo*. New York: St. Martin's Press.

Berger, J. (1980) "Why Look at Animals?" *About Looking*. New York: Pantheon, 1–26.

Birke, L. (2010) "War Horse." *Huminalia: Journal of Human/Animal Interface Studies* 1 no. 2: 122–32.

Brantley, B. (2011) "A Boy and His Steed, Far From Humane Society." *New York Times*, April 15. C1.

DeGrazia, D. (1996) *Taking Animals Seriously: Mental Life and Moral Status*. Cambridge: Cambridge UP.

Denning, K. (2008) "Regarding the Zoo: On the Deployment of a Metaphor." *International Journal of Heritage* 14 no. 1: 60–73. Online.

Derrida, J. (2008) *The Animal That Therefore I Am*, ed. M-L. Mallet, trans. D. Wills. New York: Fordham UP.

Joseph, R. (2010) *Bengal Tiger at the Baghdad Zoo*, in *Three Plays*. Berkeley, CA: Soft Skull Press.

Mangum, T. and Creekmur, C. (2007) "Review: A Graphic Novel Depicting War as an Interspecies Event: Pride of Baghdad." *Society and Animals* 15 no. 4: 401–8.

Morpurgo, M. (2007) *War Horse*. London: Egmont.

Morton, T. (2010) "Guest Column: Queer Ecology." *PMLA* 125 no. 2 (March): 273–82.

Trouem-Trend, J. (2006) *Birding Babylon: A Soldier's Journal from Iraq*. San Francisco, CA: Sierra Club Books.

Vaughan, B.K. and Henrichon, N. (2006) *Pride of Baghdad*. New York: Vertigo/DC Comics.

Chapter 11

Interspecies Diplomacy in Anthropocenic Waters

Performing an Ocean-Oriented Ontology

"The animal, what a word!" Jacques Derrida famously exclaimed, calling out the totalization of animal life by a self-serving and arrogant humanist tradition.[1] Today, the concept of the Anthropocene suggests an inverse scandal, and evokes the equivalent of another exclamation: "the *Anthropos*—what a prefix!"[2] many seem to be saying, objecting to the term's potential elision of national and economic differences, its tendency to shift ecological responsibility away from the West's carbon-based industrial capitalism and onto a totalized and featureless humanity. Yet, undifferentiated though they are, both the Anthropocene and "the animal" are galvanizing concepts for two fields, the environmental humanities and animal studies respectively, whose subjects involve urgent realities that can make certain differences seem less relevant. When terrestrial species are undergoing something called "the Sixth Extinction," and when CO_2 levels are over 400 parts per million, "big picture" constructs like "the animal" and "the Anthropocene" can be valuable not just for political activation, but also for fresh thinking about the species and ecospheres that climate change is plunging into a state of emergency.

The art practice I discuss in this essay responds to this emergency in a way that balances species-specificity with global ecological awareness. Its intense focus on a single species is motivated by a concern for—rather than disinterest in—the fate of all species. And it understands that fate in a way that is best described as "anthropocenic," to mark the vital need, at this rapidly unfolding juncture, for concerted and universal human attention to the environment, no matter what the historical causes of—and specific culprits behind—the current crisis.

The Dolphin Dance Project was initiated in 2009 by New York-based dancer and choreographer Chisa Hidaka and her partner, filmmaker Benjamin Harley. The artists describe the project as bringing together "human dancers and wild dolphins to co-create underwater dances in the open ocean" (*Dolphin Dance Project*). The dances are filmed, most recently in 3D, with the intention of offering viewers the "extraordinary experience of participating in an intimate movement-based conversation with completely wild animals, in whose eyes we recognize shared intelligence, creativity, and rich, meaningful emotional lives." In pursuit of this inspiring goal, the Dolphin Dance Project inevitably encounters many of the ethical and ideological challenges that beset even the most benign and well intentioned of interactions between humans and any of the other animals. Indeed, for some people, the project arouses anxiety and distrust—even outright anger, as was the case with one of my friends, whose immediate comment upon hearing the mere name of the project was: "Leave those dolphins the fuck alone!" This friend is an accomplished artist, a lifelong birdwatcher, highly conversant with the field of animal studies, and deeply committed to safeguarding wild species. I do not dismiss his instinctive reaction; on the contrary, I believe it is based upon the very values that motivate the Dolphin Dance Project itself: urgent concern for increasingly endangered animal species, respect for wild habitats, and unwillingness to excuse or further tolerate the long-standing and deeply exploitive practices of animal exhibition and entertainment.

I interpret the Dolphin Dance Project as a complex corrective and alternative to the whole shameful history of marine exhibition, the history which results in such media sensations—and personal tragedies—as the death of the veteran Sea World trainer Dawn Brancheau, the history whose systemic violence is documented in recent films like *Blackfish* and *The Cove*. The latter shows how tourist practices like the many "Swim with Dolphins" programs that flourish all over the world are implicated in hideous practices like the annual dolphin massacre in Taiji, Japan. Without question, such interspecies violence deserves universal condemnation and legal opposition. Yet it is also important to seriously consider the fact that marine animal displays and interactive programs draw thousands of spectators and participants worldwide. Clearly, they promise a kind of interspecies experience that many people crave, and they afford powerful affective rewards. To disregard this reality and focus exclusively on the harm that results may be to miss an important opportunity to discover new and better answers to the question posed in that fertile early site of animal studies, John Berger's classic essay "Why Look at Animals?"

The consideration of human–animal encounter, interaction, and representation which that essay initiated, especially its bold claim that modernity had replaced actual animals with their effigies, continues to be both highly contested and enormously generative. My friend's vehement reaction to the Dolphin Dance Project, reflecting a growing cultural awareness of the price other species pay for our curiosity, implies a revision of Berger's question along the lines of "Why Not *Stop* Looking at Animals?"—a reflexively ironic idea coming from a birdwatcher. But that irony arises from the fact that Berger's catchy title has distorted his deeper argument, which was not primarily about looking but rather about encountering animals, about *exchanging* looks with the animal, about *being with* the animal. What Berger bemoans about modernity's animal practices is that they substitute looking at for being with, installing a regime of alienated visuality where once there was embodied co-presence.

If the interspecies fascination that fosters animal shows and touristic animal encounters is not just an idle, self-indulgent curiosity but something else, perhaps a deep-rooted and nature-affirming need to be better connected to the earthly realities that our so-called civilization deprives us of, then these practices may be sites for fostering a much needed biophilia, along with the enhanced ecological and interspecies consciousness that the Anthropocene demands. I read the Dolphin Dance Project as a thoughtful, painstaking attempt to navigate the conundrum arising, on the one hand, from a vital need for interspecies encounter and, on the other, from the potential damage that the fulfillment of this need unwittingly inflicts on the non-human species involved. The effort is undertaken in a spirit of remediation and reparation, with deliberate attention to egregious past errors and a desire to revise the values from which they arose. The Dolphin Dance Project's work answers a different revision of Berger's question: "How might we—how should we—be with animals? Especially now, in the Anthropocene, when their lives and habitats are so threatened by the activities of our species?"

The Dolphin Dance Project combines two art forms—dance and film—to provide a rich, though indirect, experience of interspecies encounter. The "actuality deficit" that the project deliberately incurs—the fact that while the dancers enjoy the thrilling *presence* of actual dolphins, their audiences do not—is carefully compensated for by several features of the project, which work to heighten one aspect of the traditional artist-to-audience relationship: that of messenger between worlds. This aspect of the Dolphin Dance Project would seem to affiliate it with such paradigms as the shamanism, or neo-shamanism, that many contemporary artists have become interested in, but the discourse framing the project points in a different direction, toward a possible "interspecies diplomacy."

I am well aware that the concept of diplomacy carries many negative associations and unpalatable connotations. In a recent interview with Bruno Latour, Heather Davis expresses her hesitation about diplomacy as a political modality, saying that it "seems already to presume two, or more, opposing sides. And the diplomat [...] is slippery, not quite trustworthy" (Latour 51). Latour agrees, adding "it is someone who betrays" (51). But then he offers this provocative, and counter-intuitive elaboration: the diplomat, he says, "betrays those who have sent him or her precisely because he or she modifies their values. He or she sees that the official attachment is not one to be ready to die for." By thus refusing to grant preeminence to the values of the group he or she represents, the diplomat "introduces a margin and a space to manoeuver. [...] So, to say that there is a horizon of diplomacy is to say we have to state our agreement or disagreement" (51). The "horizon of diplomacy" produced by the Dolphin Dance Project emerges from acknowledging species similarity and difference rather than ideological agreement or disagreement; it is shaped by the dialectical character of the discursive framework within which the work is presented to audiences: a framework that carefully balances showing and telling, presence and absence, doing and not doing, knowing and not knowing.

I should note that the artists themselves do not use the term "diplomacy," nor do they make any explicit claim about engaging in interspecies diplomacy. However, their website does have a section entitled "Dolphin Etiquette," where their key principles are articulated. Each of the sentences in the following excerpt exemplifies crucial elements of what I interpret as an interspecies diplomacy:

> We only work with wild dolphins in the open ocean, on the dolphins' terms. We never feed dolphins, nor attempt to coerce or train them in any way. As a rule, the dolphins approach us out of their own curiosity. We do our best to be well-informed about the most current scientific research on the natural behavior of dolphins so that we can interact with them in ways

that are safe and appropriate for humans and dolphins. We understand that we are visitors in the dolphins' environment and we never attempt to interact with dolphins if they are resting or feeding or show any signs of disinterest or annoyance.

(Dolphin Dance Project)

To take the last sentence first: understanding the human as visitor effectively reverses the deeply fraudulent claim—ubiquitous in zoo publications and websites—that animals in zoos and aquariums are "ambassadors" from the wild. The Dolphin Project's principle of carefully prepared and "well-informed" visitation counters the practices of violent territorial intrusion that make the institutions of the zoo and the aquarium possible. If there are any ambassadors here, it is the human dancers, and this role is highlighted through the discourse that frames and accompanies the presentation of the filmed dances to audiences. The contextualizing discourse—on the project's website, within the films themselves, and in discussions following screenings—implicitly theorizes the project's ideological and imaginative operations.

Whenever the artists present the project, they always mention two "rules" they have imposed on themselves: one, the dancers never touch the dolphins; and two, the project team never discloses the location of their dances. Each of these rules, fairly simple and straightforward at first glance, is in fact one of the pillars of an ethos of restraint that the Dolphin Dance Project is invested in. Each rule also revises certain pervasive assumptions about the ocean and its inhabitants that are inaccurate or outdated, as well as ecologically dangerous.

The first rule—no touching—can perhaps most readily be unpacked with the help of Susan Davis's analysis of the Sea World slogan and advertisement entitled "Touch the Magic." Davis shows how the ad's designation of the ocean world and its inhabitants as an otherworldly realm of enchantment and wonder is crucially linked to the promise of tactile contact, "the fantastic wish for a total merging with [a] wild nature" that has long been constructed as a distant spectacle (211). The possibility of touching something also brings with it the temptation or fantasy of "grasping" it—physically, emotionally, intellectually. The Dolphin project rejects this hubristic fantasy, holding itself to an ethos of self-restraint that is also a statement of respect for its animal partners as well as an acknowledgment of the limits of human knowledge.

The Dolphin project's injunction against touching the animals—even when the dolphins initiate physical contact, as they sometimes do—is especially interesting in light of the fact that the project leaders and dances are rooted in the dance form known as "contact improvisation," which relies heavily on physical contact as a form of information and communication, and where the patterns of the choreographies emerge not only from touch but from full body contact. In the context of their work with the dolphins, the dancers derive this information from the movement and behavior of the animals, as well as from a different kind of contact: eye contact, about which the artists often speak in stirring terms. In one of the films, Hidaka says:

> When you're eye to eye with a dolphin, you really see a person, regarding you. They're going, "Wow, there's a real person there, or there's a real dolphin there." That's a real paradigm shift. Because we're so used to thinking of ourselves as being separate and different from everything else. You know? There's humans, and then there's animals? Well, all of a sudden, you realize: there are these persons in the ocean.

This description of the experience and meaning of the interspecies gaze explicates—better than any other I've come across—Berger's enigmatic formulation of its unique value. Discussing the intersubjective drama that unfolds when the human being and the animal look at each other across the "narrow abyss of incomprehension" he made famous, Berger writes:

> [W]hen he is being seen by the animal he is *being seen as his surroundings are seen by him*. His recognition of this is what makes the look of the animal familiar. And yet, the animal is distinct and can never be confused with man. Thus a power is ascribed to the animal, comparable to human power but never coinciding with it. The animal has secrets, which, unlike the secrets of caves, mountains, seas, are specifically addressed to man.
>
> (3, emphasis added)

The interspecies gaze is, for Berger, the recognition that there are other subjectivities from whose perspective the human is an "Other"; in Hidaka's more straightforward terms, it is the recognition that other members of other species are "persons" too.

The remainder of Berger's article tracks the transformation of the animal from interacting equal to inert spectacle, and inaugurates a great suspicion—ongoing in contemporary animal studies—about the sense of sight and regimes of visuality. The Dolphin Dance Project intervenes in that history by locating its use of eyesight within a revised sensorium that arises from a mindful engagement with the alien world and the inhospitable element which the animals inhabit, and which the dancers enter as visitors. Both the new kind of interspecies gaze the project achieves and the revised sensorium that makes it possible are part of an ocean-oriented ontology that we can begin to glimpse through the second basic rule of the project, keeping the performance sites secret.

The refusal to disclose where the dolphin dances take place is motivated firstly, of course, by a desire to keep dolphin habitats commercially undisturbed, free of the intrusions from the "Swim with Dolphins"-style of tourist entertainments. But it has another meaning as well, a symbolic resonance that corrects current (mis) alignments between oceanic realities and human knowledge. Through a kind of negative mimesis, it performs the ocean's essential unknowability, its resistance to easy mapping. It stands as a rebuke, for example, to the kind of assumptions that came into view in 2014, when a lost Malaysia Airlines flight proved impossible to locate. The expression of public outrage and incredulity that accompanied the inability of authorities to find the plane, in spite of a massive international effort, suggested that things like GPS and Google Earth have done some serious cognitive damage in that they have convinced us that we can go anywhere and see anything on this planet.

While this may be close to the truth for terrestrial areas, it is nowhere near the reality of our current command over the ocean, which is feeble, if not non-existent. A vast array of statistics and facts could be marshaled to convey the current state of ocean knowledge; I prefer, however, to offer an image drawn from a recent book of popular science writing, James Nestor's account of the sport of free diving: "If you compare the ocean to a human body, the current exploration of the ocean is the equivalent of snapping a photograph of a finger to figure out how our bodies work" (9). Another statistic confirms this limit now and for the future: the U.S. budget for space exploration (NASA) is 150 times larger than that for ocean exploration (NOAA, the National Oceanic and Atmospheric Administration) (Conathan). This deficit is also responsible for a widespread and profound misunderstanding about the ocean as an earthly environment. Were maritime exploration further along, people would presumably be better informed about how thoroughly alien the oceanic environment is to human life and human physiology, a fact that Nestor's body-oriented perspective on the ocean emphasizes:

> At sea level, we are ourselves. Blood flows from the heart to the organs and extremities. The lungs take in air and expel carbon dioxide. Synapses in the brain fire at a frequency of around eight cycles per second. The heart pumps between sixty and a hundred times per minute. We see, touch, feel, taste, and smell. Our bodies are acclimatized to living here, at or above the water's surface. *At sixty feet down, we are not quite ourselves.* The heart beats at half its normal rate. Blood starts rushing from the extremities toward the more critical areas of the body's core. The lungs shrink to a third of their usual size. The senses numb, and synapses slow. The brain enters a heavily meditative state. Most humans can make it to this depth and feel these changes within their bodies. Some choose to dive deeper. *At three hundred feet, we are profoundly changed.* The pressure at these depths is ten times that of the surface. The organs collapse. The heart beats at a quarter of its normal rate, slower than the rate of a person in a coma. Senses disappear. The brain enters a dream state. At six hundred feet down, the ocean's pressure—some twenty times that of the surface—is too extreme for most human bodies to withstand. Few freedivers have ever attempted dives to this depth; fewer have survived.
>
> (8, emphasis added)

A space beyond the normal realm of the human senses, the ocean has also long been a space beyond human thought, almost beyond human imagining. The names given to its deepest layers signal our sense of fearful otherness: the second deepest layer, the abyssal zone, is etymologically linked to the mind-boggling concept of bottomlessness, while the hadal zone is named after the Greek underworld of everlasting darkness. These sunless depths are currently enjoying a moment in the media spotlight, thanks to James Cameron's dive to the Marianas Trench, but for centuries they were relegated to the status of a void. As Philip Steinberg has argued, the purported emptiness of the ocean was ideologically useful, a convenient untruth, because it allowed the ocean to be regarded as an "empty transportation *surface*, beyond the space of social relations" (113). This construction was well suited to serve the interests of industrial capitalism, enabling the "free" flow of goods that has, in our own time of globalization, reached its apotheosis in the commercial revolution known as containerization, a massive system of ocean freight using gigantic standardized "modal" steel boxes. Allan Sekula's recent film essay about the subject is aptly titled *The Forgotten Space*.

While sporadic efforts of maverick oceanographers occasionally challenged the view of the ocean as a featureless void, it was only late in the last century that a new awareness began to dawn of the vast biological treasures of marine life, as undersea expeditions dredged up not only the lost treasure they were seeking but also thousands of strange new species: "giant worms and slugs, spindly crabs and prawns, delicate sponges and sea lilies" (Broad 37). Today, with marine science still in its infancy, the ocean faces devastation from a host of human activities, including overfishing, trawling, deep-sea mining, oil spills, and toxic dumping. Ocean acidification and warming sea temperatures all but guarantee that countless species of marine animals, plants, and organisms will be rendered extinct before they are even discovered by science—a paradox on which Stacy Alaimo reflects in an essay in 2016. This combination of historical oblivion, current fascination, and overarching threat is the fraught context for artists like the Dolphin Dance Project's, and a growing number of others, who seek to perform in, about, or for the ocean today.

Interspecies diplomacy in this context begins with an acknowledgement of the ocean's alien ontology, of the vastly different sensoria of the species native to it, and their profoundly divergent modes of phenomenal experience. Differences between oceanic and terrestrial realms range from obvious ones like the elemental (water instead of air) to perplexing ones like the cartographic (the volume and mobility of seawaters thwart land-mapping techniques suited to static, two-dimensional surfaces). These differences also require us to shift or expand our modes of knowledge production to include forms of embodied experience:

> Whilst rationalists "turn away from the waves to admire the wave-born" [...] and romantics revel in the ocean's alterity [...] those who actually engage the ocean, like sailors and, perhaps

even more profoundly, surfers and swimmers, become one with the waves as the waves become one with them, in a blend of complementarity and opposition.

(Steinberg and Peters 4)

The Dolphin Dance Project makes oceanic alterity an integral part of its interspecies diplomacy, embracing the limitations that it imposes upon (and reveals in) human physiology: compared to dolphins, humans are lousy water-dancers! The Project also welcomes the ways in which this alterity can shape a mental state with enhanced interactive potential for the artists. This mental state is intimately connected to a key feature of ocean ontology, humans' inability to breathe underwater. To hold our breath for any length of time is a conscious act that can be improved with practice and technique, and one that affects our physical state. (This is something that all of us—even those of us who haven't trained for diving—have some experience of, if only through relaxation exercises or yoga classes.)

For the dancers to be able to hold their breath and remain underwater long enough to engage the dolphins in dance sequences requires, among other things, that they calm their minds, because the active brain uses more oxygen than other organs. Mindfully measured breathing is a key to this calming:

A focus on breath is core to our practice, whether we are training or actually dancing with dolphins. We hold our breath for a minute or more repetitively, with little rest in between, and this means we need to have excellent control of our breath. We need to breathe deeply and well between dives, and remain relaxed while holding our breath during the dives. We need to be keenly aware of our oxygen deficit and carbon dioxide build up so we can extend our diving times and depths safely.

(Hidaka)

The mental state that results profoundly shapes the experience of interspecies encounter, especially of the interspecies gaze. When speaking of this, Hidaka is understandably cautious; the project prizes its alignment with marine science and the artists are wary of being dismissed as New-Age kooks. Choosing her words carefully, Hidaka allows that "I know this kind of focus on breath is common in various meditation practices, but I wouldn't really call what we do 'meditative' ... The breath work does affect our mental, physical and emotional state. I would describe it as a feeling of 'openness.'" Hidaka's further observations on this state of being link sensation and affect, physicality and emotionality, linkages that in turn foster a new space for ethical interspecies encounter: "The 'open' state is also a relaxed one, and our relaxed demeanor and body posture expresses our trust (and lack of anxiety or aggression). *A sense of trust* definitely seems to be noticed and reciprocated by our dolphin partners." In this account, experience flows in both directions, inward and outward: the dancer's relaxed body (a relaxation achieved through the special breathing practices) makes her feel calm and safe, but it also communicates beyond the dancer, to the dolphins, whose demeanor in turn encourages a creative physicality and a heightened spirit of collaboration. Like the medium in which the work occurs, the dance practice involves circulations and flows, mobilizing a dynamic reciprocity of perceptions and emotions ranging from excitement, curiosity, and fascination, to enjoyment and love:

> The engagement with dolphins is very social. Sometimes dolphins look at us wide-eyed as if excited or curious. Sometimes they cast a sleepy, half-open eye towards us. Sometimes the regard expresses deep interest in us. In an "open" state we can respond with our full range of emotional and kinesthetic expressions. Sometimes we are also joyful or fascinated. Sometimes we feel a crushing tenderness, or even love. And if we are clear in our expression, our dolphin partners easily respond to us—to what we express—just as we respond to them: through eye contact and shared movement. Our meeting turns into a true exchange—a movement-based "conversation"—a dance.
>
> (Hidaka)

To conclude, I return to Latour's provocative formulation about diplomacy to ask: What values does this "movement-based conversation" modify? How does it "betray" the ways that humans have previously related to animals? As I read the project, that "betrayal" happens in two areas, which we can identify, very broadly, as knowledge production and artistic process.

The words "mysterious" and "unfamiliar" recur in Hidaka's discussions of the work, often closely connected to "openness." She notes, for instance, that "the 'open' state helps me accept the unfamiliar without rushing to 'figure it out' or give it an overly anthropomorphic meaning. I don't have to feel anxious about what I don't know" (Hidaka). In place of the inquiring mind of scientific investigation, the calm mind of the relaxed dancer affords a tolerance for the unknown. This acceptance of the unknown and unfamiliar is, for Hidaka, linked to necessary changes in the regimes of knowledge underlying existing relationships to wild animals. According to her, the connection we need to feel in order to care enough to protect animals and their habitats has to leave room for non-humans "to have needs and desires we cannot fully know. Without allowing for that, we start to imagine—wrongly—that 'caring' for dolphins in captivity on completely human terms could be ok for them. We start to think that we can 'manage' the complex ecology of their ocean habitats with our puny knowledge" (Hidaka). The interspecies diplomacy of the project, then, includes recalibrating the relative roles of scientific certainty and epistemological humility. Balancing the known with the unknown, accepting unfamiliarity while cultivating alertness, produces a result—"I can remain alert and connected to my partner, continuing to move fluidly together"— that resonates with Latour's description of the "horizon of diplomacy" as a space where peers learn what it is to be together.

Paradoxically, the embrace of the unknown makes the ocean feel, says Hidaka, like "less of a 'void,' and exposes humans as less 'exceptional' than we might believe." This felt rejection of human exceptionalism, is, I would suggest, the bedrock principle and fundamental achievement of the project and the cornerstone of its interspecies diplomacy. It is both cause and effect of the artists' willingness to cede control to the other species, even in an area that most artists find hard to let go of: aesthetic control. To use Latour's term again, the artists "betray" the traditional centrality and agency of the artist, making the animals their guides and teachers, allowing the animals' movements to determine the dancers' movements and hence the works' choreography.

By having their choreography emerge from mirroring the animals' movements, the Dolphin Dance Project firmly rejects the principle underlying the long history of animal performances: namely, to make animals imitate *human* movement and behavior. Unlike the orcas at Sea World, the dolphins in this project are not required to wave hello, or clap their "hands," or kiss their trainers on cue. Indeed, they are not *required* to do anything. On the contrary, great care is taken to ensure they will and can do only what they chose to do: either engage creatively with the human dancers, or swim away.[3]

The imagery that emerges from this project—imagery enhanced by brilliant cinematography, complex sound design, skillful editing, and the latest video technologies—is gorgeous and stirring to behold. Yet it is never allowed to remain just that. The project's deepest goal—and the one I have tried to track and theorize here—is achieved through the discursive framing. If encountered, as intended, in the carefully introduced film screenings, followed by conversation with the artists, it is rich in potential for progressive interspecies thinking and feeling. The heavy mediation involved is part and parcel of its functioning as diplomacy, as is its species-specificity. Focusing their attention, research, training, and artistry on one species and one challengingly alien environment, the artists of the Dolphin Dance Project bring us thought-provoking, heart-stirring, and politically promising glimpses of how to look at—and be with—the other animals with whom we share this fragile, endangered world.

Notes

1 "The animal is a word, it is an appellation that men have instituted, a name they have given themselves the right and the authority to give to another living creature [à l'autre vivant]" (2008: 23).
2 "The anthropos—what is that? All of Homo sapiens sapiens? All of mankind? Well, who exactly? Fossil-fuel-burning humanity is the first short answer to that. Industrial humanity, however, is still a kind of a species-being; it doesn't even speak to all of industrial humanity, but specifically the formations of global capital and global state socialisms. Very much a part of that are the exchange networks, the financial networks, extraction practices, wealth creations, and (mal)distributions in relation to both people and other critters. It would probably be better named the Capitalocene, if one wanted a single word" (Haraway, in Haraway and Kenney, 259).
3 I am indebted to Chisa Hidaka for her generous discussion and explanation of the Dolphin Dance Project's strategies and values. On the issue of the dolphins' free choice, she elaborated as follows: "Part of what's remarkable in our process is that IF we approach in an appropriate way (no touching, and respecting the dolphins' inclinations/desires) the dolphins show us that they want to interact with us, and that they can do so in a way that shows they are taking our human capabilities and individuality into account. The dolphins show us that—for their own reasons (whatever they are—we certainly don't claim to know)—they are interested in a voluntary engagement with a shared intention to create an experience of some kind of coherence for both humans and dolphins. They show us that they don't just look at us as dangerous THINGS that they should avoid. They see us as capable of doing something meaningful for both them and us. We don't just shape ourselves to fit the dolphins. They also accommodate us—going slowly so we can stay together, not

taking us too deep or far from the boat or shore, never bumping us accidentally. Sometimes they follow our lead, diving after us. Sometimes they offer new movements for us to try. They don't just swim. They act in ways that are very specific to the context we present. In doing so they demonstrate their 'creative agency.' The dolphins show us that they see us as a 'person'—a subject capable of engaging meaningfully—and this, in turn, reveals them to us as 'persons.'"

Works cited

Alaimo, S. (2016) "The Anthropocene at Sea: Temporality, Paradox, Compression" in U. Heise, J. Christensen and M. Niemann (eds) *The Routledge Companion to the Environmental Humanities*. Oxford: Routledge.

Berger, J. (1980) "Why Look at Animals?" *About Looking*. London: Bloomsbury, 1–26.

Blackfish (2013) Film, dir. G. Cowperthwaite. Manny O Productions.

Broad, W.J. (1997) *The Universe Below: Discovering the Secrets of the Deep Sea*. New York: Touchstone.

Conathan, M. (2013) "Rockets Top Submarines: Space Exploration Dollars Dwarf Ocean Spending." *American Progress*, June 18. Online.

The Cove (2009) Film, dir. L. Psihoyos. Participant Media.

Davis, S. (1996) "Touch the Magic" in W. Cronon (ed.) *Uncommon Ground: Rethinking the Human Place in Nature*. New York: Norton, 204–31.

Derrida, J. (2008) *The Animal That Therefore I Am*, ed. M-L. Mallet, trans. D. Wills. New York: Fordham UP.

The Dolphin Dance Project (2010) "Dancing with Dolphins." Online.

Haraway, D. and Kenney, M. (2014) "Anthropocene, Capitalocene, Chthulhocene: Donna Haraway in Conversation with Martha Kenney" in H. Davis and E. Turpin (eds) *Art in the Anthropocene: Encounters Among Aesthetics, Politics, Environments and Epistemologies*. London: Open Humanities Press, 255–70.

Hidaka, C. (2014) Personal communication, May 15.

Latour, B. (2014) "Diplomacy in the Face of Gaia: Bruno Latour in Conversation with Heather Davis" in H. Davis and E. Turpin (eds) *Art in the Anthropocene: Encounters Among Aesthetics, Politics, Environments and Epistemologies*. London: Open Humanities Press, 43–56.

Nestor, J. (2014) *Deep: Freediving, Renegade Science, and What the Ocean Tells Us about Ourselves*. New York: Houghton Mifflin Harcourt.

Sekula, A. and Burch, N. (2011) *The Forgotten Space*. Icarus Films.

Steinberg, P.E. (2001) *The Social Construction of the Ocean*. Cambridge: Cambridge UP.

—— and Peters, K. (2015) "Wet Ontologies, Fluid Spaces: Giving Depth to Volume through Oceanic Thinking." *Environment and Planning D: Society and Space* 33: 247–64. Online.

Index